taste of home
soups

taste of home
BOOKS

REIMAN MEDIA GROUP, LLC • GREENDALE, WI

taste of home

Reader's Digest

EDITORIAL
Editor-in-Chief: Catherine Cassidy

Executive Editor, Print and Digital Books: Stephen C. George
Creative Director: Howard Greenberg
Editorial Services Manager: Kerri Balliet

Editor: Christine Rukavena
Associate Creative Director: Edwin Robles Jr.
Content Production Manager: Julie Wagner
Layout Designer: Catherine Fletcher
Copy Chief: Deb Warlaumont Mulvey
Copy Editor: Mary C. Hanson
Contributing Editor: Victoria Soukup Jensen
Contributing Layout Designer: Holly Patch
Recipe Content Manager: Colleen King
Recipe Testing: Taste of Home Test Kitchen
Food Photography: Taste of Home Photo Studio
Executive Assistant: Marie Brannon
Editorial Assistant: Marilyn Iczkowski

BUSINESS
Vice President, Publisher:
Jan Studin, jan_studin@rd.com
Regional Account Director:
Donna Lindskog, donna_lindskog@rd.com
Eastern Account Director: Joanne Carrara
Eastern Account Manager: Kari Nestor
Account Manager: Gina Minerbi
Midwest & Western Account Director: Jackie Fallon
Midwest Account Manager: Lorna Phillips
Western Account Manager: Joel Millikin
Michigan Sales Representative: Linda C. Donaldson

Corporate Integrated Sales Director: Steve Sottile
Digital Sales Planner: Tim Baarda

General Manager, Taste of Home Cooking Schools:
Erin Puariea

Direct Response: Katherine Zito, David Geller Associates

Executive Director, Brand Marketing: Leah West
Associate Marketing Manager: Betsy Connors
VP, Creative Director: Paul Livornese

VP, Magazine Marketing: Dave Fiegel

READER'S DIGEST NORTH AMERICA
President: Dan Lagani

VP, Business Development: Jonathan Bigham
President, Books and Home Entertaining: Harold Clarke
Chief Financial Officer: Howard Halligan
VP, General Manager, Reader's Digest Media:
Marilynn Jacobs
Chief Content Officer, Milwaukee: Mark Jannot
Chief Marketing Officer: Renee Jordan
VP, Chief Sales Officer: Mark Josephson
VP, Chief Strategy Officer: Jacqueline Majers Lachman
VP, Marketing and Creative Services: Elizabeth Tighe
VP, Chief Content Officer: Liz Vaccariello

THE READER'S DIGEST ASSOCIATION, INC.
President and Chief Executive Officer:
Robert E. Guth

For other Taste of Home books and products,
visit us at **tasteofhome.com.**

For more Reader's Digest products and information,
visit **rd.com** (in the United States) or see **rd.ca** (in Canada).

International Standard Book Number (10): 1-61765-090-0
International Standard Book Number (13): 978-1-61765-090-1
Library of Congress Control Number: 2011933613

Cover Photography
Photographer: Rob Hagen
Food Stylist: Alynna Malson
Set Styling Manager:
Stephanie Marchese
Set Stylist: Pamela Stasney

Pictured on front cover
(clockwise from top left):
No-Bean Chili, page 57; Cassoulet
for the Gang, page 170; Chicken
Bagel Melts and Classic Cream of
Asparagus Soup, page 33; Classic
Broccoli Cheese Soup, page 146;
Rustic Tortellini Soup, page 113.

Pictured on back cover
(top to bottom):
Curried Pumpkin Apple Soup and French Market Sandwiches, page 32;
Hamburger Vegetable Soup, page 57.

Pictured on spine: Cheesy Tortilla Soup, page 135.

Printed in China.
1 3 5 7 9 10 8 6 4 2

contents

Warm & *wonderful!*

soups

A good soup recipe is like a **cherished friend** that you can turn to season after season. In these pages, discover **hundreds** of beloved **soups from readers just like you**, plus dozens of delicious **sandwich pairings** and **easy breads** that will make your soup into a **special meal.**

heartwarming soups & stews

❝ I like to keep my son's heritage alive through cooking. This recipe reflects my wife's Hispanic background. ❞
—**GREG FONTENOT** THE WOODLANDS, TEXAS

soup & sandwich pairings

❝ These sandwiches make a perfect mini snack or appetizer. Your guests will adore them! ❞
—**SUSANNE ROUPE** EAST FAIRFIELD, VERMONT

so-easy breads

❝ I love easy recipes. They help me juggle working, volunteering, and keeping my family's schedule running smoothly. ❞
—**TERRI KEENEY** GREELEY, COLORADO

page 74 Greg's fabulous stew

page 37 Susanne's irresistible ham sliders paired with rich cheese soup!

page 244 Terri's super-quick corn bread

soups in a jiffy

chick-n-rice soup

(pictured above)

The ladies at a church I attended years ago served this crowd-pleaser on many occasions. It's perfect for a weeknight family meal.

SARA NELSON FREEPORT, MICHIGAN

8	cups water
1-1/2	cups sliced celery
1	cup thinly sliced fresh carrots
4	cups cubed cooked chicken
1	package (6.9 ounces) chicken-flavored rice and vermicelli mix
4	teaspoons chicken bouillon granules

☐ In a large saucepan, bring water, celery and carrots to a boil. Stir in the chicken, rice mix and bouillon. Return to a boil. Reduce heat; cover and simmer for 15-20 minutes or until rice is tender.

Yield: 10 servings.

NUTRITION FACTS: 1 cup equals 184 calories, 5 g fat (1 g saturated fat), 50 mg cholesterol, 683 mg sodium, 17 g carbohydrate, 1 g fiber, 18 g protein.

beef minestrone

My sister-in-law had this soup simmering on her stove to welcome our family to her home in Oklahoma. We not only gobbled it up, we left with the recipe!

BEVERLY MOSS PHOENIX, ARIZONA

1	pound ground beef
1	small onion, chopped
2	cans (10-3/4 ounces each) condensed minestrone soup, undiluted
2-1/2	cups water
1	can (10 ounces) diced tomatoes and green chilies

☐ In a large saucepan, cook beef and onion over medium heat until meat is no longer pink; drain. Add the soup, water and tomatoes. Cook, uncovered, over medium heat until heated through.

Yield: 8 servings (2 quarts).

NUTRITION FACTS: 1 serving equals 122 calories, 6 g fat (2 g saturated fat), 29 mg cholesterol, 436 mg sodium, 6 g carbohydrate, 2 g fiber, 11 g protein.

fast vegetable soup

I dress up canned minestrone to make a shortcut soup that's loaded with colorful veggies. Serve steaming bowls with a sandwich or salad for a satisfying yet fast meal.
JENNIFER SHIELDS CHESNEE, SOUTH CAROLINA

- 1 can (19 ounces) ready-to-serve minestrone soup
- 1 package (16 ounces) frozen mixed vegetables
- 1 can (14-3/4 ounces) whole kernel corn, drained
- 1 can (15 ounces) black beans, rinsed and drained
- 1 can (14-1/2 ounces) Italian diced tomatoes, undrained

▨ In a 2-1/2 quart microwave-safe bowl, combine all the ingredients. Cover and microwave on high for 8-10 minutes or until heated through, stirring twice.

Yield: 9 servings.

NUTRITION FACTS: 1 cup equals 149 calories, 1 g fat (trace saturated fat), 1 mg cholesterol, 625 mg sodium, 27 g carbohydrate, 7 g fiber, 6 g protein.

EDITOR'S NOTE: This recipe was tested in a 1,100-watt microwave oven.

broccoli wild rice soup

I love soup and serve it often. My sister gave me this delicious recipe that's surprisingly low in fat. It cooks up in no time.
MARTHA POLLOCK OREGONIA, OHIO

- 5 cups water
- 1 package (6 ounces) long grain and wild rice mix
- 1 can (10-3/4 ounces) reduced-fat reduced-sodium condensed cream of chicken soup, undiluted
- 1-1/2 cups fat-free milk
- 1 package (8 ounces) fat-free cream cheese, cubed
- 1/4 teaspoon salt
- 3 cups frozen chopped broccoli
- 1 large carrot, shredded
- 1/4 cup sliced almonds, toasted

▨ In a large saucepan, combine the water and rice mix with contents of seasoning packet; bring to a boil. Reduce heat; cover and simmer for 20 minutes.

▨ Add the soup, milk, cream cheese and salt; stir until cheese is melted. Add broccoli and carrot; cook over medium-low heat for 5-6 minutes or until vegetables and rice are tender. Sprinkle with almonds.

Yield: 6 servings.

NUTRITION FACTS: 1-1/2 cups equals 232 calories, 5 g fat (1 g saturated fat), 10 mg cholesterol, 927 mg sodium, 35 g carbohydrate, 3 g fiber, 14 g protein. **DIABETIC EXCHANGES:** 1-1/2 starch, 1 lean meat, 1 vegetable, 1/2 fat-free milk.

EDITOR'S NOTE: This recipe was tested with Uncle Ben's Original Long Grain and Wild Rice mix.

reuben chowder

If you like Reuben sandwiches, you'll be delighted with the flavor of my unusual chowder. Crunchy rye bread croutons top a hearty blend of convenient canned soups, sauerkraut, corned beef and mozzarella cheese.
IOLA EGLE BELLA VISTA, ARKANSAS

1	tablespoon butter
3	slices rye bread
1	can (11 ounces) condensed nacho cheese soup, undiluted
1	can (10-3/4 ounces) condensed cream of mushroom soup, undiluted
3	cups milk
1	can (14 ounces) sauerkraut, rinsed and drained
3/4	pound deli corned beef, diced
1	cup (4 ounces) shredded part-skim mozzarella cheese

▢ Butter bread on both sides; cube. Place on an ungreased baking sheet. Bake at 375° for 6-8 minutes or until browned.

▢ Meanwhile, in a large saucepan, combine the soups, milk, sauerkraut and corned beef; cook and stir over medium heat for 8-10 minutes or until heated through. Add cheese; stir until melted. Top with croutons.

Yield: 8 servings (2 quarts).

NUTRITION FACTS: 1 cup equals 266 calories, 14 g fat (8 g saturated fat), 57 mg cholesterol, 1,532 mg sodium, 19 g carbohydrate, 3 g fiber, 16 g protein.

veggie beef soup

As a full-time teacher, I have time to cook from scratch only a few nights each week. This convenient recipe makes a big enough batch to feed my family for two nights.
JULIE KRUGER ST. CLOUD, MINNESOTA

1	can (46 ounces) V8 juice
2	packages (16 ounces each) frozen mixed vegetables
1	pound ground beef, cooked and drained
1	can (10-3/4 ounces) condensed cream of mushroom soup, undiluted
2	teaspoons dried minced onion

Salt and pepper to taste

▢ In a 5-qt. slow cooker, combine the first five ingredients; mix well. Cover and cook on high for 4-5 hours or until heated through. Season with salt and pepper.

Yield: 12 servings (3 quarts).

NUTRITION FACTS: 1 cup equals 125 calories, 5 g fat (2 g saturated fat), 20 mg cholesterol, 494 mg sodium, 12 g carbohydrate, 2 g fiber, 9 g protein.

tomato tortellini soup

(pictured above)

No one will guess that you cheated by using canned tomato soup. My lovely soup tastes homemade all the way!
SANDRA FICK LINCOLN, NEBRASKA

1	package (9 ounces) refrigerated cheese tortellini
2	cans (10-3/4 ounces each) reduced-sodium condensed tomato soup, undiluted
2	cups vegetable broth
2	cups 2% milk
2	cups half-and-half cream
1/2	cup chopped oil-packed sun-dried tomatoes
1	teaspoon onion powder
1	teaspoon garlic powder
1	teaspoon dried basil
1/2	teaspoon salt
1/2	cup shredded Parmesan cheese

Additional shredded Parmesan cheese, optional

☐ Cook tortellini according to package directions.

☐ Meanwhile, in a Dutch oven, combine the soup, broth, milk, cream, tomatoes and seasonings. Heat through, stirring frequently. Drain tortellini; carefully add to soup. Stir in cheese. Sprinkle each serving with additional cheese if desired.

Yield: 10 servings (2-1/2 quarts).

NUTRITION FACTS: 1 cup (calculated without additional cheese) equals 245 calories, 11 g fat (6 g saturated fat), 42 mg cholesterol, 756 mg sodium, 27 g carbohydrate, 2 g fiber, 10 g protein.

hearty hamburger soup

This thick soup, chock-full of beef, veggies and noodles, satisfies my husband's appetite after a busy day on the farm.
JULIE GREEN HULL, IOWA

2	pounds ground beef
1/2	cup chopped onion
6	cups water
1	package (10 ounces) frozen mixed vegetables
1	can (14 -1/2 ounces) diced tomatoes, undrained
1	package (6-3/4 ounces) beef pasta dinner mix
1	bay leaf
1/4	to 1/2 teaspoon salt
1/4	teaspoon pepper

☐ In a Dutch oven, cook beef and onion over medium heat until meat is no longer pink; drain. Stir in the remaining ingredients; bring to a boil. reduce heat; cover and simmer until pasta is tender. Discard bay leaf.

Yield: 12 servings (3 quarts).

NUTRITION FACTS: 1 cup equals 178 calories, 9 g fat (4 g saturated fat), 52 mg cholesterol, 186 mg sodium, 7 g carbohydrate, 2 g fiber, 16 g protein.

barbecued turkey chili

(pictured at left)

My so-simple chili takes just minutes to mix together, and the slow cooker does the rest. Friends and family often request it when we all get together.
MELISSA WEBB ELLSWORTH, SOUTH DAKOTA

- 1 can (16 ounces) kidney beans, rinsed and drained
- 1 can (16 ounces) hot chili beans, undrained
- 1 can (15 ounces) turkey chili with beans
- 1 can (14-1/2 ounces) diced tomatoes, undrained
- 1/3 cup barbecue sauce

In a 3-qt. slow cooker, combine all the ingredients. Cover and cook on high for 4 hours or until heated through and flavors are blended.

Yield: 6 servings.

NUTRITION FACTS: 1 cup equals 215 calories, 2 g fat (1 g saturated fat), 10 mg cholesterol, 936 mg sodium, 36 g carbohydrate, 10 g fiber, 14 g protein.

campfire stew

This speedy, single-pan meal brings back childhood memories of my days at Girl Scout camp. The stew is so hearty and flavorful, it will be an instant hit with your family.
EVA KNIGHT NASHUA, NEW HAMPSHIRE

- 1 pound ground beef
- 1 can (15 ounces) mixed vegetables, drained
- 1 can (10-3/4 ounces) condensed tomato soup, undiluted
- 1 can (10-1/2 ounces) condensed vegetable beef soup, undiluted
- 1/4 cup water
- 1/4 teaspoon garlic powder
- 1/4 teaspoon onion powder
- 1/4 teaspoon salt
- 1/8 teaspoon pepper

In a large saucepan, cook beef over medium heat until no longer pink; drain. Stir in the remaining ingredients. Bring to a boil. Reduce heat; cover and simmer for 8-10 minutes or until heated through.

Yield: 4 servings.

NUTRITION FACTS: 1 serving equals 353 calories, 15 g fat (6 g saturated fat), 78 mg cholesterol, 1,428 mg sodium, 24 g carbohydrate, 4 g fiber, 29 g protein.

macaroni vegetable soup

With just minutes of prep time, this hearty soup truly couldn't be easier to make. Simply open up the ingredients, pour 'em in and dinner's practically done!
METZEL TURLEY SOUTH CHARLESTON, WEST VIRGINIA

- 1 package (1.4 ounces) vegetable soup mix
- 1 envelope (.6 ounce) cream of chicken soup mix
- 2 cans (5-1/2 ounces each) spicy tomato juice
- 4 cups water
- 2 cans (15 ounces each) mixed vegetables, drained

Dash crushed red pepper flakes

Dash dried minced garlic

- 1/2 cup uncooked elbow macaroni

In a Dutch oven, combine soup mixes and tomato juice. Stir in the water, mixed vegetables, pepper flakes and garlic; bring to a boil. Add macaroni. Reduce heat; cook, uncovered, for 10-15 minutes or until macaroni is tender, stirring occasionally.

Yield: 7 servings.

NUTRITION FACTS: 1 cup equals 94 calories, 1 g fat (trace saturated fat), trace cholesterol, 944 mg sodium, 19 g carbohydrate, 3 g fiber, 4 g protein.

beef soup in a hurry

(pictured above)

I nicknamed my quick and easy beef recipe "throw-together soup" because it calls for just a few canned goods and cooks up fast in the microwave. Serve it with a green salad and hot rolls for a hearty meal.
LOELLEN HOLLEY TOPOCK, ARIZONA

- 1   can (24 ounces) beef stew
- 1   can (14-1/2 ounces) stewed tomatoes, cut up
- 1   can (10-3/4 ounces) condensed vegetable beef soup, undiluted
- 1   can (8-3/4 ounces) whole kernel corn, drained
- 1/8 teaspoon hot pepper sauce

▨ Combine all ingredients in a microwave-safe bowl. Cover and microwave on high for 3-5 minutes or until heated through, stirring once.

Yield: 6 servings.

NUTRITION FACTS: 1 cup equals 188 calories, 7 g fat (3 g saturated fat), 20 mg cholesterol, 1,030 mg sodium, 22 g carbohydrate, 3 g fiber, 9 g protein.

EDITOR'S NOTE: This recipe was tested in a 1,100-watt microwave oven.

shrimp chowder

With only three ingredients, this chowder is as simple as it gets! I like recipes that get me out of the kitchen in a flash.
MARTHA CASTILLE OPELOUSAS, LOUISIANA

- 1   package (11 ounces) cream of potato soup mix
- 1   cup frozen mixed vegetables
- 1   pound cooked small shrimp, peeled and deveined

▨ In a large saucepan, prepare soup mix according to package directions, adding the mixed vegetables. Stir in shrimp; cook 5-6 minutes longer or until heated through.

Yield: 12 servings (3 quarts).

NUTRITION FACTS: 1 cup equals 143 calories, 3 g fat (2 g saturated fat), 80 mg cholesterol, 584 mg sodium, 19 g carbohydrate, 3 g fiber, 12 g protein.

EDITOR'S NOTE: This recipe was tested with Bear Creek creamy potato soup mix.

presto chili

Canned soup and beans are the secrets to my chili's quick preparation. For even faster meals, I sometimes cook and freeze the ground beef in advance. Then I just combine the frozen cooked beef with the other ingredients and simmer them as usual.
JEAN WARD MONTOGOMERY, TEXAS

1	pound lean ground beef (90% lean)
1	can (10-3/4 ounces) condensed tomato soup, undiluted
1	can (16 ounces) chili beans, undrained
2	to 3 teaspoons chili powder
1/2	cup water, optional

☐ In a saucepan, brown ground beef until no longer pink; drain. Add soup, beans and chili powder. Reduce heat. Cover and simmer for 20 minutes. Add water if you prefer a thinner chili.

Yield: 4 servings.

NUTRITION FACTS: 1 serving equals 337 calories, 10 g fat (4 g saturated fat), 71 mg cholesterol, 840 mg sodium, 35 g carbohydrate, 7 g fiber, 30 g protein. **DIABETIC EXCHANGES:** 3 meat, 1-1/2 starch.

nacho potato soup

Because this recipe starts with a box of au gratin potatoes, you don't have to spend time peeling and slicing them. My husband requests this simple soup often.
SHERRY DICKERSON SEBASTOPOL, MISSISSIPPI

1	package (5-1/4 ounces) au gratin potatoes
1	can (11 ounces) whole kernel corn, drained
1	can (10 ounces) diced tomatoes and green chilies, undrained
2	cups water
2	cups 2% milk
2	cups cubed process American cheese (Velveeta)

Dash hot pepper sauce, optional
Minced fresh parsley, optional

☐ In a 3-qt. saucepan, combine the contents of potato package, corn, tomatoes and water. Bring to a boil.

☐ Reduce heat; cover and simmer for 15-18 minutes or until potatoes are tender. Add the milk, cheese and hot pepper sauce if desired; cook and stir until the cheese is melted. Garnish with parsley if desired.

Yield: 6-8 servings (2 quarts).

NUTRITION FACTS: 1 cup equals 234 calories, 10 g fat (6 g saturated fat), 26 mg cholesterol, 980 mg sodium, 25 g carbohydrate, 2 g fiber, 10 g protein.

30-minute chicken noodle soup

This great soup is perfect for a cold, wintry day. It is my favorite thing to eat when I'm not feeling well; it makes me feel so much better.
LACEY WAADT PAYSON, UTAH

4	cups water
1	can (14-1/2 ounces) chicken broth
1-1/2	cups cubed cooked chicken breast
1	can (10-3/4 ounces) condensed cream of chicken soup, undiluted
3/4	cup sliced celery
3/4	cup sliced carrots
1	small onion, chopped
1-1/2	teaspoons dried parsley flakes
1	teaspoon reduced-sodium chicken bouillon granules
1/4	teaspoon pepper
3	cups uncooked egg noodles

▢ In a Dutch oven, combine the first 10 ingredients. Bring to a boil. Reduce heat; cover and simmer for 10 minutes or until vegetables are crisp-tender. Stir in noodles; cook 5-7 minutes longer or until noodles and vegetables are tender.

Yield: 6 servings (2-1/4 quarts).

NUTRITION FACTS: 1-1/2 cups equals 196 calories, 5 g fat (1 g saturated fat), 49 mg cholesterol, 759 mg sodium, 22 g carbohydrate, 2 g fiber, 15 g protein. **DIABETIC EXCHANGES:** 2 lean meat, 1 starch, 1/2 fat.

minestrone stew

I add green chilies to spice up my slow-cooked stew. You'll like the convenience of using everyday pantry ingredients.
JANIE HOSKINS RED BLUFF, CALIFORNIA

1	pound ground beef
1	small onion, chopped
1	can (19 ounces) ready-to-serve minestrone soup
1	can (15 ounces) pinto beans, rinsed and drained
1	can (14-1/2 ounces) stewed tomatoes
1	can (11 ounces) whole kernel corn, drained
1	can (4 ounces) chopped green chilies
1	teaspoon salt
1/2	teaspoon garlic powder
1/2	teaspoon onion powder

▢ In a large skillet, cook beef and onion over medium heat until meat is no longer pink; drain. Transfer to a 3-qt. slow cooker. Stir in the remaining ingredients. Cover and cook on low for 4-6 hours or until heated through.

Yield: 8 servings (2 quarts).

NUTRITION FACTS: 1 cup equals 221 calories, 6 g fat (3 g saturated fat), 29 mg cholesterol, 901 mg sodium, 24 g carbohydrate, 5 g fiber, 15 g protein.

mac 'n' cheese soup

(pictured above)

I came across this recipe a few years ago and made some changes to suit our tastes. Because it starts with packaged macaroni and cheese, it's ready in a jiffy.

NANCY DAUGHERTY CORTLAND, OHIO

- 1 package (14 ounces) deluxe macaroni and cheese dinner mix
- 9 cups water, divided
- 1 cup fresh broccoli florets
- 2 tablespoons finely chopped onion
- 1 can (10-3/4 ounces) condensed cheddar cheese soup, undiluted
- 2-1/2 cups 2% milk
- 1 cup chopped fully cooked ham

☐ Set aside cheese sauce packet from macaroni and cheese mix. In a large saucepan, bring 8 cups water to a boil. Add macaroni; cook for 8-10 minutes or until tender.

☐ Meanwhile, in another large saucepan, bring remaining water to a boil. Add broccoli and onion; cook, uncovered, for 3 minutes. Stir in the soup, milk, ham and contents of cheese sauce packet; heat through. Drain macaroni; stir into soup.

Yield: 8 servings (2 quarts).

NUTRITION FACTS: 1 cup equals 263 calories, 9 g fat (4 g saturated fat), 28 mg cholesterol, 976 mg sodium, 32 g carbohydrate, 2 g fiber, 13 g protein.

easy corn chowder

This soup comes together faster than you can imagine! I came up with the recipe when my family had a hard time finding a corn chowder that all of us liked.

DANNA CHAMBERS TOPSHAM, MAINE

- 1 can (14-1/2 ounces) diced new potatoes, drained
- 1-1/2 cups whole milk
- 1 can (10-3/4 ounces) condensed cheddar cheese soup, undiluted
- 1 can (8-1/4 ounces) cream-style corn
- 1 cup frozen corn, thawed
- 1 cup cubed deli ham

☐ In a large microwave-safe bowl, combine all the ingredients. Cover and microwave on high for 5-8 minutes or until heated through, stirring twice.

Yield: 3 servings.

NUTRITION FACTS: 2 cups equals 392 calories, 10 g fat (5 g saturated fat), 42 mg cholesterol, 1,861 mg sodium, 61 g carbohydrate, 6 g fiber, 19 g protein.

EDITOR'S NOTE: This recipe was tested in a 1,100-watt microwave oven.

lemony turkey rice soup

(pictured above)

While growing up in Texas, I spent a lot of time helping my grandma cook. I still enjoy trying new things in the kitchen—like this deliciously different turkey soup.
MARGARITA CUELLAR EAST CHICAGO, INDIANA

6	cups chicken broth, divided
1	can (10-3/4 ounces) condensed cream of chicken soup, undiluted
2	cups cooked rice
2	cups diced cooked turkey
1/4	teaspoon pepper
2	tablespoons cornstarch
1/4	to 1/3 cup lemon juice
1/4	to 1/2 cup minced fresh cilantro

◻ In a large saucepan, combine 5-1/2 cups of broth, soup, rice, turkey and pepper. Bring to a boil; boil or 3 minutes.

◻ In a small bowl, combine cornstarch and remaining broth until smooth. Gradually stir into hot soup. Cook and stir for 1-2 minutes or until thickened and heated through. Remove from the heat; stir in lemon juice and cilantro.

Yield: 8 servings (about 2 quarts).

NUTRITION FACTS: 1 cup equals 166 calories, 4 g fat (1 g saturated fat), 30 mg cholesterol, 1,012 mg sodium, 17 g carbohydrate, 1 g fiber, 14 g protein.

potato soup in bread bowls

This heartwarming main course helps my husband get a swift yet filling meal on the table when I'm at work. He loves clam chowder, and with this simple recipe he can prepare it in just a few minutes.
CHERYL COR AUBURN, WASHINGTON

2	cans (18.8 ounces each) ready-to-serve chunky baked potato with cheddar and bacon bits soup
2	cans (6-1/2 ounces each) chopped clams, drained
1	bacon strip, cooked and crumbled
1	teaspoon minced chives
1	teaspoon dried parsley flakes
1	teaspoon dried rosemary, crushed
1/4	teaspoon pepper
5	round loaves (8 ounces each) sourdough bread

◻ In a large saucepan, combine first seven ingredients; heat through.

◻ Meanwhile, cut a thin slice off the top of each loaf; set aside. Hollow out loaves, leaving 3/4-in. shells (discard removed bread or save for another use). Ladle soup into bread bowls; replace tops.

Yield: 5 servings.

NUTRITION FACTS: 1 serving equals 512 calories, 9 g fat (3 g saturated fat), 26 mg cholesterol, 1,850 mg sodium, 85 g carbohydrate, 4 g fiber, 23 g protein.

shortcut split pea soup

Pair my hearty soup with a simple tossed salad for an easy meal that's as well-rounded and nourishing as it is quick.
DONNA NOEL GRAY, MAINE

3	cups water
2	teaspoons reduced-sodium chicken bouillon granules
1/2	teaspoon dried thyme
4	celery ribs and leaves
2	medium carrots, thinly sliced
2	cans (11-1/2 ounces each) condensed split pea soup, undiluted
1	cup cubed fully cooked ham

Shaved Parmesan cheese, optional

▢ In a large saucepan, bring the water, bouillon granules and thyme to a boil. Thinly slice celery ribs and finely chop the leaves; set leaves aside.

▢ Add celery ribs and carrots to water mixture; simmer, uncovered, for 5-8 minutes or until tender. Stir in the soup, ham and celery leaves; heat through. Top each serving with cheese if desired.

Yield: 5 servings.

NUTRITION FACTS: 1-1/3 cups (calculated without cheese) equals 249 calories, 7 g fat (3 g saturated fat), 23 mg cholesterol, 1,502 mg sodium, 32 g carbohydrate, 4 g fiber, 16 g protein.

tortellini beef soup

Here's a soup that's delicious, pretty and unbelievably fast to make. For a creamy variation, I sometimes substitute cream of mushroom soup for the French onion soup. If there are any leftovers, they taste even better the next day.
MARSHA FARLEY BANGOR, MAINE

1	pound ground beef
3-1/2	cups water
1	can (28 ounces) diced tomatoes, undrained
1	can (10-1/2 ounces) condensed French onion soup, undiluted
1	package (9 ounces) frozen cut green beans
1	package (9 ounces) refrigerated cheese tortellini
1	medium zucchini, chopped
1	teaspoon dried basil

▢ In a large saucepan, cook beef over medium heat until no longer pink; drain. Add the remaining ingredients; bring to a boil. Cook, uncovered, for 7-9 minutes or until tortellini is tender.

Yield: 6-8 servings.

NUTRITION FACTS: 1 serving equals 241 calories, 9 g fat (4 g saturated fat), 43 mg cholesterol, 608 mg sodium, 25 g carbohydrate, 4 g fiber, 16 g protein.

hot dog potato soup

(pictured at left)

To vary this yummy soup, you can use leftover meatballs instead of hot dogs and leftover corn in place of frozen. It also works with any cheese blend you have on hand.
JEANNIE KLUGH LANCASTER, PENNSYLVANIA

- 2 cans (18.8 ounces each) ready-to-serve chunky baked potato with cheddar and bacon bits soup
- 4 hot dogs, halved lengthwise and sliced
- 1 cup (4 ounces) shredded cheddar-Monterey Jack cheese
- 1 cup frozen corn
- 1 cup milk

▦ In a large microwave-safe bowl, combine all the ingredients. Cover and microwave soup on high for 8-10 minutes or until heated through, stirring soup every 2 minutes.

Yield: 5 servings.

NUTRITION FACTS: 1-1/3 cups equals 400 calories, 26 g fat (13 g saturated fat), 57 mg cholesterol, 1,301 mg sodium, 29 g carbohydrate, 2 g fiber, 15 g protein.

EDITOR'S NOTE: This recipe was tested in a 1,100-watt microwave oven.

buffalo chicken wing soup

My husband and I love buffalo chicken wings, so we created a soup with the same zippy flavor. It's very popular with guests. Start with a small amount of hot sauce, then add more if needed to suit your family's preferences.
PAT FARMER FALCONER, NEW YORK

- 6 cups 2% milk
- 3 cans (10-3/4 ounces each) condensed cream of chicken soup, undiluted
- 3 cups shredded cooked chicken (about 1 pound)
- 1 cup (8 ounces) sour cream
- 1/4 to 1/2 cup Louisiana-style hot sauce

▦ Combine all ingredients in a 5-qt. slow cooker. Cover and cook on low for 4-5 hours or until heated through.

Yield: 8 servings (2 quarts).

NUTRITION FACTS: 1 cup equals 311 calories, 17 g fat (9 g saturated fat), 97 mg cholesterol, 486 mg sodium, 12 g carbohydrate, trace fiber, 24 g protein.

fiesta chicken chowder

A restaurant-style soup that starts with cans? It's possible with this creamy, comforting dish.
DANA ROOD OREANA, ILLINOIS

- 2 cans (10-3/4 ounces each) condensed cream of potato soup, undiluted
- 2 cans (10-3/4 ounces each) condensed cream of chicken soup, undiluted
- 2 cups 2% milk
- 1 can (14-1/2 ounces) reduced-sodium chicken broth
- 1 can (11 ounces) Mexicorn, drained
- 1 package (9 ounces) ready-to-serve roasted chicken breast strips, chopped
- 1 can (4 ounces) chopped green chilies
- 3 flour tortillas (8 inches), cut into 2-inch x 1/2-inch strips
- 1 cup (4 ounces) shredded cheddar cheese
Additional shredded cheddar cheese, optional

▦ In a large saucepan, combine the soups, milk and broth. Heat through, stirring frequently. Add the corn, chicken and chilies; bring to a boil. Stir in tortilla strips. Reduce heat; simmer, uncovered, for 5 minutes. Stir in cheese until melted. Sprinkle each serving with additional cheese if desired.

Yield: 10 servings (2-1/2 quarts).

NUTRITION FACTS: 1 cup (calculated without additional cheese) equals 280 calories, 11 g fat (5 g saturated fat), 42 mg cholesterol, 1,569 mg sodium, 30 g carbohydrate, 2 g fiber, 15 g protein.

zesty potato cheese soup

(pictured above)

I really prefer to make potato cheese soup from scratch. But one night we were in a hurry, so I added a few ingredients to a can of potato soup instead. It was so good that now I always keep a few cans on hand.
KAREN PIGMON CORNING, CALIFORNIA

- 3 cans (10-3/4 ounces each) condensed cream of potato soup, undiluted
- 2 cans (12 ounces each) evaporated milk
- 3/4 cup shredded cheddar cheese
- 3/4 cup pepper jack cheese
- 6 slices ready-to-serve fully cooked bacon, crumbled

▢ In a large saucepan, combine the potato soup and milk. Cook over medium heat for 5-7 minutes or until heated through. Ladle into serving bowls. Sprinkle with cheeses and bacon.

Yield: 6 servings.

NUTRITION FACTS: 1 cup equals 387 calories, 20 g fat (13 g saturated fat), 72 mg cholesterol, 1,113 mg sodium, 31 g carbohydrate, 3 g fiber, 18 g protein.

golden onion soup

Mozzarella cheese gives this savory onion soup extra richness. It's simple to make and a joy to eat.
SALVATORE BERTOLINO INDIANA, PENNSYLVANIA

- 1/2 cup butter, cubed
- 2 cups thinly sliced onions, quartered
- 1/4 cup all-purpose flour
- 2 cups chicken broth
- 2 cups milk
- 2 cups (8 ounces) shredded mozzarella cheese

▢ In a saucepan over medium-low heat, melt butter. Add onions; cook and stir until tender. Stir in flour until blended. Add broth and milk. Bring to a boil over medium heat, stirring constantly; cook and stir soup for 1 minute.

▢ Reduce heat. Add cheese; heat just until cheese is melted (do not boil).

Yield: 6 servings.

NUTRITION FACTS: 1 cup equals 334 calories, 26 g fat (16 g saturated fat), 79 mg cholesterol, 702 mg sodium, 12 g carbohydrate, 1 g fiber, 12 g protein.

chicken wild rice soup

Because this warming soup uses several convenience items, it's quick to make. It's perfect for casual entertaining, because you can keep it warm in a slow cooker. Whenever I make it, the crock is always scraped clean.
GAYLE HOLDMAN HIGHLAND, UTAH

5-2/3	cups water
1	package (4.3 ounces) long grain and wild rice mix
1	envelope chicken noodle soup mix
1	celery rib, chopped
1	medium carrot, chopped
1/3	cup chopped onion
2	cans (10-3/4 ounces each) condensed cream of chicken soup, undiluted
1	cup cubed cooked chicken

▢ In a large saucepan, combine water, rice with contents of seasoning packet, and soup mix. Bring to a boil. Reduce heat; cover and simmer for 10 minutes. Stir in the celery, carrot and onion.

▢ Cover and simmer for 10 minutes. Stir in chicken soup and chicken. Cook 8 minutes longer or until rice and vegetables are tender.

Yield: 5 servings.

NUTRITION FACTS: 1 cup equals 242 calories, 6 g fat (2 g saturated fat), 33 mg cholesterol, 1,239 mg sodium, 32 g carbohydrate, 2 g fiber, 14 g protein.

lemon chicken soup

For years, I made Greek chicken soup from scratch. My daughter created this super-simple version that her family can enjoy whenever time is short. Lemon juice gives it a bright, fresh flavor.
JOAN FOTOPOULOS TURAH, MONTANA

1	can (11-1/2 ounces) condensed chicken with rice soup, undiluted
1	can (10-3/4 ounces) condensed cream of chicken soup, undiluted
2-1/4	cups water
1	cup diced cooked chicken, optional
1	to 2 tablespoons lemon juice

Pepper to taste
Minced fresh parsley, optional

▢ In a large saucepan, combine soups and water; cook until heated through. Add the chicken if desired. Stir in lemon juice and pepper. Garnish with parsley if desired.

Yield: 4-5 servings.

NUTRITION FACTS: 1 cup equals 91 calories, 5 g fat (2 g saturated fat), 8 mg cholesterol, 949 mg sodium, 9 g carbohydrate, 1 g fiber, 3 g protein.

jazzed-up clam chowder

(pictured at left)

No one ever guesses that my dressed-up and delicious chowder came from cans! It takes only 10 minutes.
JOSEPHINE PIRO EASTON, PENNSYLVANIA

- 1 can (19 ounces) chunky New England clam chowder
- 1 can (8-1/4 ounces) cream-style corn
- 2/3 cup 2% milk
- 2 tablespoons shredded cheddar cheese
- 2 tablespoons bacon bits
- 2 tablespoons minced chives

▢ In a 1-1/2-qt. microwave-safe dish, combine the clam chowder, corn and milk.

▢ Cover and microwave on high for 4-6 minutes or until heated through, stirring every 2 minutes. Sprinkle each serving with cheese, bacon and chives.

Yield: 4 servings.

NUTRITION FACTS: 1 cup equals 211 calories, 10 g fat (5 g saturated fat), 14 mg cholesterol, 780 mg sodium, 24 g carbohydrate, 2 g fiber, 8 g protein.

EDITOR'S NOTE: This recipe was tested in a 1,100-watt microwave oven.

kids' favorite hot dog stew

Everyone, especially children, will be thrilled with this hearty stew brimming with hot dogs and beans.
DOROTHY ERICKSON BLUE EYE, MISSOURI

- 1 package (14 ounces) reduced-fat beef hot dogs, sliced
- 1 can (11-1/2 ounces) condensed bean and bacon soup, undiluted
- 1 can (10-3/4 ounces) reduced-sodium condensed tomato soup, undiluted
- 1 can (15 ounces) pork and beans
- 1 teaspoon chili powder
- 1 teaspoon dried minced onion
- 1/4 teaspoon pepper
- 1/4 teaspoon liquid smoke
- 2/3 cup fat-free evaporated milk

▢ In a nonstick saucepan, brown hot dogs over medium heat. Add the next seven ingredients. Cover and cook over low heat until heated through. Stir in milk; heat through.

Yield: 6 servings.

NUTRITION FACTS: 1 cup equals 275 calories, 6 g fat (2 g saturated fat), 36 mg cholesterol, 1,605 mg sodium, 37 g carbohydrate, 7 g fiber, 20 g protein. **DIABETIC EXCHANGES:** 2-1/2 starch, 2 lean meat.

flavorful tomato soup

A cookbook recipe called for ingredients I didn't have on hand, so I improvised and came up with this. I often make it for friends at church, and I've shared the recipe many times.
JEAN SULLIVAN DENVER, COLORADO

- 1/4 cup finely chopped onion
- 1 tablespoon butter
- 1/4 teaspoon dried basil
- 1/4 teaspoon paprika
- 1/8 teaspoon garlic powder
- 1 can (10-3/4 ounces) condensed tomato soup, undiluted
- 1 cup 2% milk

▢ In a saucepan, saute onion in butter until tender. Add basil, paprika and garlic powder. Stir in soup and milk until well blended. Cook over medium heat for 6 minutes or until heated through.

Yield: 2 servings.

NUTRITION FACTS: 1 serving equals 233 calories, 8 g fat (5 g saturated fat), 24 mg cholesterol, 989 mg sodium, 33 g carbohydrate, 2 g fiber, 7 g protein.

cheesy wild rice soup

(pictured above)

We often turn to easily prepared soups when there's not a lot of time to cook. I replaced the wild rice in the original recipe with a boxed rice mix to make it even faster.

LISA HOFER HITCHCOCK, SOUTH DAKOTA

1	package (6.2 ounces) fast-cooking long grain and wild rice mix
4	cups 2% milk
1	can (10-3/4 ounces) condensed cream of potato soup, undiluted
8	ounces process cheese (Velveeta), cubed
1/2	pound bacon strips, cooked and crumbled

▢ In a large saucepan, prepare rice mix according to package directions. Add the milk, soup and cheese. Cook and stir until cheese is melted. Garnish with bacon.

Yield: 8 servings.

NUTRITION FACTS: 1 cup equals 464 calories, 29 g fat (14 g saturated fat), 70 mg cholesterol, 1,492 mg sodium, 29 g carbohydrate, 1 g fiber, 21 g protein.

venison chili

Here's a nicely seasoned venison chili that my friends really like. It's so simple to make.

GARY URNESS KENYON, MINNESOTA

1	pound boneless venison steak, cubed
1/2	cup chopped onion
2	tablespoons olive oil
1	can (15 ounces) chili without beans
1/2	cup water
1/2	teaspoon garlic powder
1/2	teaspoon celery salt

▢ In a large saucepan, cook venison and onion in oil until meat is browned. Stir in the remaining ingredients. Bring to a boil. Reduce heat; cover and simmer for 1 hour or until meat is tender.

Yield: 3-4 servings.

NUTRITION FACTS: 1 cup equals 292 calories, 13 g fat (3 g saturated fat), 112 mg cholesterol, 681 mg sodium, 10 g carbohydrate, 2 g fiber, 34 g protein.

mock chicken dumpling soup

A few additions to canned cream of chicken soup make for amazing comfort food. No one will guess that the dumplings are actually tortilla strips.
CAROLYN GRIFFIN MACON, GEORGIA

1	can (10-3/4 ounces) condensed cream of chicken soup, undiluted
4	cups water
2	cups cubed cooked chicken
4	flour tortillas (6 inches), cut into 2-1/2-inch strips

Minced fresh parsley, optional

 In a 3-qt. saucepan, bring the soup and water to a boil. Stir in chicken and tortilla strips; reduce heat to medium-low. Cook, uncovered, for 25-30 minutes, stirring occasionally. Sprinkle with parsley if desired.

Yield: 6 servings.

NUTRITION FACTS: 1 cup equals 149 calories, 2 g fat (0 saturated fat), 32 mg cholesterol, 426 mg sodium, 21 g carbohydrate, 0 fiber, 10 g protein. **DIABETIC EXCHANGES:** 1 starch, 1 lean meat.

favorite kielbasa bean soup

Here is a satisfying soup that we get hungry for often. Good kielbasa is plentiful in Nebraska, and it makes a wonderful base for this soup!
MARY E. CORDES OMAHA, NEBRASKA

2	cups water
1	medium potato, peeled and diced
2	medium carrots, peeled and sliced
1	medium onion, chopped
1/3	cup chopped celery
8	ounces smoked kielbasa, thinly sliced
1	can (11-1/2 ounces) condensed bean and bacon soup, undiluted

Minced fresh parsley, optional

In a large saucepan, bring water and vegetables to a boil. Cover and simmer for 10-15 minutes or until vegetables are tender. Add kielbasa and soup; heat through. Sprinkle with parsley if desired.

Yield: 6 servings.

NUTRITION FACTS: 1 cup equals 234 calories, 12 g fat (5 g saturated fat), 27 mg cholesterol, 799 mg sodium, 21 g carbohydrate, 5 g fiber, 9 g protein.

quick cauliflower soup

My aunt always made her rich-tasting cauliflower soup whenever I came to visit. I could smell it simmering as soon as I arrived. Now I think of her whenever I have a bowlful.
HEATHER KASPRICK KEEWATIN, ONTARIO

1	medium head cauliflower, cut into florets
2	cans (10-3/4 ounces each) condensed cream of chicken soup, undiluted
1	can (10-3/4 ounces) condensed cheddar cheese soup, undiluted
1	can (14-1/2 ounces) chicken broth
2	cups milk

Place cauliflower in a saucepan with 1 in. of water; bring to a boil. Reduce heat; cover and simmer for 5-10 minutes or until crisp-tender.

Meanwhile, in another saucepan, combine soups, broth and milk; heat through. Drain the cauliflower; stir into soup.

Yield: 9 servings.

NUTRITION FACTS: 1 cup equals 107 calories, 6 g fat (3 g saturated fat), 14 mg cholesterol, 749 mg sodium, 11 g carbohydrate, 2 g fiber, 5 g protein.

broccoli cheese soup

I've been making this dish since a friend gave me the recipe years ago. No one can believe how fast and easy it is to prepare. It often comes to the rescue when our children and grandchildren unexpectedly stop in for lunch.
JANIS CORKERY INDEPENDENCE, IOWA

2	cans (10-3/4 ounces each) condensed cheddar cheese soup, undiluted
3	cups milk
3	cups frozen chopped broccoli
1	cup frozen O'Brien potatoes, thawed
1/2	teaspoon salt

▨ In a large saucepan, combine all ingredients. Bring to a boil. Reduce heat; simmer, uncovered, for 5 minutes or until heated through.

Yield: 7 servings.

NUTRITION FACTS: 1 cup equals 127 calories, 6 g fat (3 g saturated fat), 19 mg cholesterol, 572 mg sodium, 15 g carbohydrate, 2 g fiber, 6 g protein.

mom's monday lunch potato soup

I love making this soup for friends who visit for lunch. It's a great way to use up Sunday's mashed potatoes.
EVELYN BONAR PENSACOLA, FLORIDA

8	bacon strips, diced
1	small onion, chopped
1-1/2	cups leftover mashed potatoes
1	can (10-3/4 ounces) condensed cream of chicken soup, undiluted
2	cups milk
1/2	teaspoon salt, optional
1/8	teaspoon pepper
2	tablespoons chopped fresh parsley

▨ In a 3-qt. saucepan, cook bacon over medium heat until crisp. Remove to paper towels with a slotted spoon; drain, reserving 2 tablespoons drippings. Saute onion in drippings until tender. Add potatoes and soup; stir until blended. Gradually stir in milk. Cook and stir over medium heat until heated through.

▨ Stir in bacon, salt if desired and pepper. Sprinkle with parsley.

Yield: 3-4 servings.

NUTRITION FACTS: 1 cup (calculated without salt) equals 514 calories, 33 g fat (13 g saturated fat), 67 mg cholesterol, 1,538 mg sodium, 36 g carbohydrate, 4 g fiber, 17 g protein.

pantry-shelf salmon chowder

I always joke that if you can open a can, you can prepare this hearty chowder! It takes mere minutes to make, but people will think you fussed a lot longer.
KATHRYN AWE INTERNATIONAL FALLS, MINNESOTA

1	small onion, thinly sliced
1	tablespoon butter
1	can (10-3/4 ounces) condensed cream of celery soup, undiluted
1-1/3	cups milk
1	can (15 ounces) cream-style corn
1	can (7-1/2 ounces) salmon, drained, bones and skin removed
1	tablespoon minced fresh parsley

▨ In a large saucepan, saute onion in butter until tender. Stir in the soup, milk and corn; bring to a boil. Reduce heat; add salmon and parsley. Simmer, uncovered, until heated through.

Yield: 4 servings.

NUTRITION FACTS: 1 cup equals 295 calories, 13 g fat (6 g saturated fat), 45 mg cholesterol, 1,212 mg sodium, 31 g carbohydrate, 2 g fiber, 17 g protein.

soup & sandwich

Here's an irresistible take on Mexican comfort food: **Chiles Rellenos** are toasted up in a rich sandwich. **Vegetarian Chili** makes it a meal so satisfying, no one will miss the meat!

vegetarian chili

Hominy, green chilies and chickpeas are deliciously different additions to my chili. You don't have to be a vegetarian to savor this hearty recipe.
KAREN HUNT BELLVUE, COLORADO

- 2 cans (15 ounces each) pinto beans, rinsed and drained
- 1 can (28 ounces) crushed tomatoes
- 1 can (16 ounces) kidney beans, rinsed and drained
- 1 can (15-1/2 ounces) hominy, rinsed and drained
- 1 can (15 ounces) garbanzo beans or chickpeas, rinsed and drained
- 1 can (6 ounces) tomato paste
- 1 can (4 ounces) chopped green chilies, undrained
- 2 small zucchini, halved and thinly sliced
- 1 medium onion, chopped
- 1-1/2 to 2 cups water
- 1 to 2 tablespoons chili powder
- 1 teaspoon ground cumin
- 1 teaspoon salt, optional
- 1/2 teaspoon garlic powder
- 1/2 teaspoon sugar
- 1/2 cup shredded Monterey Jack cheese

▢ In a Dutch oven, combine the first 15 ingredients. Bring to a boil. Reduce heat; cover and simmer for 30-35 minutes or until vegetables are tender. Sprinkle with cheese.

Yield: 12 servings (about 3 quarts).

NUTRITION FACTS: 1 cup equals 210 calories, 3 g fat (1 g saturated fat), 4 mg cholesterol, 524 mg sodium, 37 g carbohydrate, 9 g fiber, 11 g protein. **DIABETIC EXCHANGES:** 2 vegetable, 1-1/2 starch, 1 lean meat.

chiles rellenos sandwiches

Since I retired over 30 years ago, I don't cook as much as I used to. But I still love to make these zesty sandwiches.
GLADYS HILL QUILIN, MISSOURI

- 1 can (4 ounces) chopped green chiles, drained
- 6 slices bread
- 3 slices Monterey Jack cheese
- 2 eggs
- 1 cup milk
- 2 to 4 tablespoons butter

Salsa, optional

▢ Mash chilies with a fork; spread on three slices of bread. Top with cheese and remaining bread. In a shallow bowl, beat eggs and milk; dip the sandwiches.

▢ Melt 2 tablespoons of butter in a large skillet. Cook sandwiches until golden brown on both sides and cheese is melted, adding additional butter if necessary. Serve with salsa if desired.

Yield: 3 servings.

NUTRITION FACTS: 1 sandwich equals 388 calories, 22 g fat (12 g saturated fat), 194 mg cholesterol, 713 mg sodium, 31 g carbohydrate, 2 g fiber, 16 g protein.

portobello-gouda grilled cheese

Take a simple grilled cheese sandwich to the next level with the earthy, rustic flavors of portobello mushrooms and Gouda cheese.

SHERYL BERGMAN SHADY SIDE, MARYLAND

- 1   cup sliced baby portobello mushrooms
- 1   tablespoon plus 4 teaspoons butter, divided
- 4   ounces smoked Gouda cheese, sliced
- 4   slices rye bread
- 1   plum tomato, sliced

In a large skillet, saute mushrooms in 1 tablespoon butter until tender. Place cheese on two bread slices; top with mushrooms, tomato and remaining bread. Spread outsides of sandwiches with remaining butter.

In a small skillet over medium heat, toast sandwiches for 2-3 minutes on each side or until cheese is melted.

Yield: 2 servings.

NUTRITION FACTS: 1 sandwich equals 498 calories, 31 g fat (19 g saturated fat), 100 mg cholesterol, 984 mg sodium, 35 g carbohydrate, 5 g fiber, 21 g protein.

tomato bisque

This bisque is the perfect antidote to cool weather. I love to serve it with a slice of homemade bread.

B.B. MALLORY IRVING, TEXAS

- 2   cans (14-1/2 ounces each) diced tomatoes, undrained
- 2   teaspoons beef bouillon granules
- 1   tablespoon sugar
- 1   to 2 teaspoons salt
- 1   teaspoon onion powder
- 1   bay leaf
- 1/4 teaspoon dried basil
- 1/4 teaspoon white pepper
- 1/2 cup butter, cubed
- 1/3 cup all-purpose flour
- 4   cups milk

In a saucepan, combine the first eight ingredients; bring to a boil. Reduce heat; simmer, uncovered, for 30 minutes.

Discard bay leaf; press mixture through sieve and set aside. In a large saucepan, melt butter; stir in flour until smooth. Gradually stir in milk. Bring to a boil over medium heat, stirring constantly; cook and stir for 2 minutes. Reduce heat. Gradually stir in tomato mixture until smooth; heat through.

Yield: 8 servings (2 quarts).

NUTRITION FACTS: 1 cup equals 171 calories, 12 g fat (8 g saturated fat), 38 mg cholesterol, 624 mg sodium, 11 g carbohydrate, trace fiber, 4 g protein.

Crispy, cool **Cucumber-Egg Salad Sandwiches** and chilled **So-Easy Gazpacho** make the perfect summertime meal: garden-fresh and almost no cooking required!

so-easy gazpacho

My daughter got this recipe from a college friend and shared it with me. Now I serve it often as an appetizer. It certainly is the talk of the party.

LORNA SIRTOLI CORTLAND, NEW YORK

2	cups tomato juice
4	medium tomatoes, peeled and finely chopped
1/2	cup chopped seeded peeled cucumber
1/3	cup finely chopped onion
1/4	cup olive oil
1/4	cup cider vinegar
1	teaspoon sugar
1	garlic clove, minced
1/4	teaspoon salt
1/4	teaspoon pepper

▨ In a large bowl, combine all ingredients. Cover and refrigerate for at least 4 hours or until chilled.

Yield: 5 servings.

NUTRITION FACTS: 1 cup equals 146 calories, 11 g fat (2 g saturated fat), 0 cholesterol, 387 mg sodium, 11 g carbohydrate, 2 g fiber, 2 g protein.

cucumber-egg salad sandwiches

Cucumber adds a summery crunch to these tasty egg sandwiches. I sometimes substitute rye bread for sourdough and add chopped celery to the salad.

KELLY MCCUNE WESTERVILLE, OHIO

1/2	cup chopped red onion
1/2	cup mayonnaise
1/4	cup sour cream
2	tablespoons Dijon mustard
1/2	teaspoon pepper
1/4	teaspoon salt
8	hard-cooked eggs, chopped
1	large cucumber, sliced
1	tablespoon dill weed
12	slices sourdough bread, toasted

▨ In a small bowl, combine the first six ingredients. Add eggs; stir gently to combine. In another bowl, toss cucumber and dill. Spread egg salad over six slices of toast; top with cucumbers and remaining toast.

Yield: 6 servings.

NUTRITION FACTS: 1 sandwich equals 458 calories, 25 g fat (6 g saturated fat), 296 mg cholesterol, 823 mg sodium, 41 g carbohydrate, 2 g fiber, 17 g protein.

International intrigue! **French Market Sandwiches** and **Curried Pumpkin Apple Soup** create an upscale, adventurous meal. A hint of curry in the sandwiches brings the pairing together.

curried pumpkin apple soup

Sweet apples and spicy curry combine in this rich soup, which is perfect for fall. A small serving is all you need to satisfy.
JANE SHAPTON IRVINE, CALIFORNIA

2	medium apples, peeled and chopped
1	medium onion, chopped
1	medium leek (white portion only), sliced
2	tablespoons butter
3	garlic cloves, minced
2	to 3 teaspoons curry powder
1	can (15 ounces) solid-pack pumpkin
4	cups chicken broth
1	cup heavy whipping cream

Salt to taste

In a large saucepan, saute the apples, onion and leek in butter until tender. Add garlic and curry; cook 1 minute longer. Add pumpkin and broth; bring to a boil. Reduce heat; cover and simmer for 20 minutes. Stir in cream; heat through (do not boil).

Remove from the heat; cool slightly. In a blender, process soup in batches until smooth. Season with salt.

Yield: 8 servings (2 quarts).

NUTRITION FACTS: 1 cup equals 187 calories, 15 g fat (9 g saturated fat), 48 mg cholesterol, 511 mg sodium, 13 g carbohydrate, 4 g fiber, 3 g protein.

french market sandwiches

I first tasted these sandwiches at a luncheon, and they quickly became a favorite. I keep some in the freezer for fast meals. My bridge club enjoys them with soup and fresh fruit.
FLORENCE MCNULTY MONTEBELLO, CALIFORNIA

1/2	cup butter, softened
1/2	cup Dijon mustard
2	tablespoons chopped green onions
1/2	teaspoon poppy seeds
1/4	teaspoon curry powder
10	croissants, split
1-1/4	pounds thinly sliced deli ham
10	slices Swiss cheese

In a small bowl, combine the butter, mustard, onions, poppy seeds and curry powder. Spread over cut sides of croissants. Place a slice of ham and cheese on each croissant; replace tops. Wrap individually in foil. Bake at 325° for 15-20 minutes or until heated through.

Yield: 10 servings.

NUTRITION FACTS: 1 sandwich equals 476 calories, 30 g fat (18 g saturated fat), 108 mg cholesterol, 1,303 mg sodium, 31 g carbohydrate, 2 g fiber, 21 g protein.

chicken bagel melts

I love experimenting with sandwiches, and my wonderful husband is often my guinea pig when I try something new. Here's a great way to use up leftover chicken. It's a little on the spicy side, but not too much.

SHANNON BROWN OMAHA, NEBRASKA

1/2	cup mayonnaise
4	Asiago cheese bagels, split
1/2	pound sliced rotisserie chicken
8	strips ready-to-serve fully cooked bacon
1/2	medium sweet red pepper, sliced
4	slices cheddar cheese
1/4	cup chipotle mustard

▢ Spread mayonnaise over bagel bottoms; layer with chicken, bacon, red pepper and cheese. Place on an ungreased baking sheet.

▢ Broil 2-4 in. from the heat for 2-3 minutes or until cheese is melted. Spread mustard over bagel tops; place over cheese. Serve immediately.

Yield: 4 servings.

NUTRITION FACTS: 1 sandwich equals 838 calories, 45 g fat (15 g saturated fat), 100 mg cholesterol, 1,332 mg sodium, 61 g carbohydrate, 2 g fiber, 43 g protein.

classic cream of asparagus soup

I developed this recipe myself by substituting asparagus for broccoli in cream of broccoli soup. It's a big favorite at our house!

WESTELLE GRISWA MONROE, CONNECTICUT

4	cups fresh asparagus, trimmed and cut in 1/2-inch pieces
2	cups water, divided
1/4	cup finely chopped green onions or 1 teaspoon onion powder
5	tablespoons butter, cubed
5	tablespoons all-purpose flour
1/2	to 1 teaspoon salt
1/4	teaspoon white pepper
4	cups milk
1	tablespoon chicken bouillon granules

▢ Place asparagus in a large saucepan and cover with 1 cup water. Bring to a boil, cover and cook for 3-5 minutes or until crisp-tender. Drain, reserving liquid.

▢ In another saucepan, saute onions in butter until tender. Stir in the flour, salt and pepper until blended. Gradually stir in the milk, bouillon, reserved cooking liquid and remaining water. Bring to a boil. Cook and stir for 2 minutes or until thickened and bubbly. Stir in asparagus; heat through.

Yield: 6 servings.

NUTRITION FACTS: 1 cup equals 232 calories, 15 g fat (9 g saturated fat), 48 mg cholesterol, 795 mg sodium, 17 g carbohydrate, 2 g fiber, 8 g protein.

You'll find Chinese, Thai and even Vietnamese influences in this party-perfect menu. Use chicken patties in the **Asian Meatless Wraps** if you prefer. Arrange garnishes for **Red Curry Carrot Soup** on a beautiful platter for all to share.

asian meatless wraps

This recipe, an impromptu creation on a busy weeknight, turned out so well that my husband never knew it wasn't "real" chicken! Good for vegetarian friends.
HEIDI HEIMGARTNER BLOOMING PRAIRIE, MINNESOTA

4	frozen vegetarian chicken patties
1	cup coleslaw mix
1/3	cup Asian toasted sesame salad dressing
4	flour tortillas (10 inches), warmed
1/2	cup chow mein noodles
1/4	cup sliced almonds

▢ Microwave patties according to the package directions. Meanwhile, combine coleslaw mix and dressing; set aside.

▢ Cut patties in half; place two halves off center on each tortilla; top with 3 tablespoons coleslaw mixture, 2 tablespoons chow mein noodles and 1 tablespoon almonds. Fold sides and ends over filling and roll up.

Yield: 4 servings.

NUTRITION FACTS: 1 wrap equals 491 calories, 19 g fat (3 g saturated fat), 0 cholesterol, 1,202 mg sodium, 58 g carbohydrate, 9 g fiber, 17 g protein.

EDITOR'S NOTE: This recipe was tested in a 1,100-watt microwave.

red curry carrot soup

With its mix of delicious colors, textures and tastes, this easy soup is something special. The meatballs make it substantial enough to serve as a light entree.
DILNAZ HECKMAN BUCKLEY, WASHINGTON

5	packages (3 ounces each) ramen noodles
3	garlic cloves, minced
2	tablespoons peanut oil
1	can (13.66 ounces) coconut milk, divided
2	tablespoons red curry paste
1-1/2	teaspoons curry powder
1/2	teaspoon ground turmeric
32	frozen fully cooked homestyle meatballs (1/2 ounce each)
4	cups chicken broth
1	medium zucchini, finely chopped
1	medium carrot, halved and sliced
1/4	cup shredded cabbage
2	teaspoons fish or soy sauce

Optional garnishes: bean sprouts, chow mein noodles, chopped fresh basil and green onions

▢ Cook noodles according to package directions (discard seasoning packets or save for another use).

▢ Meanwhile, in a Dutch oven, saute garlic in oil for 1 minute. Spoon 1/2 cup cream from top of coconut milk and place in the pan. Add the curry paste, curry powder and turmeric; cook and stir for 5 minutes or until oil separates from coconut milk mixture.

▢ Stir in the meatballs, broth, zucchini, carrot, cabbage, fish sauce and remaining coconut milk. Bring to a boil. Reduce heat; simmer, uncovered, for 15-20 minutes or until carrot is tender and meatballs are heated through. Drain noodles; stir into soup.

▢ Garnish with bean sprouts, chow mein noodles, basil and onions if desired.

Yield: 8 servings (2-1/2 quarts).

NUTRITION FACTS: 1-1/4 cups (calculated without optional garnishes) equals 572 calories, 38 g fat (22 g saturated fat), 26 mg cholesterol, 1,204 mg sodium, 43 g carbohydrate, 3 g fiber, 15 g protein.

EDITOR'S NOTE: This recipe was tested with regular (full-fat) coconut milk. Light coconut milk contains less cream.

Quick and nutritious is the name of the game with this family-friendly pairing. Kids of all ages love **Pizza Joes**, and veggie-packed **Microwave Minestrone** practically cooks itself! Use a food processor to shave prep time.

pizza joes

These Italian-style sloppy joes are just great! They can be prepared and held until everyone's ready and all set to eat.
JOANNE SCHLABACH SHREVE, OHIO

1	pound lean ground beef (90% lean)
1	can (15 ounces) pizza sauce
1	teaspoon dried oregano
1/2	medium onion
1/2	medium green pepper
1	ounce sliced pepperoni
6	hamburger buns, split
1/2	cup shredded mozzarella cheese
1/2	cup sliced fresh mushrooms

☐ In a large skillet, brown ground beef until no pink remains; drain. Stir in pizza sauce and oregano.

☐ In a food processor, combine the onion, pepper, pepperoni; cover and process until chopped. Add to beef mixture. Simmer 20-25 minutes or until vegetables are tender. Spoon mixture onto buns. Top with cheese and mushrooms.

Yield: 6 servings.

NUTRITION FACTS: 1 sandwich equals 320 calories, 12 g fat (5 g saturated fat), 57 mg cholesterol, 594 mg sodium, 29 g carbohydrate, 3 g fiber, 22 g protein.

microwave minestrone

Next time you make pasta, cook up a little extra so you have some on hand for this flavorful soup. By the time I set the table, it's ready. What a great way to get your veggies!
EMMA MAGIELDA AMSTERDAM, NEW YORK

1	cup each sliced carrots, celery and zucchini
1/2	cup diced sweet yellow pepper
1	small onion, chopped
1	tablespoon olive oil
1	can (15 ounces) cannellini or white kidney beans, rinsed and drained
1	can (14-1/2 ounces) beef broth
1	can (14-1/2 ounces) diced tomatoes, undrained
1	cup medium pasta shells, cooked and drained
1/2	to 1 teaspoon dried basil
1/2	teaspoon salt
1/4	teaspoon pepper

☐ Place carrots, celery, zucchini, yellow pepper and onion in a microwave-safe bowl. Drizzle with oil; toss to coat. Cover and microwave on high for 3 minutes. Stir in the remaining ingredients. Cover and cook on high for 9-11 minutes or until vegetables are tender.

Yield: 5 servings.

NUTRITION FACTS: 1 cup equals 220 calories, 4 g fat (1 g saturated fat), 0 cholesterol, 765 mg sodium, 39 g carbohydrate, 7 g fiber, 9 g protein.

EDITOR'S NOTE: This recipe was tested in a 1,100-watt microwave.

Rich and velvety **Chill-Chasing Cheese Soup** is perfect for holiday entertaining, especially when paired with irresistible **BBQ Ham Sliders**. They're so sweet, tangy and little, no one will want to stop at just one! Kids will love 'em.

bbq ham sliders

These flavorful sandwiches make a perfect mini snack or appetizer. Your guests will adore them!
SUSANNE ROUPE EAST FAIRFIELD, VERMONT

1	cup chili sauce
1/2	cup water
2	tablespoons sugar
2	tablespoons cider vinegar
1	tablespoon Worcestershire sauce
1	teaspoon onion powder
1	pound fully cooked ham, very thinly sliced
24	dinner rolls, split

▢ In a large saucepan, combine the first six ingredients. Bring to a boil. Reduce heat; simmer, uncovered, for 6-8 minutes or until slightly thickened. Stir in ham; heat through. Serve on rolls.

Yield: 2 dozen.

NUTRITION FACTS: 1 slider equals 143 calories, 3 g fat (1 g saturated fat), 24 mg cholesterol, 513 mg sodium, 23 g carbohydrate, 1 g fiber, 7 g protein.

chill-chasing cheese soup

Here's a creative twist on cheese soup that uses veggies and chicken broth. It tastes a bit lighter than most cheese soups, and is great for entertaining.
SHARON DELANEY-CHRONIS
SOUTH MILWAUKEE, WISCONSIN

4	medium carrots, chopped
2	celery ribs, chopped
1	large onion, chopped
1	medium green pepper, chopped
1/2	cup butter
3/4	cup all-purpose flour
1	teaspoon salt
3	quarts 2% milk
1-1/3	cups reduced-sodium chicken broth
1	package (8 ounces) process cheese (Velveeta), cubed
1-1/2	cups (6 ounces) shredded cheddar cheese

▢ In a Dutch oven, saute the carrots, celery, onion and green pepper in butter until tender. Stir in flour and salt until blended; gradually add milk and broth. Bring to a boil; cook and stir for 2 minutes or until thickened. Reduce heat to low; stir in cheeses until melted.

Yield: 12 servings (3 quarts).

NUTRITION FACTS: 1 cup equals 349 calories, 21 g fat (14 g saturated fat), 68 mg cholesterol, 783 mg sodium, 24 g carbohydrate, 1 g fiber, 16 g protein.

Cold-weather comfort abounds with **Easy Tortellini Soup** and melty, delicious **Hot Antipasto Sandwiches**. Since each recipe serves eight, this pair is perfect for holiday entertaining or game night! Men will really go for the rich, satisfying flavors.

easy tortellini soup

You can pick up everything for this hearty soup at the supermarket on the way home, then put it together in minutes. It's perfect for company and is actually quite easy. Pureed roasted peppers make the broth extra rich.

GILDA LESTER MILLSBORO, DELAWARE

1/2	pound sliced fresh mushrooms
2	teaspoons olive oil
4-1/2	cups water
1	can (14-1/2 ounces) no-salt-added diced tomatoes, undrained
3	tablespoons grated Romano cheese
5	teaspoons sodium-free chicken bouillon granules
1	tablespoon prepared pesto
1	jar (7 ounces) roasted sweet red peppers, drained
1	package (9 ounces) refrigerated cheese tortellini

GARNISH:

8	thin slices prosciutto or deli ham
8	teaspoons grated Romano cheese

▢ In a Dutch oven, saute mushrooms in oil until tender. Add the water, tomatoes, cheese, bouillon and pesto.

▢ Place peppers in a food processor; cover and process until blended. Add to mushroom mixture and bring to a boil. Reduce heat; cover and simmer for 10 minutes.

▢ Stir in the tortellini; return to a boil. Cook for 7-9 minutes or until tender, stirring occasionally. Cut prosciutto into thin strips; garnish each serving with prosciutto and cheese.

Yield: 8 servings (2 quarts).

NUTRITION FACTS: 1 cup equals 201 calories, 8 g fat (3 g saturated fat), 32 mg cholesterol, 609 mg sodium, 20 g carbohydrate, 2 g fiber, 12 g protein. **DIABETIC EXCHANGES:** 1 starch, 1 medium-fat meat, 1 vegetable.

hot antipasto sandwiches

I usually make this popular dish as an appetizer for holiday get-togethers. But I also like to serve it with salad as a satisfying meal.

LISA BERRY FAYETTEVILLE, WEST VIRGINIA

2	tubes (8 ounces each) refrigerated crescent rolls
1/4	pound each sliced deli ham, pepperoni and hard salami
1/4	pound sliced provolone cheese
2	eggs
Dash pepper	
1	jar (7 ounces) roasted sweet red peppers, drained, patted dry and chopped
2	tablespoons grated Parmesan cheese
1	egg yolk, lightly beaten

▢ Unroll crescent roll dough into two rectangles; seal seams and perforations. Press one rectangle onto the bottom and 3/4 in. up the sides of a greased 13-in. x 9-in. baking dish. Layer with meats and provolone cheese.

▢ Whisk eggs and pepper; pour over cheese. Top with roasted peppers and Parmesan cheese. Place remaining crescent dough rectangle over the top; pinch edges to seal. Brush with egg yolk.

▢ Cover and bake at 350° for 30 minutes. Uncover; bake 15-20 minutes longer or until golden brown. Cut into eight triangles; serve warm.

Yield: 8 servings.

NUTRITION FACTS: 1 sandwich equals 450 calories, 30 g fat (11 g saturated fat), 123 mg cholesterol, 1,420 mg sodium, 24 g carbohydrate, trace fiber, 19 g protein.

Make the pizza lovers in your house cheer! So-easy **Pizza Soup** and fun **Pepperoni Quesadillas** will hit the spot after a day of ice skating or playing in the snow.

12	slices pepperoni
1/4	cup shredded Parmesan cheese
1/2	teaspoon dried oregano

▢ In a small saucepan, cook spaghetti sauce over medium-low heat for 3-4 minutes or until heated through.

▢ Meanwhile, spread butter over one side of each tortilla. Sprinkle unbuttered side of two tortillas with mozzarella cheese; top with salami and pepperoni. Sprinkle with Parmesan cheese and oregano. Top with remaining tortillas, buttered side up.

▢ Cook on a griddle over medium heat for 2-3 minutes on each side or until cheese is melted. Cut into wedges; serve with warmed spaghetti sauce.

Yield: 2 servings.

NUTRITION FACTS: 1 quesadilla equals 887 calories, 39 g fat (18 g saturated fat), 95 mg cholesterol, 2,732 mg sodium, 76 g carbohydrate, 14 g fiber, 43 g protein.

pizza soup

This family favorite is ready in no time at all. I like to serve it with garlic bread, and I'll sometimes use bacon or salami instead of pepperoni (just like a pizza!).
JANET BELDMAN LONDON, ONTARIO

1	pound ground beef
1	small onion, chopped
1	cup sliced fresh mushrooms
1	medium green pepper, cut into strips
1	can (28 ounces) diced tomatoes, undrained
1	cup beef broth
1	cup sliced pepperoni
1	teaspoon dried basil

Shredded mozzarella cheese

▢ In a large saucepan, cook the beef, onion, mushrooms and green pepper over medium heat until meat is no longer pink and vegetables are almost tender; drain. Stir in the tomatoes, broth, pepperoni and basil; heat through. Sprinkle with cheese.

Yield: 6 servings.

NUTRITION FACTS: 1 cup equals 245 calories, 15 g fat (6 g saturated fat), 59 mg cholesterol, 621 mg sodium, 9 g carbohydrate, 3 g fiber, 18 g protein.

pepperoni quesadillas

When my husband and I needed a quick meal, I came up with this recipe using what I had on hand. Unlike traditional quesadillas, these use Italian meats, cheeses and seasoning.
BARBARA RUPERT EDGEFIELD, SOUTH CAROLINA

1	cup meatless spaghetti sauce
2	teaspoons butter, softened
4	flour tortillas (10 inches)
1	cup (4 ounces) shredded part-skim mozzarella cheese
8	thin slices hard salami

Rich and creamy **Quick Clam Chowder** is so easy, you can enjoy it anytime. **Spinach Po' Boy** is a contemporary take on a coastal favorite. Here is an excellent Friday night dinner!

spinach po' boy

I like to make this warm and cheesy sandwich for a simple dinner, served with fresh fruit on the side.
JAN BRIGGS GREENFIELD, WISCONSIN

1	loaf (8 ounces) French bread, split
1/2	cup butter, divided
1/3	cup chopped green onions
6	cups fresh spinach, coarsely chopped
1/2	teaspoon garlic powder
1/8	teaspoon hot pepper sauce
1/2	cup shredded sharp cheddar cheese
1/2	cup shredded mozzarella cheese

▣ Spread bread with half of the butter; set aside. In a skillet, cook onions in remaining butter over medium heat until tender. Add spinach, garlic powder and pepper sauce; cook and stir until spinach is tender.

▣ Spread mixture over bread bottom; top with cheeses. Replace bread top. Wrap in foil; place on a pan. Bake at 375° for 20 minutes. Open foil; bake 5 minutes longer.

Yield: 6 servings.

NUTRITION FACTS: 1 serving equals 314 calories, 21 g fat (13 g saturated fat), 58 mg cholesterol, 494 mg sodium, 24 g carbohydrate, 2 g fiber, 10 g protein.

quick clam chowder

Not only is this soup a quick fix, but it's oh-so-tasty! Enjoy the comfort of clam chowder with a fraction of the work.
JUDY JUNGWIRTH ATHOL, SOUTH DAKOTA

1	can (10-3/4 ounces) condensed cream of celery soup, undiluted
1	can (10-3/4 ounces) condensed cream of potato soup, undiluted
2	cups half-and-half cream
2	cans (6-1/2 ounces each) minced/chopped clams, drained
1/4	teaspoon ground nutmeg

Pepper to taste

▣ In a saucepan, combine all ingredients; heat through.

Yield: 5 servings.

NUTRITION FACTS: 1 cup equals 251 calories, 14 g fat (7 g saturated fat), 65 mg cholesterol, 985 mg sodium, 18 g carbohydrate, 3 g fiber, 10 g protein.

Take a classic comfort pairing to tasty new heights with **Green Chili Tomato Soup** and **Two-Tone Grilled Cheese**. This meal is a snap to make.

green chili tomato soup

Here's an easy way to jazz up canned tomato soup. I modeled this recipe after a soup I tried in a restaurant. My version is so simple and very tasty.
CHRIS CHRISTOPHER ALBUQUERQUE, NEW MEXICO

1	can (10-3/4 ounces) condensed tomato soup, undiluted
3/4	cup 2% milk
1	can (4 ounces) chopped green chilies
1/2	cup shredded cheddar cheese

▨ In a small saucepan, combine the soup, milk and chilies until blended. Cook and stir over medium heat until heated through. Sprinkle with cheese.

Yield: 2 servings.

NUTRITION FACTS: 1 serving equals 270 calories, 10 g fat (7 g saturated fat), 37 mg cholesterol, 1,328 mg sodium, 33 g carbohydrate, 2 g fiber, 12 g protein.

two-tone grilled cheese

My family loves these quick-to-fix sandwiches with two kinds of bread and two kinds of cheese. They're fun!
RHONDA BECKETT INDEPENDENCE, MISSOURI

2	tablespoons butter, softened
4	slices whole wheat bread
2	to 4 tablespoons mayonnaise
4	slices white bread
4	slices process American cheese
4	slices Swiss cheese

▨ Spread one side of whole wheat bread with butter. Spread mayonnaise over white bread.

▨ Place whole wheat bread, buttered side down, on a hot griddle. Layer with cheeses; top with white bread, mayonnaise side up. Cook until golden brown.

Yield: 4 servings.

NUTRITION FACTS: 1 grilled cheese equals 389 calories, 24 g fat (13 g saturated fat), 56 mg cholesterol, 674 mg sodium, 26 g carbohydrate, 3 g fiber, 15 g protein.

meaty macaroni soup

As an elementary school librarian and church choir director, I've come to rely on—and thoroughly enjoy—the homemade convenience of slow-cooked meals.
ANN BOST ELKHART, TEXAS

1	can (28 ounces) diced tomatoes, undrained
2	cans (8 ounces each) tomato sauce
2	cups water
1/2	pound ground beef, cooked and drained
1/2	pound bulk pork sausage, cooked and drained
2	tablespoons dried minced onion
2	teaspoons chicken bouillon granules
3/4	teaspoon garlic salt
3/4	cup uncooked elbow macaroni

Shredded cheddar cheese, optional

▨ In a 3-qt. slow cooker, combine the first eight ingredients; mix well. Cover and cook on low for 8-10 hours. Add macaroni and mix well.

▨ Cover and cook 30 minutes longer or until macaroni is tender. Garnish with cheese if desired.

Yield: 10 servings (2-1/2 quarts).

NUTRITION FACTS: 1 cup (calculated without cheese) equals 128 calories, 7 g fat (2 g saturated fat), 19 mg cholesterol, 672 mg sodium, 10 g carbohydrate, 2 g fiber, 8 g protein.

bacon cheeseburger roll-ups

My husband and I both love these roll-ups. I often serve them with broccoli and cheese. They must be good, because this recipe won a first place prize at the Iowa State Fair!
JESSICA CAIN DES MOINES, IOWA

1	pound ground beef
6	bacon strips, diced
1/2	cup chopped onion
1	package (8 ounces) process cheese (Velveeta), cubed
1	tube (16.3 ounces) large refrigerated buttermilk biscuits
1/2	cup ketchup
1/4	cup yellow mustard

▨ In a skillet, cook the beef, bacon and onion over medium heat until meat is no longer pink; drain. Add cheese; cook and stir until melted. Remove from heat.

▨ Flatten each biscuit into a 5-in. circle; spoon 1/3 cup beef mixture onto each biscuit. Fold sides and ends over filling and roll up. Place seam side down on a greased baking sheet.

▨ Bake at 400° for 18-20 minutes or until golden brown. In a small bowl, combine ketchup and mustard; serve with roll-ups.

Yield: 8 servings.

NUTRITION FACTS: 1 roll-up with 4-1/2 teaspoons sauce equals 429 calories, 24 g fat (10 g saturated fat), 63 mg cholesterol, 1,372 mg sodium, 32 g carbohydrate, 1 g fiber, 21 g protein.

Shake up your lunch box routine with a wholesome, incredibly easy **ABC Soup** and **Turkey Ranch Wraps**. They're so easy and fun to make, children will want to help.

abc soup

Instead of opening a can of alphabet soup, why not make some from scratch? Kids of all ages love this traditional soup with a tomato base, ground beef and alphabet pasta.
SHARON BROCKMAN APPLETON, WISCONSIN

1	pound ground beef
1	medium onion, chopped
2	quarts tomato juice
1	can (15 ounces) mixed vegetables, undrained
1	cup water
2	beef bouillon cubes
1	cup alphabet pasta or small pasta

Salt and pepper to taste

▨ In a Dutch oven, cook beef and onion over medium heat until the meat is no longer pink; drain. Add tomato juice, vegetables, water and bouillon; bring to a boil. Add pasta. Cook, uncovered, for 6-8 minutes or until pasta is tender, stirring frequently. Add salt and pepper.

Yield: 11 servings (2-3/4 quarts).

NUTRITION FACTS: 1 cup equals 148 calories, 4 g fat (2 g saturated fat), 19 mg cholesterol, 858 mg sodium, 19 g carbohydrate, 2 g fiber, 10 g protein.

turkey ranch wraps

Here's a cool idea that's ready to gobble up in no time. Load up these wraps with deli turkey, veggies, cheese and ranch dressing for a flavorful, low-fat blend.
TASTE OF HOME TEST KITCHEN

8	thin slices cooked turkey
4	flour tortillas (6 inches), warmed
1	large tomato, thinly sliced
1	medium green pepper, cut into thin strips
1	cup shredded lettuce
1	cup (4 ounces) shredded cheddar cheese
1/3	cup fat-free ranch salad dressing

▨ Place two slices of turkey on each tortilla. Layer with tomato, green pepper, lettuce and cheese. Drizzle with salad dressing. Roll up tightly.

Yield: 4 servings.

NUTRITION FACTS: 1 wrap equals 335 calories, 14 g fat (7 g saturated fat), 73 mg cholesterol, 676 mg sodium, 25 g carbohydrate, 1 g fiber, 27 g protein.

greek salad pitas

This healthy meal-in-a-pocket combines fresh Greek salad with a yummy homemade hummus. You can use store-bought hummus if you like. Or make extra hummus to serve later with veggie sticks as a healthy snack.

NICOLE FILIZETTI JACKSONVILLE, FLORIDA

3/4	cup canned garbanzo beans or chickpeas, rinsed and drained
2	tablespoons lemon juice
1	tablespoon sliced green olives with pimientos
1	teaspoon olive oil
1	garlic clove, minced
1	cup fresh baby spinach
1/4	cup chopped seeded peeled cucumber
1/4	cup crumbled feta cheese
2	tablespoons chopped marinated quartered artichoke hearts
2	tablespoons sliced Greek olives
1/4	teaspoon dried oregano
2	whole wheat pita pocket halves

▢ Place the first five ingredients in a food processor; cover and process until smooth. In a small bowl, combine the spinach, cucumber, cheese, artichokes, olives and oregano.

▢ Spread bean mixture into pita halves; add salad. Serve immediately.

Yield: 2 servings.

NUTRITION FACTS: 1 serving equals 292 calories, 12 g fat (3 g saturated fat), 8 mg cholesterol, 687 mg sodium, 38 g carbohydrate, 7 g fiber, 10 g protein. **DIABETIC EXCHANGES:** 2 starch, 1 lean meat, 1 fat.

lemony chicken velvet soup

Here's the perfect warmer-upper on a chilly spring day. The lively flavor of lemon perks up a rich chicken soup accented with sugar snap peas.

CELESTE BUCKLEY REDDING, CALIFORNIA

2	tablespoons butter
2	tablespoons all-purpose flour
1	can (14-1/2 ounces) chicken broth
3	tablespoons lemon juice
1-1/2	cups cubed cooked chicken breast
10	fresh or frozen sugar snap peas
2	tablespoons minced fresh parsley
1	teaspoon grated lemon peel
3	tablespoons heavy whipping cream

▢ In a small saucepan, melt butter. Stir in flour until smooth; gradually add broth and lemon juice. Bring to a boil; cook and stir for 1-2 minutes or until thickened.

▢ Stir in the chicken, peas, parsley and lemon peel; cook 2-3 minutes longer or until chicken is heated through and peas are crisp-tender. Stir in cream; heat through (do not boil).

Yield: 2 servings.

NUTRITION FACTS: 1-1/4 cups equals 352 calories, 18 g fat (10 g saturated fat), 131 mg cholesterol, 730 mg sodium, 13 g carbohydrate, 2 g fiber, 37 g protein.

Dainty **Summer Tea Sandwiches** will have friends thinking you fussed. For carefree entertaining, serve the **Pretty Pea Soup Cups** in small disposable "cut crystal" glasses with clear plastic spoons. Just add drinks and your garden party's ready!

summer tea sandwiches

These dainty finger sandwiches are perfect for casual picnics or ladies' luncheons. Tarragon-seasoned chicken complements cucumber and cantaloupe slices.

TASTE OF HOME TEST KITCHEN

1/2	teaspoon dried tarragon
1/2	teaspoon salt, divided
1/4	teaspoon pepper
1	pound boneless skinless chicken breasts
1/2	cup reduced-fat mayonnaise
1	tablespoon finely chopped red onion
1	teaspoon dill weed
1/2	teaspoon lemon juice
24	slices soft multigrain bread, crusts removed
1	medium cucumber, thinly sliced
1/4	medium cantaloupe, cut into 12 thin slices

▢ Combine the tarragon, 1/4 teaspoon salt and pepper; rub over chicken. Place on a baking sheet coated with cooking spray.

▢ Bake at 350° for 20-25 minutes or until a thermometer reads 170°. Cool to room temperature; thinly slice.

▢ In a small bowl, combine the mayonnaise, onion, dill, lemon juice and remaining salt; spread over 12 bread slices. Top with cucumber, chicken, cantaloupe and remaining bread. Cut sandwiches in half diagonally.

Yield: 12 servings.

NUTRITION FACTS: 2 sandwich halves equals 212 calories, 6 g fat (1 g saturated fat), 24 mg cholesterol, 450 mg sodium, 27 g carbohydrate, 4 g fiber, 13 g protein.

pretty pea soup cups

Here's an irresistibly elegant idea for your next party.

TASTE OF HOME TEST KITCHEN

1	package (16 ounces) frozen peas, thawed
1	cup chicken broth
1/4	cup minced fresh mint
1	tablespoon lime juice
1	teaspoon ground cumin
1/4	teaspoon salt
1-1/2	cups plain yogurt

SHRIMP SALAD:

2	tablespoons minced fresh mint
4	teaspoons lime juice
4	teaspoons canola oil
2	teaspoons red curry paste
1/8	teaspoon salt
1	cup chopped cooked shrimp

▢ Place the peas, broth, mint, lime juice, cumin and salt in a blender. Cover and process until smooth. Add yogurt; process until blended. Refrigerate for at least 1 hour.

▢ In a small bowl, whisk the mint, lime juice, oil, curry paste and salt. Add shrimp; toss gently to coat. Chill.

▢ To serve, pour soup into small cups or glasses; garnish with shrimp salad.

Yield: 1 dozen.

NUTRITION FACTS: 1/4 cup soup with 1 tablespoon shrimp salad equals 79 calories, 3 g fat (1 g saturated fat), 23 mg cholesterol, 252 mg sodium, 7 g carbohydrate, 2 g fiber, 6 g protein.

turkey focaccia club

This sandwich is pure heaven, thanks to the cranberry-pecan mayo. It's delicious any day of the year!
JUDY WILSON SUN CITY WEST, ARIZONA

CRANBERRY PECAN MAYONNAISE:
- 1/2 cup mayonnaise
- 1/2 cup whole-berry cranberry sauce
- 2 tablespoons Dijon mustard
- 2 tablespoons chopped pecans, toasted
- 1 tablespoon honey

SANDWICH:
- 1 loaf (8 ounces) focaccia bread
- 3 lettuce leaves
- 1/2 pound thinly sliced cooked turkey
- 1/4 pound sliced Gouda cheese
- 8 slices tomato
- 6 bacon strips, cooked

☐ In a small bowl, combine the mayonnaise, cranberry sauce, mustard, pecans and honey.

☐ Cut bread in half horizontally; spread with cranberry pecan mayonnaise. Layer with lettuce, turkey, cheese, tomato and bacon; replace bread top. Cut into wedges.

Yield: 4 servings.

NUTRITION FACTS: 1 wedge equals 707 calories, 41 g fat (10 g saturated fat), 96 mg cholesterol, 1,153 mg sodium, 53 g carbohydrate, 2 g fiber, 32 g protein.

beer cheese soup

We had this soup many times at a family friend's, and I just had to have the recipe! It tastes like a restaurant treat.
SHARON LOCK FORMAN, NORTH DAKOTA

- 2 tablespoons finely chopped onion
- 1/2 teaspoon butter
- 2 cans (10-3/4 ounces each) condensed cream of celery soup, undiluted
- 1 cup beer or nonalcoholic beer
- 1 cup milk
- 1 teaspoon Worcestershire sauce
- 1/2 teaspoon dried parsley flakes
- 1/4 teaspoon paprika
- 3/4 pound process cheese (Velveeta), cubed

☐ In a large saucepan, saute onion in butter until tender. Stir in the soup, beer, milk, Worcestershire sauce, parsley and paprika.

☐ Reduce heat; stir in cheese until melted. Heat through (do not boil).

Yield: 6 servings.

NUTRITION FACTS: 1 cup equals 269 calories, 18 g fat (11 g saturated fat), 45 mg cholesterol, 1,077 mg sodium, 12 g carbohydrate, trace fiber, 13 g protein.

quick italian wedding soup

My husband and two children love the combination of meatballs, spinach and shredded chicken in my hearty soup.
SHERRI PERFETT MOON TOWNSHIP, PENNSYLVANIA

10	cups chicken broth
2	bone-in chicken breast halves (8 ounces each), skin removed
1	egg, lightly beaten
1/4	cup dry bread crumbs
4	tablespoons grated Parmesan cheese, divided
1-1/2	teaspoons Italian seasoning, divided
1	pound ground beef
1/2	cup uncooked orzo pasta
1/4	teaspoon pepper
1	package (10 ounces) frozen chopped spinach, thawed and drained

☐ In a large saucepan, bring broth and chicken to a boil. Reduce heat; simmer, uncovered, for 15-20 minutes or until chicken is no longer pink. Remove the chicken and set aside.

☐ In a large bowl, combine the egg, bread crumbs, 2 tablespoons cheese and 1 teaspoon Italian seasoning. Crumble beef over mixture and mix well.

☐ Shape into 1-in. balls; add to broth. Bring to a boil. Reduce heat; simmer, uncovered, for 10 minutes or until meatballs are no longer pink. Skim fat.

☐ Add pasta, pepper and remaining Italian seasoning to soup. Bring to a boil. Reduce heat; simmer, uncovered, for 12-15 minutes or until pasta is tender. Remove chicken from bones; discard bones and shred meat. Add the chicken, spinach and remaining cheese to soup and heat through.

Yield: 8 servings (2-1/2 quarts).

NUTRITION FACTS: 1-1/4 cups equals 175 calories, 6 g fat (3 g saturated fat), 54 mg cholesterol, 1,056 mg sodium, 12 g carbohydrate, 1 g fiber, 17 g protein.

pesto skillet panini

I created this recipe for my students in the foods and nutrition class I teach. The kids like it so much, they often go home and make it for their families. It's a healthier alternative to grilled cheese made with mayonnaise and butter.
BETH HIOTT YORK, SOUTH CAROLINA

8	slices Italian bread
4	tablespoons prepared pesto
4	slices provolone cheese
4	slices part-skim mozzarella cheese
5	teaspoons olive oil

Marinara sauce warmed, optional

☐ Spread four bread slices with pesto. Layer with cheeses; top with remaining bread. Spread outsides of sandwiches with oil.

☐ In a large skillet over medium heat, toast sandwiches for 3-4 minutes on each side or until cheese is melted. Serve with marinara if desired.

Yield: 4 servings.

NUTRITION FACTS: 1 sandwich (calculated without marinara) equals 445 calories, 27 g fat (10 g saturated fat), 35 mg cholesterol, 759 mg sodium, 32 g carbohydrate, 2 g fiber, 20 g protein.

hearty chili with a twist

This thick chili is ideal for tailgate parties or on cold winter evenings. I like to top it with crushed saltine crackers and shredded cheddar cheese.
LOUISE JACINO EAST MORICHES, NEW YORK

1	pound ground beef
1	pound bulk Italian sausage
2	large onions, chopped
4	garlic cloves, minced
2	cans (16 ounces each) kidney beans, rinsed and drained
2	cans (14-1/2 ounces each) Italian diced tomatoes, undrained
2	cans (10-3/4 ounces each) condensed tomato soup, undiluted
2	cans (6 ounces each) Italian tomato paste
1	can (8-1/2 ounces) peas, drained
2	tablespoons chili powder
2	teaspoons ground cumin
2	teaspoons dried oregano
1	teaspoon hot pepper sauce
3/4	teaspoon salt
1/2	teaspoon pepper

☐ In a large skillet, cook the beef, sausage and onions over medium heat until the meat is no longer pink. Add garlic; cook 1 minute longer. Drain.

☐ Transfer to a 5-qt. slow cooker. Stir in the beans, tomatoes, soup, tomato paste, peas, chili powder, cumin, oregano, pepper sauce, salt and pepper. Cover and cook on low for 6-8 hours or until heated through.

Yield: 12 servings (3 quarts).

NUTRITION FACTS: 1 cup equals 318 calories, 10 g fat (3 g saturated fat), 38 mg cholesterol, 1,353 mg sodium, 36 g carbohydrate, 7 g fiber, 19 g protein.

tailgate sausages

Try these sausages for a crowd-pleasing casual meal. Make the tomato sauce loaded with green peppers, then keep it hot in a foil pan on the grill and let your friends serve themselves.
MIKE YAEGER BROOKINGS, SOUTH DAKOTA

4	large green peppers, thinly sliced
1/2	cup chopped onion

2	tablespoons olive oil
4	garlic cloves, minced
1	can (15 ounces) tomato sauce
1	can (12 ounces) tomato paste
1	cup water
1	tablespoon sugar
2	teaspoons dried basil
1	teaspoon salt
1	teaspoon dried oregano
20	uncooked Italian sausage links
20	sandwich buns

Shredded part-skim mozzarella cheese, optional

☐ In a saucepan, saute peppers and onion in oil until crisp-tender. Drain. Add garlic; cook 1 minute longer. Stir in the tomato sauce, tomato paste, water, sugar, basil, salt and oregano. Bring to a boil. Reduce heat; cover and simmer for 30 minutes or until heated through.

☐ Meanwhile, grill sausages, covered, over medium heat for 10-16 minutes or until a thermometer reads 160°, turning occasionally. Serve on buns with sauce and cheese if desired.

Yield: 20 servings.

NUTRITION FACTS: 1 sandwich equals 525 calories, 28 g fat (10 g saturated fat), 60 mg cholesterol, 1,327 mg sodium, 45 g carbohydrate, 2 g fiber, 25 g protein.

Treat that special someone to elegant **Bistro Breakfast Panini** paired with a chilled **Strawberry Soup** you smartly whipped up the night before. This unforgettable lazy-day meal is sure to impress.

bistro breakfast panini

I tried an omelet that contained Brie, bacon and apples and thought it would be tasty as a breakfast panini...so I created this recipe!
KATHY HARDING RICHMOND, MISSOURI

6	bacon strips
1	teaspoon butter
4	eggs, beaten
4	slices sourdough bread (3/4 inch thick)
1/8	teaspoon salt
1/8	teaspoon pepper
3	ounces Brie cheese, thinly sliced
8	thin slices apple
1/2	cup fresh baby spinach
2	tablespoons butter, softened

▢ In a large skillet, cook bacon over medium heat until crisp. Remove to paper towels to drain. Meanwhile, heat butter in a large skillet over medium heat. Add eggs; cook and stir until set.

▢ Place eggs on two slices of bread; sprinkle with salt and pepper. Layer with cheese, apple, bacon, spinach and remaining bread. Butter outsides of sandwiches.

▢ Cook on a panini maker or indoor grill for 3-4 minutes or until bread is browned and cheese is melted.

Yield: 2 servings.

NUTRITION FACTS: 1 sandwich equals 710 calories, 44 g fat (22 g saturated fat), 522 mg cholesterol, 1,510 mg sodium, 42 g carbohydrate, 3 g fiber, 36 g protein.

strawberry soup

Try my refreshing chilled soup for a lovely addition to any special-occasion brunch or luncheon just for two.
LUCIA JOHNSON MASSENA, NEW YORK

1	pint fresh strawberries, hulled
1/2	cup white wine or apple juice
1/3	to 1/2 cup sugar
2	tablespoons lemon juice
1	teaspoon grated lemon peel

▢ In a blender, combine all ingredients. Cover and process until smooth. Pour into two bowls; cover and refrigerate until thoroughly chilled, about 1-2 hours.

Yield: 2 servings.

NUTRITION FACTS: 1 cup equals 281 calories, 1 g fat (trace saturated fat), 0 cholesterol, 5 mg sodium, 62 g carbohydrate, 3 g fiber, 1 g protein.

beef

sally's west coast chili

We often have chili cook-offs at our church, so we trade lots of different recipes. I was always experimenting, trying to come up with an original recipe that would be a little different. That's how I developed this one, and I never fail to get compliments on it!

SALLY GRISHAM MURRAY, KENTUCKY

1	pound sliced bacon, diced
2	pounds beef stew meat, cut into 1/4-inch cubes
2	medium onions, chopped
4	garlic cloves, minced
3	cans (14-1/2 ounces each) diced tomatoes, undrained
1	cup barbecue sauce
1	cup chili sauce
1/2	cup honey
4	teaspoons beef bouillon granules
1	bay leaf
1	tablespoon chili powder
1	tablespoon baking cocoa
1	tablespoon Worcestershire sauce
1	tablespoon Dijon mustard
1-1/2	teaspoons ground cumin
1/4	teaspoon cayenne powder, optional
3	cans (16 ounces each) kidney beans, rinsed and drained

Shredded cheddar cheese

☐ In a Dutch oven, cook bacon until crisp; remove to paper towels to drain. Reserve 3 tablespoons drippings.

☐ Brown beef in drippings. Add onions; cook until tender. Add garlic; cook 1 minute longer. Return bacon to pan. Stir in the next 12 ingredients.

☐ Bring to a boil. Reduce heat; cover and simmer until meat is tender, about 3 hours.

☐ Add beans and heat through. Discard bay leaf. Garnish with cheddar cheese.

Yield: 12 servings (4 quarts).

NUTRITION FACTS: 1 cup (calculated without cheese) equals 264 calories, 12 g fat (4 g saturated fat), 46 mg cholesterol, 898 mg sodium, 23 g carbohydrate, 2 g fiber, 17 g protein.

bacon-beef barley soup

Served over creamy mashed potatoes, this quick, comforting soup will really hit the spot.
CATHY PETERSON MENOMINEE, MICHIGAN

4	bacon strips, chopped
1-1/2	pounds beef stew meat, cut into 1/2-inch pieces
1	medium onion, chopped
4	medium red potatoes, cut into 1/2-inch cubes
1-1/2	cups fresh baby carrots, cut in half lengthwise
1	cup frozen corn
1/4	cup medium pearl barley
2	cans (14-1/2 ounces each) beef broth
1	can (14-1/2 ounces) diced tomatoes with basil, oregano and garlic, undrained
1	jar (12 ounces) home-style beef gravy
1/2	teaspoon pepper

Mashed potatoes, optional

▢ In a large skillet, cook bacon over medium heat until crisp. Using a slotted spoon, remove to paper towels to drain. In the drippings, cook beef and onion until meat is no longer pink; drain.

▢ In a 5-qt. slow cooker, layer the potatoes, carrots, corn and barley. Top with beef mixture and bacon. Combine the broth, tomatoes, gravy and pepper; pour over top (do not stir).

▢ Cover and cook on low for 8-10 hours or until meat and vegetables are tender. Stir before serving. Serve over mashed potatoes if desired.

Yield: 7 servings.

NUTRITION FACTS: 1-1/3 cups (calculated without mashed potatoes) equals 319 calories, 10 g fat (3 g saturated fat), 68 mg cholesterol, 1,218 mg sodium, 32 g carbohydrate, 4 g fiber, 26 g protein.

hamburger minestrone

Any kind of convenient frozen mixed vegetables and whatever small pasta you choose will work well in this dish.
TASTE OF HOME TEST KITCHEN

1/2	cup small uncooked pasta shells
1	pound ground beef
1/2	cup chopped onion
3	cans (14-1/2 ounces each) beef broth
1	package (16 ounces) frozen mixed vegetables
1	can (16 ounces) kidney beans, rinsed and drained
1	can (14-1/2 ounces) diced tomatoes, undrained
1	can (6 ounces) tomato paste
3	teaspoons Italian seasoning
1	teaspoon salt
1/4	teaspoon dried thyme
1/4	teaspoon dried basil
1/4	teaspoon pepper

▢ Cook pasta according to package directions. Meanwhile, in a large saucepan, cook beef and onion over medium heat until meat is no longer pink; drain.

▢ Stir in the remaining ingredients. Bring to a boil. Reduce heat; simmer, uncovered, for 15 minutes. Drain pasta and add to the pan. Cook 5 minutes longer or until heated through.

Yield: 6 servings.

NUTRITION FACTS: 1-1/2 cups equals 324 calories, 8 g fat (4 g saturated fat), 37 mg cholesterol, 1,427 mg sodium, 40 g carbohydrate, 10 g fiber, 25 g protein.

rich 'n' hearty burger soup

Two generations of my family—so far!—have made this soup a cold-weather specialty.
IVAN HOCHSTETLER SHIPSHEWANA, INDIANA

1	pound ground beef
1	medium onion, chopped
2	cups tomato juice
1	cup finely chopped carrot
1	cup finely chopped peeled potato
1-1/2	teaspoons salt
1/4	teaspoon pepper
1	teaspoon seasoned salt

WHITE SAUCE:

1/4	cup butter, cubed
1/3	cup all-purpose flour
4	cups milk

◻ In a large skillet, cook beef and onion over medium heat until meat is no longer pink; drain. Add the tomato juice, carrot and potato. Stir in seasonings. Bring to a boil. Reduce heat; cover and simmer for 10-15 minutes or until vegetables are tender.

◻ Meanwhile, in a large saucepan, melt butter. Stir in flour until smooth; gradually add milk. Bring to a boil; cook and stir for 1-2 minutes or until thickened. Stir in vegetable mixture; heat through.

Yield: 8 servings (2 quarts).

NUTRITION FACTS: 1 cup equals 274 calories, 15 g fat (8 g saturated fat), 60 mg cholesterol, 1,014 mg sodium, 20 g carbohydrate, 2 g fiber, 16 g protein.

tip!

SECRETS TO SUCCESS FOR WHITE SAUCE

Most white sauces begin with stirring flour into melted butter over medium heat until the mixture is smooth and bubbly. To help prevent lumps, you may prefer to use a wire whisk for stirring. The whisk evenly distributes the flour and prevents it from sinking to the bottom of the pan, where it can burn. Be sure to add the liquid very slowly, whisking constantly, especially in the beginning. Let the mixture thicken after each addition of liquid to ensure a lump-free sauce. Once all liquid has been added, cook and whisk until sauce comes to a boil. Then cook 1-2 minutes longer.

aloha chili

Pineapple and brown sugar give this unusual chili a tropical taste. Every person who samples it is pleasantly surprised, and often requests a second bowl.
DYAN CORNIES VERNON, BRITISH COLUMBIA

2	pounds ground beef
1	large onion, finely chopped
1	can (20 ounces) pineapple chunks, undrained
1	can (16 ounces) kidney beans, rinsed and drained
1	can (15-3/4 ounces) pork and beans
1	cup ketchup
1/4	cup packed brown sugar
1/4	cup white vinegar

◻ In a Dutch oven, cook beef and onion over medium heat until no meat is no longer pink; drain.

◻ Stir in the remaining ingredients. Bring to a boil. Reduce heat; cover and simmer for 20 minutes to allow flavors to blend.

Yield: 8 servings (about 2 quarts).

NUTRITION FACTS: 1 cup equals 371 calories, 11 g fat (5 g saturated fat), 56 mg cholesterol, 711 mg sodium, 44 g carbohydrate, 7 g fiber, 27 g protein.

no-bean chili

I like to combine the ingredients for this zesty chili the night before. In the morning, I load up the slow cooker and let it do the rest of the work for me.
MOLLY BUTT GRANVILLE, OHIO

1-1/2	pounds lean ground beef (90% lean)
1	can (14-1/2 ounces) stewed tomatoes, undrained
1	can (8 ounces) tomato sauce
1	small onion, chopped
1	small green pepper, chopped
1	can (4 ounces) chopped green chilies
1/2	cup minced fresh parsley
1	tablespoon chili powder
1	garlic clove, minced
1-1/4	teaspoons salt
1/2	teaspoon paprika
1/4	teaspoon pepper

Hot cooked rice or pasta
Optional toppings: Shredded cheddar cheese, sour cream and sliced green onions

▢ Crumble beef into a 3-qt. slow cooker. Add the next 11 ingredients and mix well. Cover and cook on high for 4-6 hours or until meat is no longer pink. Serve with rice or pasta and the toppings of your choice.

Yield: 6 servings.

NUTRITION FACTS: 1 serving (calculated without rice and optional toppings) equals 217 calories, 9 g fat (3 g saturated fat), 56 mg cholesterol, 954 mg sodium, 11 g carbohydrate, 2 g fiber, 24 g protein.

hamburger vegetable soup

Soup is pure comfort food, and a favorite in our family. It's the dish I take most often to friends who are in need of a helping hand.
ELEANOR BELL UTICA, PENNSYLVANIA

1	pound ground beef
1	cup chopped onion
1	cup diced peeled potatoes
1	cup sliced carrots
1	cup shredded cabbage
1	cup sliced celery
2	cans (14-1/2 ounces each) diced tomatoes, undrained
1/4	cup uncooked long grain rice
3	cups water
2	teaspoons salt
1/4	teaspoon dried basil
1/4	teaspoon dried thyme
1	bay leaf

▢ In a Dutch oven, cook beef and onion over medium heat until the meat is no longer pink; drain. Add the remaining ingredients; bring to a boil. Reduce heat; cover and simmer for 1 hour or until vegetables are tender, stirring occasionally. Discard bay leaf.

Yield: 8 servings (2 quarts).

NUTRITION FACTS: 1 serving equals 157 calories, 5 g fat (2 g saturated fat), 28 mg cholesterol, 752 mg sodium, 15 g carbohydrate, 2 g fiber, 12 g protein.

texas taco soup

(pictured at left)

My popular taco soup offers a bright assortment of colors and flavors. Garnish with shredded cheese, sour cream or sliced jalapenos if you like.

JENNIFER VILLARREAL TEXAS CITY, TEXAS

1-1/2 pounds ground beef
   1 envelope taco seasoning
   2 cans (15-1/4 ounces each) whole kernel corn, undrained
   2 cans (15 ounces each) Ranch Style beans (pinto beans in seasoned tomato sauce)
   2 cans (14-1/2 ounces each) diced tomatoes, undrained
Crushed tortilla chips and shredded cheddar cheese
Flour tortillas, warmed

▢ In a Dutch oven, cook beef over medium heat until no longer pink; drain. Stir in the taco seasoning, corn, beans and tomatoes. Cover and simmer for 15 minutes or until heated through, stirring occasionally. Place tortilla chips in soup bowls; ladle soup over top. Sprinkle with cheese. Serve with tortillas.

Yield: 8 servings (about 2 quarts).

NUTRITION FACTS: 1 cup (calculated without chips, cheese and tortillas) equals 380 calories, 13 g fat (5 g saturated fat), 53 mg cholesterol, 1,395 mg sodium, 38 g carbohydrate, 9 g fiber, 23 g protein.

big red soup

We're Nebraska Cornhusker football fans, and on the days when Big Red is playing, I make up a big pot of this soup. The whole family gathers around the TV to eat it while watching the game.

SHELLY KORELL BAYARD, NEBRASKA

   2 pounds beef stew meat, cut into 1-inch cubes
   2 tablespoons canola oil
  3/4 cup chopped onion
   2 cloves garlic, minced
   2 cans (14-1/2 ounces each) diced tomatoes in sauce
   1 can (10-1/2 ounces) condensed beef broth, undiluted
   1 can (10-1/2 ounces) condensed chicken broth, undiluted
   1 can (10-3/4 ounces) condensed tomato soup, undiluted
  1/4 cup water
   1 teaspoon ground cumin
   1 teaspoon chili powder
   1 teaspoon salt
  1/2 teaspoon lemon-pepper seasoning

   2 teaspoons Worcestershire sauce
  1/3 cup picante sauce
   8 corn tortillas, cut into quarters
   1 cup (4 ounces) shredded cheddar cheese

▢ In a large skillet, brown beef in oil. Transfer to a 5-qt. slow cooker; add the remaining ingredients except for tortillas and cheese. Cover and cook on low for 8-10 hours or until meat is tender.

▢ To serve, place enough tortilla quarters to cover bottom of each bowl. Pour soup over tortilla pieces; sprinkle with cheese.

Yield: 12 servings (3 quarts).

NUTRITION FACTS: 1 cup equals 247 calories, 11 g fat (4 g saturated fat), 57 mg cholesterol, 989 mg sodium, 16 g carbohydrate, 2 g fiber, 20 g protein.

taco soup

(pictured above)

My spicy, satisfying soup is a nice change of pace. Teenagers love it, and it's fast to make.
DEBBIE MOFFITT ALBANY, OREGON

- 1 pound ground beef
- 1 envelope (1-1/4 ounces) taco seasoning
- 1 can (14-1/2 ounces) stewed tomatoes
- 1 can (15 ounces) kidney beans, rinsed and drained
- 1 cup water

Shredded cheddar cheese
Sliced green onions, sour cream and corn chips or tortilla chips, optional

▢ In a large saucepan, cook beef over medium heat until no longer pink; drain. Add the taco seasoning, tomatoes, beans and water; bring to a boil. Reduce heat; cook until heated through.

▢ Ladle into individual bowls; top with shredded cheese. If desired, also top each serving with onions, sour cream and chips.

Yield: 5 servings.

NUTRITION FACTS: 1 cup (calculated without toppings) equals 262 calories, 8 g fat (4 g saturated fat), 44 mg cholesterol, 994 mg sodium, 25 g carbohydrate, 5 g fiber, 22 g protein.

zucchini beef soup

My garden produces a bumper crop of zucchini, and I hate to see even one go to waste. This satisfying soup is a simple solution. The broth is delicious.
ROBERT KEITH ROCHESTER, MINNESOTA

- 1 pound beef stew meat, cut into 1-inch cubes
- 1 tablespoon canola oil
- 6 cups water
- 1 can (8 ounces) tomato sauce
- 1 medium onion, chopped
- 1-1/2 teaspoons salt
- 3/4 teaspoon dried oregano
- 1/4 teaspoon pepper
- 2 cups thinly sliced zucchini
- 1 cup broken uncooked spaghetti

▢ In a Dutch oven, brown beef in oil; drain. Add the water, tomato sauce, onion, salt, oregano and pepper. Bring to a boil. Reduce heat; cover and simmer for 2 hours. Add zucchini and spaghetti; return to a boil. Cover and cook for 15-18 minutes or until zucchini and spaghetti are tender.

Yield: 8 servings (2 quarts).

NUTRITION FACTS: 1 cup equals 155 calories, 6 g fat (2 g saturated fat), 35 mg cholesterol, 598 mg sodium, 12 g carbohydrate, 1 g fiber, 13 g protein.

ravioli soup

My family's love of pasta inspired me to create this rich, special-looking dish. We really enjoy the flavorful tomato base and tender, cheese-filled ravioli.

SHELLEY WAY CHEYENNE, WYOMING

1	pound ground beef
2	cups water
2	cans (one 28 ounces, one 14-1/2 ounces) crushed tomatoes
1	can (6 ounces) tomato paste
1-1/2	cups chopped onions
1/4	cup minced fresh parsley
2	garlic cloves, minced
3/4	teaspoon dried basil
1/2	teaspoon sugar
1/2	teaspoon dried oregano
1/2	teaspoon onion salt
1/2	teaspoon salt
1/4	teaspoon pepper
1/4	teaspoon dried thyme
1	package (9 ounces) refrigerated cheese ravioli
1/4	cup grated Parmesan cheese

Additional minced fresh parsley, optional

▣ In a Dutch oven, cook beef over medium heat until no longer pink; drain. Add the water, tomatoes, tomato paste, onions, parsley, garlic, basil, sugar, oregano, onion salt, salt, pepper and thyme; bring to a boil. Reduce heat; cover and simmer for 30 minutes.

▣ Cook ravioli according to package directions; drain. Stir into soup with the Parmesan cheese. Sprinkle with additional parsley if desired.

Yield: 10 servings (2-1/2 quarts).

NUTRITION FACTS: 1 cup equals 235 calories, 8 g fat (4 g saturated fat), 42 mg cholesterol, 542 mg sodium, 25 g carbohydrate, 4 g fiber, 17 g protein.

cabbage soup

My husband was never too fond of cabbage until the first time he tried this recipe from my aunt. Now it's regularly on the menu at our house.

NANCY STEVENS MORRISON, ILLINOIS

1	medium head cabbage, chopped
1	cup chopped celery
1	cup chopped onion
8	cups water
1	teaspoon beef bouillon granules
1	tablespoon salt
2	teaspoons pepper
1-1/2	pounds ground beef, browned and drained
2	cans (15 ounces each) tomato sauce
1	tablespoon brown sugar
1/4	cup ketchup

▣ In a stockpot, cook the cabbage, celery and onion in water until tender. Add bouillon, salt, pepper, beef and tomato sauce. Bring to a boil; reduce heat and simmer 10 minutes. Stir in brown sugar and ketchup; simmer 10 minutes longer to allow flavors to blend.

Yield: 20 servings (5 quarts).

NUTRITION FACTS: 1 cup equals 80 calories, 3 g fat (1 g saturated fat), 17 mg cholesterol, 567 mg sodium, 6 g carbohydrate, 2 g fiber, 7 g protein.

best lasagna soup

All the traditional flavors of lasagna come together in this heartwarming meal in a bowl. It's comforting and really satisfies a hearty appetite.
SHERYL OLENICK DEMAREST, NEW JERSEY

1	pound lean ground beef (90% lean)
1	large green pepper, chopped
1	medium onion, chopped
2	garlic cloves, minced
2	cans (14-1/2 ounces each) reduced-sodium beef broth
2	cans (14-1/2 ounces each) diced tomatoes
1	can (8 ounces) tomato sauce
1	cup frozen corn
1/4	cup tomato paste
2	teaspoons Italian seasoning
1/4	teaspoon pepper
2-1/2	cups uncooked spiral pasta
1/2	cup shredded Parmesan cheese

▢ In a large saucepan, cook the beef, green pepper and onion over medium heat until meat is no longer pink. Add garlic; cook 1 minute longer. Drain.

▢ Stir in the broth, tomatoes, tomato sauce, corn, tomato paste, Italian seasoning and pepper. Bring to a boil. Stir in pasta. Return to a boil. Reduce heat; cover and simmer for 10-12 minutes or until pasta is tender. Sprinkle with cheese.

Yield: 8 servings.

NUTRITION FACTS: 1-1/3 cups equals 280 calories, 7 g fat (3 g saturated fat), 41 mg cholesterol, 572 mg sodium, 35 g carbohydrate, 4 g fiber, 20 g protein. **DIABETIC EXCHANGES:** 2 lean meat, 2 vegetable, 1-1/2 starch.

forgotten minestrone

This soup gets its name because the broth simmers for hours, allowing me to work on my freelance writing. But after one taste, you and your family will agree this full-flavored soup is truly unforgettable!
MARSHA RANSOM SOUTH HAVEN, MICHIGAN

1	pound beef stew meat, cut into 1/2-inch cubes
1	can (28 ounces) diced tomatoes, undrained
1	medium onion, chopped
2	tablespoons minced dried parsley
2-1/2	teaspoons salt, optional
1-1/2	teaspoons ground thyme
1	beef bouillon cube
1/2	teaspoon pepper
6	cups water
1	medium zucchini, halved and thinly sliced
2	cups chopped cabbage
1	can (15 ounces) garbanzo beans or chickpeas, rinsed and drained
1	cup uncooked elbow macaroni
1/4	cup grated Parmesan cheese, optional

▢ In a 5-qt. slow cooker, combine the first nine ingredients. Cover and cook on low for 8-10 hours or until meat is tender.

▢ Add the zucchini, cabbage, beans and macaroni; cover and cook on high for 30-45 minutes or until macaroni and vegetables are tender. Sprinkle servings with cheese if desired.

Yield: 8 servings (2 quarts).

NUTRITION FACTS: 1 cup (calculated without salt and cheese) equals 203 calories, 5 g fat (2 g saturated fat), 35 mg cholesterol, 335 mg sodium, 24 g carbohydrate, 5 g fiber, 16 g protein. **DIABETIC EXCHANGES:** 2 lean meat, 2 vegetable, 1 starch.

so-easy vegetable beef soup

My easy soup is packed with homemade flavor. Thanks to convenience products, it's perfect for a weeknight supper, but would also make a tasty lunch some snowy Saturday.
JOANNE MEEHAN SHIPPENSBURG, PENNSYLVANIA

1	package (17 ounces) refrigerated beef roast au jus
2	cans (14-1/2 ounces each) Italian diced tomatoes, undrained
1	package (16 ounces) frozen mixed vegetables
5-1/2	cups water
1/4	teaspoon salt
1-1/2	cups uncooked mini penne pasta

◻ Shred beef with two forks; transfer to a Dutch oven. Add the tomatoes, vegetables, water and salt. Bring to a boil.

◻ Stir in pasta. Reduce heat; simmer, uncovered, for 15 minutes or until flavors are blended and pasta is tender.

Yield: 8 servings (about 2-1/2 quarts).

NUTRITION FACTS: 1-1/3 cups equals 238 calories, 5 g fat (2 g saturated fat), 37 mg cholesterol, 705 mg sodium, 33 g carbohydrate, 4 g fiber, 17 g protein. **DIABETIC EXCHANGES:** 1 starch, 1 lean meat, 1 vegetable.

autumn chili

(pictured at left)

A touch of baking cocoa gives my chili a rich flavor without adding sweetness. When I was growing up in the North, we served chili over rice. But after I married a Texan, I began serving it with chopped onions, shredded cheese and, of course, corn bread!

AUDREY BYRNE LILLIAN, TEXAS

- 1 large onion, chopped
- 2 cans (16 ounces each) kidney beans, rinsed and drained
- 2 cans (14-1/2 ounces each) diced tomatoes
- 2 cups cooked and crumbled ground beef
- 1 can (8 ounces) tomato sauce
- 1 medium green pepper
- 3 tablespoons chili powder
- 1 tablespoon ground cumin
- 2 garlic cloves, minced
- 1 teaspoon baking cocoa
- 1 teaspoon dried oregano
- 1 teaspoon Worcestershire sauce, optional

Salt and pepper to taste

▨ In a large saucepan coated with cooking spray, saute onion until tender. Add the remaining ingredients; bring to a boil. Reduce heat; cover and simmer for 2 hours, stirring occasionally.

Yield: 4 servings.

NUTRITION FACTS: 1 serving equals 540 calories, 16 g fat (6 g saturated fat), 86 mg cholesterol, 1,026 mg sodium, 58 g carbohydrate, 18 g fiber, 43 g protein.

hearty beef vegetable soup

My stew-like soup is loaded with nutritious ingredients, yet it's so easy to prepare. I make homemade bread or breadsticks to serve with it.

SHERMAN SNOWBALL SALT LAKE CITY, UTAH

- 3 tablespoons all-purpose flour
- 1/2 teaspoon salt
- 1/4 teaspoon pepper
- 1 pound beef stew meat, cut into 1/2-inch cubes
- 2 tablespoons olive oil
- 1 can (14-1/2 ounces) Italian diced tomatoes
- 1 can (8 ounces) tomato sauce
- 2 tablespoons red wine vinegar
- 2 tablespoons Worcestershire sauce
- 3 garlic cloves, minced
- 1 teaspoon dried oregano
- 3 cups water
- 4 medium potatoes, peeled and cubed
- 6 medium carrots, sliced
- 2 medium turnips, peeled and cubed
- 1 medium zucchini, halved lengthwise and sliced
- 1 medium green pepper, julienned
- 1 cup sliced fresh mushrooms
- 1 medium onion, chopped
- 1 can (4 ounces) chopped green chilies
- 2 tablespoons sugar

▨ In a large resealable plastic bag, combine the flour, salt and pepper. Add beef, a few pieces at a time, and shake to coat.

▨ In a Dutch oven, brown beef in oil. Stir in the tomatoes, tomato sauce, vinegar, Worcestershire sauce, garlic and oregano. Bring to a boil. Reduce heat; cover and simmer for 1 hour.

▨ Stir in the remaining ingredients. Bring to a boil. Reduce heat; cover and simmer for 1 hour or until meat and vegetables are tender.

Yield: 8 servings (2-1/2 quarts).

NUTRITION FACTS: 1-1/2 cups equals 276 calories, 8 g fat (2 g saturated fat), 35 mg cholesterol, 638 mg sodium, 38 g carbohydrate, 5 g fiber, 15 g protein.

three's-a-charm shamrock soup

(pictured above)

There's no better way to use up leftover St. Patrick's Day corned beef and cabbage than to make another hearty meal. This soup is one of my best.

DEBORAH MCMIRTREY ESTES PARK, COLORADO

6	celery ribs, chopped
4	medium carrots, sliced
2	cups cubed peeled potatoes
5	cups water
3	cups diced cooked corned beef
2	cups chopped cooked cabbage
1	teaspoon dill weed
1	teaspoon salt
1	teaspoon seasoned salt
1/2	teaspoon white pepper

◻ In a large soup kettle, bring the celery, carrots, potatoes and water to a boil. Reduce heat; cover and simmer until vegetables are tender, about 20 minutes.

◻ Stir in the remaining ingredients. Cover and simmer for 15-20 minutes or until heated through.

Yield: 10 servings (2-1/2 quarts).

NUTRITION FACTS: 1 cup equals 132 calories, 7 g fat (2 g saturated fat), 34 mg cholesterol, 818 mg sodium, 11 g carbohydrate, 2 g fiber, 7 g protein.

slow-cooked hamburger soup

I work full-time, but my family sits down to a home-cooked meal just about every night, thanks in part to simple recipes like this that I can make in the slow cooker.

THERESA JACKSON CICERO, NEW YORK

1	pound ground beef
1	medium onion, chopped
2	garlic cloves, minced
4	cups V8 juice
1	can (14-1/2 ounces) stewed tomatoes
2	cups coleslaw mix
2	cups frozen green beans
2	cups frozen corn
2	tablespoons Worcestershire sauce
1	teaspoon dried basil
1/2	teaspoon salt
1/4	teaspoon pepper

◻ In a large saucepan, cook beef and onion over medium heat until meat is no longer pink. Add garlic; cook 1 minute longer. Drain. Place in a 5-qt. slow cooker; add the remaining ingredients. Cover and cook on low for 8-10 hours or until the vegetables are tender.

Yield: 10 servings (2-1/2 quarts).

NUTRITION FACTS: 1 cup equals 164 calories, 6 g fat (2 g saturated fat), 28 mg cholesterol, 538 mg sodium, 19 g carbohydrate, 3 g fiber, 11 g protein.

home-style veggie beef soup

I developed this recipe as a way to use my homegrown vegetables. When you don't have abundant garden-fresh produce, frozen veggies can stand in.
LESLIE LUTHE PARKERSBURG, ILLINOIS

4	large potatoes, peeled and cubed
2	cups water
3	large carrots, sliced
1	large onion, chopped

Salt and pepper to taste

4	cups fresh or frozen cut green beans
4	cups tomato juice
1-1/2	pounds ground beef, cooked and drained
2	cups fresh or frozen corn
1	teaspoon Italian seasoning
1/2	teaspoon garlic powder
2	bay leaves

▨ In a large saucepan, combine the potatoes, water, carrots, onion, salt and pepper; bring to a boil. Reduce heat; cover and simmer for 25 minutes or until tender. Add the remaining ingredients.

▨ Cover and simmer 30 minutes longer or until heated through, stirring occasionally. Discard bay leaves.

Yield: 10-12 servings (2-3/4 quarts).

NUTRITION FACTS: 1 cup equals 246 calories, 6 g fat (2 g saturated fat), 28 mg cholesterol, 350 mg sodium, 36 g carbohydrate, 5 g fiber, 15 g protein.

beef & potato soup

One of our Christmas Eve traditions is to put this soup in the slow cooker to enjoy after the evening service at church.
SHEILA HOLDERMAN BERTHOLD, NORTH DAKOTA

1-1/2	pounds lean ground beef (90% lean)
3/4	cup chopped onion
1/2	cup all-purpose flour
2	cans (14-1/2 ounces each) reduced-sodium chicken broth, divided
5	medium potatoes, peeled and cubed
5	medium carrots, chopped
3	celery ribs, chopped
3	teaspoons dried basil
2	teaspoons dried parsley flakes
1	teaspoon garlic powder
1/2	teaspoon pepper
12	ounces reduced-fat process cheese (Velveeta), cubed
1-1/2	cups 2% milk
1/2	cup reduced-fat sour cream

▨ In a large skillet, cook beef and onion over medium heat until meat is no longer pink; drain. Combine flour and 1 can broth until smooth. Add to beef mixture. Bring to a boil; cook and stir for 2 minutes or until thickened.

▨ Transfer to a 5-qt. slow cooker. Stir in the potatoes, carrots, celery, seasonings and remaining broth. Cover and cook on low for 6-8 hours or until vegetables are tender.

▨ Stir in cheese and milk. Cover and cook 30 minutes longer or until cheese is melted. Just before serving, stir in sour cream.

Yield: 10 servings (3 quarts).

NUTRITION FACTS: 1-1/4 cups equals 327 calories, 11 g fat (5 g saturated fat), 61 mg cholesterol, 832 mg sodium, 32 g carbohydrate, 3 g fiber, 25 g protein.

freeze-ahead veggie beef soup

On cool nights, it's so nice to enjoy a bowl of hot homemade soup. You can opt for chicken (and chicken broth) instead of beef and substitute your favorite veggies to create your own customized version.
TASTE OF HOME TEST KITCHEN

1	pound lean ground beef (90% lean)
1/3	cup chopped onion
1/3	cup chopped green pepper
2	cans (14-1/2 ounces each) reduced-sodium beef broth
1	can (14-1/2 ounces) diced tomatoes, undrained
1	cup cubed peeled potatoes
3/4	cup fresh or frozen cut green beans
1/2	cup chopped carrot
1/2	cup water
1	garlic clove, minced
1	teaspoon Italian seasoning
1/8	teaspoon pepper

▨ In a Dutch oven, cook the beef, onion and green pepper over medium heat until meat is no longer pink; drain. Stir in the remaining ingredients. Bring to a boil. Reduce heat; cover and simmer for 30 minutes or until vegetables are tender.

▨ Serve immediately or transfer to freezer containers. May be frozen for up to 3 months.

▨ To use frozen soup: Thaw in the refrigerator overnight. Transfer to a saucepan. Cover and cook over medium heat until heated through.

Yield: 6 servings.

NUTRITION FACTS: 1-1/3 cups equals 173 calories, 6 g fat (2 g saturated fat), 40 mg cholesterol, 394 mg sodium, 13 g carbohydrate, 3 g fiber, 17 g protein.

santa fe stew

This recipe has been well-received everywhere I've served it, from a simple family dinner to events at my church.
PATTI HENSON LINDEN, TEXAS

2	tablespoons canola oil
1	beef eye round roast (2 to 3 pounds), cut into 1/2-inch cubes
2	medium onions, sliced
1	can (15 ounces) pinto beans, rinsed and drained
1	can (10-1/2 ounces) condensed beef broth, undiluted
1	can (10 ounces) diced tomatoes with mild green chilies, undrained
2	cans (4 ounces each) chopped green chilies
1	cup water
1	medium green pepper, chopped
1	tablespoon sugar
1	to 2 teaspoons ground cumin
1	garlic clove, minced

Salt to taste
Shredded Monterey Jack cheese

▨ In a Dutch oven, heat oil over medium-high heat. Brown beef on all sides. Stir in the remaining ingredients except cheese.

▨ Bring to a boil. Reduce heat; cover and simmer for 1-1/2 hours or until meat is tender. Sprinkle with cheese.

Yield: 8 servings (2 quarts).

NUTRITION FACTS: 1 cup (calculated without cheese) equals 251 calories, 8 g fat (2 g saturated fat), 52 mg cholesterol, 565 mg sodium, 18 g carbohydrate, 4 g fiber, 27 g protein.

MAKE YOUR OWN ITALIAN SEASONING

If you don't have Italian seasoning, you can substitute a mixture of equal parts basil, thyme, rosemary and oregano. You can add a little marjoram, savory or sage if you have it, too. Add to or reduce the amounts to suit your taste and what you have on hand.

roast beef soup

If your family's like mine, you have to disguise leftovers before anyone will eat them! This special soup turns those humble leftovers into a lively meal.
KATHY JENSEN EDMONDS, WASHINGTON

2	pounds cubed cooked roast beef
1-1/4	cups chopped onion
2	tablespoons canola oil
4-1/2	cups water
1	jar (12 ounces) beef au jus gravy
1	cup leftover beef gravy or 1 can (10-1/4 ounces) beef gravy
1	envelope brown gravy mix
2	bay leaves
1/4	teaspoon garlic salt
1/4	teaspoon pepper
1/4	teaspoon hot pepper sauce
1	cup dried lentils, rinsed
1	cup frozen mixed vegetables

▦ In a 3-qt. saucepan, saute beef and onion in oil until onion is tender. Add the next eight ingredients; cover and simmer for 1 hour.

▦ Stir in lentils; cover and simmer for 30 minutes. Add vegetables; cover and simmer for 10 minutes or until lentils and vegetables are tender. Remove bay leaves.

Yield: 6-8 servings (2 quarts).

NUTRITION FACTS: 1 cup equals 409 calories, 12 g fat (3 g saturated fat), 103 mg cholesterol, 747 mg sodium, 24 g carbohydrate, 9 g fiber, 50 g protein.

kentucky chili

This chili tastes extra-special with spaghetti stirred in. I love it so much I named it after my home state.
TINA SULLIVAN CORNITH, KENTUCKY

1-1/2	pounds ground beef
1	medium onion, chopped
2	cans (32 ounces each) tomato juice
1	cup water
1	can (16 ounces) chili beans, undrained
1	tablespoon chili powder
1	teaspoon salt
1/2	teaspoon pepper
8	ounces uncooked spaghetti, broken in half

▦ In a Dutch oven, cook beef and onion over medium heat until meat is no longer pink; drain. Add the tomato juice, water, chili beans, chili powder, salt and pepper. Bring to a boil. Reduce heat; cover and simmer for 15-20 minutes.

▦ Meanwhile, cook spaghetti according to package directions. Drain and stir into chili.

Yield: 12 servings (3 quarts).

NUTRITION FACTS: 1 cup equals 232 calories, 8 g fat (3 g saturated fat), 38 mg cholesterol, 606 mg sodium, 26 g carbohydrate, 3 g fiber, 16 g protein.

spicy potato soup

My sister-in-law, who is from Mexico, shared this wonderful recipe with me. Since she prefers food much spicier than we do, I've cut back on the heat by reducing the amount of pepper sauce.
AUDREY WALL INDUSTRY, PENNSYLVANIA

1	pound ground beef
4	cups cubed peeled potatoes (1/2-inch cubes)
1	small onion, chopped
3	cans (8 ounces each) tomato sauce
4	cups water
2	teaspoons salt
1-1/2	teaspoons pepper
1/2	to 1 teaspoon hot pepper sauce

▦ In a Dutch oven, brown ground beef over medium heat until no longer pink; drain. Add the potatoes, onion and tomato sauce. Stir in the water, salt, pepper and hot pepper sauce; bring to a boil. Reduce heat and simmer for 1 hour or until the potatoes are tender and the soup has thickened.

Yield: 6-8 servings (2 quarts).

NUTRITION FACTS: 1 cup equals 159 calories, 5 g fat (2 g saturated fat), 28 mg cholesterol, 764 mg sodium, 16 g carbohydrate, 2 g fiber, 12 g protein.

zesty hamburger soup

(pictured at left)

You'll have plenty of energy in the afternoon if you make this wonderful soup part of your lunch. Freeze leftovers in small batches so you can enjoy it anytime.
KELLY MILAN LAKE JACKSON, TEXAS

1	pound lean ground beef (90% lean)
2	cups sliced celery
1	cup chopped onion
2	teaspoons minced garlic
4	cup water
2	medium red potatoes, peeled and cubed
2	cups frozen corn
1-1/2	cups uncooked small shell pasta
4	pickled jalapeno slices, chopped
4	cups V8 juice
2	cans (10 ounces each) diced tomatoes with green chilies
1	to 2 tablespoons sugar

▢ In a Dutch oven, cook the beef, celery and onion over medium heat until meat is no longer pink. Add garlic; cook 1 minute longer. Drain. Stir in the water, potatoes, corn, pasta and jalapeno.

▢ Bring to a boil. Reduce heat; cover and simmer for 10-15 minutes or until pasta is tender. Add remaining ingredients; cook and stir until heated through.

Yield: 10 servings (3-3/4 quarts).

NUTRITION FACTS: 1-1/2 cups equals 222 calories, 5 g fat (2 g saturated fat), 28 mg cholesterol, 542 mg sodium, 33 g carbohydrate, 4 g fiber, 14 g protein. **DIABETIC EXCHANGES:** 2 vegetable, 1-1/2 starch, 1 lean meat.

steak soup

One of the nice things about this thick soup is that you can make it in an afternoon without too much fuss. It's perfect for soccer-practice night.
MARY DICE CHEMAINUS, BRITISH COLUMBIA

2	tablespoons butter
2	tablespoons canola oil
1-1/2	to 2 pounds beef eye round roast, cut into 1/2-inch cubes
1/4	cup chopped onion
3	tablespoons all-purpose flour
1	tablespoon paprika
1	teaspoon salt
1/4	teaspoon pepper
4	cups beef stock or broth
2	cups water
1	bay leaf
4	sprigs fresh parsley, chopped
2	sprigs celery leaves, chopped
1/2	teaspoon dried marjoram
1-1/2	cups cubed peeled potatoes
1-1/2	cups sliced carrots
1-1/2	cups chopped celery
1	can (6 ounces) tomato paste

▢ In a Dutch oven, melt butter over medium heat; add oil. Brown beef and onion. Combine flour, paprika, salt and pepper; sprinkle over beef and mix well. Stir in stock and water. Add bay leaf, parsley, celery leaves and marjoram. Bring to a boil; reduce heat and simmer, covered, about 1 hour or until tender.

▢ Add the potatoes, carrots and celery. Simmer, covered, for 30-45 minutes or until vegetables are tender and soup begins to thicken. Stir in tomato paste; simmer, uncovered, 15 minutes or until heated through. Discard bay leaf.

Yield: 6 servings.

NUTRITION FACTS: 1 cup equals 319 calories, 13 g fat (4 g saturated fat), 56 mg cholesterol, 1,112 mg sodium, 21 g carbohydrate, 4 g fiber, 30 g protein.

beef vegetable soup

(pictured above)

Convenient frozen veggies and hash browns make this meaty soup a snap to mix up. Simply brown the ground beef, then stir everything together to simmer in the slow cooker all day. It's wonderful served with bread and a salad.

CAROL CALHOUN SIOUX FALLS, SOUTH DAKOTA

- 1 pound ground beef
- 1 can (46 ounces) tomato juice
- 1 package (16 ounces) frozen mixed vegetables, thawed
- 2 cups frozen cubed hash brown potatoes, thawed
- 1 envelope onion soup mix

In a large skillet, cook beef over medium heat until no longer pink; drain. Transfer beef to a 5-qt. slow cooker. Stir in the tomato juice, mixed vegetables, potatoes and soup mix.

Cover and cook on low for 8-10 hours or until the soup is heated through.

Yield: 10 servings (2-1/2 quarts).

NUTRITION FACTS: 1 cup equals 139 calories, 4 g fat (2 g saturated fat), 22 mg cholesterol, 766 mg sodium, 16 g carbohydrate, 3 g fiber, 11 g protein.

stovetop beef stew

I jazz up a packaged pot roast with just a few ingredients to give my super-fast stew a slow-cooked flavor. You might think this is too good to be true, but believe it!

MITZI SENTIFF ANNAPOLIS, MARYLAND

- 1 package (24 ounces) frozen Yankee pot roast skillet dinner
- 1 can (14-1/2 ounces) diced tomatoes with roasted garlic, undrained
- 1 cup reduced-sodium beef broth
- 1/2 cup dry red wine or additional reduced-sodium beef broth
- 1/2 cup sliced celery
- 1/2 teaspoon pepper
- 1/8 to 1/4 teaspoon dried marjoram
- 1 package (9 ounces) frozen peas and pearl onions
- 2 tablespoons minced fresh parsley

In a large saucepan, bring the first seven ingredients to a boil. Reduce heat; cover and simmer for 8 minutes. Stir in peas and onions; cook 7-9 minutes longer or until onions are tender. Sprinkle with parsley.

Yield: 4 servings.

NUTRITION FACTS: 1-3/4 cups equals 263 calories, 4 g fat (2 g saturated fat), 21 mg cholesterol, 1,274 mg sodium, 38 g carbohydrate, 5 g fiber, 13 g protein.

EDITOR'S NOTE: This recipe was tested with Stouffer's Skillets Yankee Pot Roast.

southwest beef stew

I made this stew in the slow cooker for my ladies' group at church, and everyone loved it! I started the soup before leaving for work in the morning, and it was ready to go for my church group when I got home.
ANITA ROBERSON WILLIAMSTON, NORTH CAROLINA

1-1/2	pounds lean ground beef (90% lean)
1	large onion, chopped
2	cans (14-1/2 ounces each) diced tomatoes, undrained
1	package (16 ounces) frozen corn
1	can (15 ounces) black beans, rinsed and drained
1	can (14-1/2 ounces) chicken broth
1	can (10 ounces) diced tomatoes and green chilies, undrained
1	teaspoon garlic powder
1-1/2	teaspoons salt-free Southwest chipotle seasoning blend
1-1/2	cups cooked rice
1/4	cup shredded cheddar cheese

▨ In a large skillet, cook beef and onion over medium heat until meat is no longer pink; drain.

▨ Transfer to a 5-qt. slow cooker. Stir in the tomatoes, corn, black beans, broth, tomatoes, garlic powder and seasoning blend. Cover and cook on low for 6-8 hours or until heated through.

▨ Stir in rice; heat through. Sprinkle each serving of stew with cheese.

Yield: 11 servings (2-3/4 quarts).

NUTRITION FACTS: 1 cup equals 228 calories, 6 g fat (3 g saturated fat), 42 mg cholesterol, 482 mg sodium, 26 g carbohydrate, 4 g fiber, 17 g protein. **DIABETIC EXCHANGES:** 2 lean meat, 1-1/2 starch, 1 vegetable.

stuffed pepper soup

While talking about stuffed peppers with the other cooks at the restaurant where I work, we decided to stir up similar ingredients for a soup. Customer response to our creation was overwhelmingly positive.
KRISTA MUDDIMAN MEADVILLE, PENNSYLVANIA

2	pounds ground beef
2	quarts water
1	can (28 ounces) tomato sauce
1	can (28 ounces) diced tomatoes, undrained
2	cups cooked long grain rice
2	cups chopped green peppers
1/4	cup packed brown sugar
2	teaspoons salt
2	teaspoons beef bouillon granules
1	teaspoon pepper

▨ In a Dutch oven, cook beef over medium heat until no longer pink; drain. Stir in the remaining ingredients; bring to a boil. Reduce heat; cover and simmer for 30-40 minutes or until peppers are tender.

Yield: 10 servings (2-1/2 quarts).

NUTRITION FACTS: 1 cup equals 248 calories, 8 g fat (4 g saturated fat), 45 mg cholesterol, 1,158 mg sodium, 24 g carbohydrate, 3 g fiber, 19 g protein.

and blackened. Immediately place poblanos in a small bowl; cover and let stand for 20 minutes.

▢ Peel off and discard charred skins. Remove stems and seeds. Coarsely chop poblanos.

▢ In a Dutch oven, brown beef in oil in batches. Remove and keep warm. In the same pan, saute onion until tender. Add garlic; cook 1 minute longer.

▢ Gradually add broth; stir in the tomatoes, cilantro, chili powder, salt, cumin, pepper, poblanos and beef. Bring to a boil. Reduce heat; cover and simmer 1-1/2 hours or until beef is tender. Add the potatoes; cook 10-15 minutes longer or until potatoes are tender. Skim off fat.

Yield: 8 servings (3 quarts).

NUTRITION FACTS: 1-1/2 cups equals 337 calories, 15 g fat (5 g saturated fat), 74 mg cholesterol, 808 mg sodium, 24 g carbohydrate, 4 g fiber, 27 g protein. **DIABETIC EXCHANGES:** 3 lean meat, 1 starch, 1 vegetable, 1 fat.

meatball minestrone

Just thinking about this soup simmering on the stove gets me hungry for some! It's fairly easy to make, but looks impressive on the dinner table.
ESTHER PEREA VAN NUYS, CALIFORNIA

1	pound ground beef
1	egg, lightly beaten
1/2	cup chopped onion
1/4	cup dry bread crumbs
1	teaspoon salt
1/4	teaspoon pepper
1	can (15 ounces) tomato sauce
2-1/2	cups water
1	can (15-1/2 ounces) kidney beans, undrained
1/2	teaspoon dried oregano
1/4	teaspoon dried thyme
1	cup sliced celery
1/4	cup uncooked elbow macaroni
1/4	cup chopped fresh parsley

▢ In a large bowl, combine the beef, egg, onion, crumbs, salt and pepper. Shape into 1-in. balls.

▢ In large saucepan, brown meatballs on all sides until no longer pink. Drain. Add remaining ingredients except macaroni and parsley; cover and simmer 20 minutes. Add macaroni; simmer 10 minutes or until tender. Stir in the parsley.

Yield: 8 servings (2 quarts).

NUTRITION FACTS: 1 cup equals 210 calories, 8 g fat (3 g saturated fat), 64 mg cholesterol, 706 mg sodium, 17 g carbohydrate, 4 g fiber, 17 g protein.

roasted poblano beef stew

I like to keep my son's heritage alive through cooking. This recipe reflects my wife's Hispanic background. Try serving it in flour tortillas.
GREG FONTENOT THE WOODLANDS, TEXAS

5	poblano peppers
1	boneless beef chuck roast (2 to 3 pounds), cut into 1-inch cubes
2	tablespoons olive oil
1	medium onion, chopped
3	garlic cloves, minced
1	carton (32 ounces) beef broth
2	medium tomatoes, chopped
1/3	cup minced fresh cilantro
1	tablespoon chili powder
1	teaspoon salt
1	teaspoon ground cumin
1/2	teaspoon pepper
2	large potatoes, peeled and cut into 1-inch cubes

▢ Broil poblano peppers 4 in. from the heat until skins blister, about 5 minutes. With tongs, rotate peppers a quarter turn. Broil and rotate until all sides are blistered

wintertime meatball soup

If you like, you can vary the vegetables added to this soup. I sometimes add a bit of chopped jalapeno pepper for some heat, and I love to serve it with corn bread.
EUNICE JUSTICE CODY, WYOMING

2	cans (16 ounces each) chili beans, undrained
2	cans (14-1/2 ounces each) beef broth
1	jar (26 ounces) spaghetti sauce
1/4	cup chopped onion
3	garlic cloves, minced
1	tablespoon Worcestershire sauce
1	teaspoon Italian seasoning
1	package (32 ounces) frozen fully cooked Italian meatballs
1	package (16 ounces) frozen mixed vegetables
4	cups chopped cabbage

▢ In a 6-qt. slow cooker, combine the beans, broth, spaghetti sauce, onion, garlic, Worcestershire sauce and Italian seasoning. Stir in the meatballs, mixed vegetables and cabbage. Cover and cook on low for 8-10 hours or until vegetables are tender.

Yield: 15 servings (3-3/4 quarts).

NUTRITION FACTS: 1 cup equals 295 calories, 16 g fat (7 g saturated fat), 30 mg cholesterol, 1,147 mg sodium, 25 g carbohydrate, 7 g fiber, 16 g protein.

peasant's delight soup

Beef, beans, barley and a cornucopia of vegetables come together in this delightfully hearty soup. It's a tasty way to chase away the chill of winter.
MARY SULLIVAN SPOKANE, WASHINGTON

1	pound beef stew meat, cut into 3/4-inch cubes
1	tablespoon olive oil
2	cups chopped onions
1	cup sliced celery
2	garlic cloves, minced
5	cups water
5	cups beef broth
2	cups sliced carrots
1-1/2	cups medium pearl barley
1	can (15 ounces) garbanzo beans or chickpeas, rinsed and drained
1	can (15 ounces) kidney beans, rinsed and drained
4	cups sliced zucchini
3	cups diced plum tomatoes
2	cups chopped cabbage
1/4	cup minced fresh parsley
1	teaspoon dried thyme
1-1/2	teaspoons Italian seasoning

Salt and pepper to taste
Grated Parmesan cheese, optional

▢ In a stockpot, brown meat in oil. Add onions and celery. Cook until beef is no longer pink. Add garlic and cook 1 minute longer. Add water and broth; bring to a boil. Add carrots and barley. Reduce heat; cover and simmer for 45-60 minutes or until barley is tender.

▢ Add the beans, zucchini, tomatoes, cabbage, parsley and seasonings; simmer 15-20 minutes or until vegetables are tender. Top each serving with Parmesan cheese if desired.

Yield: 20 servings (5 quarts).

NUTRITION FACTS: 1 cup (calculated without cheese) equals 159 calories, 3 g fat (1 g saturated fat), 14 mg cholesterol, 292 mg sodium, 24 g carbohydrate, 6 g fiber, 10 g protein.

pasta pizza soup

(pictured at left)

A steaming bowl of my soup hits the spot on rainy or snowy days, which we have in abundance here. Oregano adds fast flavor to the pleasant combination of tender vegetables, pasta spirals and ground beef.
LINDA FOX SOLDOTNA, ALASKA

1	pound ground beef
1-3/4	cups sliced fresh mushrooms
1	medium onion, chopped
1	celery rib, thinly sliced
1	garlic clove, minced
4	cups water
1	can (14-1/2 ounces) Italian diced tomatoes, undrained
2	medium carrots, sliced
4	teaspoons beef bouillon granules
1	bay leaf
1-1/2	teaspoons dried oregano
1-1/2	cups cooked tricolor spiral pasta

▨ In a large saucepan over medium heat, cook the beef, mushrooms, onion and celery until meat is no longer pink. Add garlic; cook 1 minute longer. Drain.

▨ Stir in the water, tomatoes, carrots, bouillon, bay leaf and oregano. Bring to a boil. Reduce heat; cover and simmer for 20-25 minutes or until carrots are tender. Stir in pasta; heat through. Discard bay leaf.

Yield: 8 servings (about 2 quarts).

NUTRITION FACTS: 1 cup equals 180 calories, 7 g fat (3 g saturated fat), 35 mg cholesterol, 639 mg sodium, 16 g carbohydrate, 2 g fiber, 13 g protein. **DIABETIC EXCHANGES:** 2 vegetable, 1 lean meat, 1/2 starch, 1/2 fat.

truly texan chili

As a native Texan, I can promise you this is the best chili recipe I've ever tasted. It's meaty and spicy. During the years we spent away from Texas because of my husband's military career, I made this chili whenever I was homesick.
BETTY BROWN SAN ANTONIO, TEXAS

3	pounds ground beef
2	garlic cloves, minced
3	tablespoons chili powder (or to taste)
1	tablespoon ground cumin
1/4	cup all-purpose flour
1	tablespoon dried oregano
2	cans (14-1/2 ounces each) beef broth
1	teaspoon salt
1/4	teaspoon pepper
1	can (15 ounces) pinto beans, rinsed and drained, optional

Optional garnishes: shredded cheddar cheese, tortilla chips, sour cream and/or lime wedges

▨ In a Dutch oven, cook beef and garlic over medium heat until no longer pink; drain. Combine the flour, chili powder, oregano and cumin; sprinkle over meat, stirring until evenly coated. Add the broth, beans if desired, salt and pepper.

▨ Bring to a boil. Reduce heat; cover and simmer for 1-1/2 to 2 hours to allow flavors to blend, stirring occasionally. Sprinkle with cheese, tortilla chips, sour cream and/or lime wedges if desired.

Yield: 8 servings.

NUTRITION FACTS: 1 serving (calculated without beans and optional garnishes) equals 343 calories, 21 g fat (8 g saturated fat), 105 mg cholesterol, 872 mg sodium, 5 g carbohydrate, 1 g fiber, 32 g protein.

beef & vegetable soup

(pictured above)

I've been making this for more than 20 years. The beer makes people stop and wonder what the unique flavor is.
TAMMY LANDRY SAUCIER, MISSISSIPPI

1	pound lean ground beef (90% lean)
1/2	cup chopped sweet onion
1	bottle (12 ounces) beer or nonalcoholic beer
1	can (10-1/2 ounces) condensed beef broth, undiluted
1-1/2	cups sliced fresh carrots
1-1/4	cups water
1	cup chopped peeled turnip
1/2	cup sliced celery
1	can (4 ounces) mushroom stems and pieces, drained
1	teaspoon salt
1	teaspoon pepper
1	bay leaf
1/8	teaspoon ground allspice

▢ In a large skillet, cook beef and onion over medium heat until meat is no longer pink; drain. Transfer to a 5-qt. slow cooker. Stir in the remaining ingredients. Cover and cook on low for 8-10 hours or until heated through. Discard bay leaf.

Yield: 6 servings.

NUTRITION FACTS: 1 cup equals 176 calories, 6 g fat (2 g saturated fat), 38 mg cholesterol, 939 mg sodium, 8 g carbohydrate, 2 g fiber, 17 g protein.

hamburger soup

I can't wait for chilly weather just so I can make this satisfying soup!
SANDRA KOCH ELYRIA, OHIO

1-1/2	pounds ground beef
2	cups diced onions
1	cup diced carrots
1	cup diced celery
3	garlic cloves, minced
3	cans (14-1/2 ounces each) chicken broth
1	can (15 ounces) crushed tomatoes
2	tablespoons Worcestershire sauce
1	teaspoon hot pepper sauce
1/4	cup butter, cubed
1/2	cup all-purpose flour

▢ In a large saucepan, cook the beef, onions, carrots, celery and garlic over medium heat until meat is no longer pink and vegetables are tender; drain. Stir in broth, tomatoes, Worcestershire sauce and hot pepper sauce. Bring to a boil. Reduce heat; cover and simmer for 15 minutes.

▢ In another saucepan, melt butter over medium-low heat. Stir in flour until smooth. Cook and stir for 6-8 minutes or until mixture turns golden brown (do not burn). Carefully stir into soup. Cover and simmer for 15 minutes or until thickened, stirring occasionally.

Yield: 10 servings (2-1/2 quarts).

NUTRITION FACTS: 1 cup equals 208 calories, 11 g fat (4 g saturated fat), 33 mg cholesterol, 366 mg sodium, 13 g carbohydrate, 2 g fiber, 14 g protein.

montana wildfire chili

This thick and chunky chili really has some kick to it. I like to top mine with shredded cheddar and serve it with a side of hot corn bread.

DONNA EVARO GREAT FALLS, MONTANA

- 2 pounds ground beef
- 1 large sweet onion, chopped
- 1 medium sweet red pepper, finely chopped
- 1 medium sweet yellow pepper, finely chopped
- 2 cans (16 ounces each) chili beans, undrained
- 2 cans (14-1/2 ounces each) stewed tomatoes, undrained
- 2 jalapeno peppers, seeded and minced
- 2 garlic cloves, minced
- 2 teaspoons ground cumin
- 2 teaspoons chili powder
- 1 teaspoon salt
- 1 teaspoon cayenne pepper

◻ In a large skillet, cook beef, onion and peppers over medium heat until meat is no longer pink; drain.

◻ Transfer to a 4-or 5-quart slow cooker. Stir in the beans, tomatoes, jalapenos, garlic, cumin, chili powder, salt and cayenne. Cover and cook on low for 5-6 hours or until heated through.

Yield: 8 servings (2-1/2 quarts).

NUTRITION FACTS: 1-1/3 cups equals 365 calories, 15 g fat (6 g saturated fat), 70 mg cholesterol, 920 mg sodium, 36 g carbohydrate, 9 g fiber, 28 g protein.

EDITOR'S NOTE: Wear disposable gloves when cutting hot peppers; the oils can burn skin. Avoid touching your face.

crowd-sized chili

Everyone who tastes my chili says it's restaurant-quality. It's especially good with homemade corn bread. I have always loved to cook, and I enjoy coming up with original recipes like this one.

SHANNON WRIGHT ERIE, PENNSYLVANIA

- 3 pounds ground beef
- 1 large onion, chopped
- 1 medium green pepper, chopped
- 2 celery ribs, chopped
- 2 cans (16 ounces each) kidney beans, rinsed and drained
- 1 can (29 ounces) tomato puree
- 1 jar (16 ounces) salsa
- 1 can (14-1/2 ounces) diced tomatoes, undrained
- 1 can (10-1/2 ounces) condensed beef broth, undiluted

- 1 to 2 cups water
- 1/4 cup chili powder
- 2 tablespoons Worcestershire sauce
- 1 tablespoon dried basil
- 2 teaspoons ground cumin
- 2 teaspoons steak sauce
- 1 teaspoon garlic powder
- 1 teaspoon salt
- 1 teaspoon coarsely ground pepper
- 1-1/2 teaspoons browning sauce, optional

Additional chopped onion, optional

◻ In a stockpot, cook the beef, onion, green pepper and celery over medium heat until meat is no longer pink and vegetables are tender; drain.

◻ Stir in the beans, tomato puree, salsa, tomatoes, broth, water, seasonings and browning sauce if desired. Bring to a boil. Reduce heat; simmer, uncovered, for 30 minutes or until chili reaches desired thickness. Garnish with chopped onion if desired.

Yield: 16 servings (4 quarts).

NUTRITION FACTS: 1 cup equals 242 calories, 11 g fat (4 g saturated fat), 57 mg cholesterol, 611 mg sodium, 13 g carbohydrate, 4 g fiber, 21 g protein.

quick vegetable beef soup

I send my husband off to the farm every day with lunch in a cooler. It's hard to have a variety of meals, especially hot ones. But a thermos full of this soup keeps him going all day long!
JUNE FORMANEK BELLE PLAINE, IOWA

1-1/2	pounds ground beef
1/3	cup dried minced onion
1	can (46 ounces) tomato juice
2	packages (10 ounces each) frozen mixed vegetables
2	teaspoons beef bouillon granules
1	teaspoon sugar
1/2	teaspoon pepper

☐ In a Dutch oven, cook the beef and onion over medium heat until meat is no longer pink; drain.

☐ Add the remaining ingredients and bring mixture to a boil. Reduce heat. Cover and simmer 20-30 minutes or until the vegetables are tender.

Yield: 10 servings (2-1/2 quarts).

NUTRITION FACTS: 1 cup equals 173 calories, 6 g fat (3 g saturated fat), 33 mg cholesterol, 742 mg sodium, 15 g carbohydrate, 3 g fiber, 15 g protein.

hearty oxtail soup

I first made a version of this soup for a friend who was coming to visit. I decided to liven up my usual vegetable soup by adding oxtails. Little did I know oxtails were her favorite and she hadn't had them for years!
MARGIE GERNDT GILLETT, WISCONSIN

2	pounds oxtails or meaty beef shanks
1-1/2	cup sliced carrots
1	cup chopped onion
1	cup chopped celery
1	cup sliced leeks
1/2	green pepper, chopped
3	tablespoons butter
1	can (28 ounces) crushed tomatoes
4	beef bouillon cubes
2	teaspoons onion powder
1-1/2	teaspoons garlic powder
1	teaspoon pepper
Salt to taste	
6	quarts water
1	cup medium pearl barley
Chopped fresh parsley	

☐ In a stockpot, saute oxtails, carrots, onion, celery, leeks and green pepper in butter until vegetables are crisp-tender. Add the tomatoes, bouillon, seasonings and water. Bring to a boil. Skim off any foam. Reduce heat; cover and simmer for 2-3 hours or until the meat is tender.

☐ Stir in barley; cover and continue to simmer until tender, about 1 hour. Add additional water if necessary.

☐ Remove oxtails; set aside until cool enough to handle. Remove meat from bones; discard bones and cut meat into cubes. Return meat to soup. Garnish with parsley.

Yield: 24 servings (6 quarts).

NUTRITION FACTS: 1 cup equals 102 calories, 4 g fat (2 g saturated fat), 15 mg cholesterol, 218 mg sodium, 11 g carbohydrate, 2 g fiber, 6 g protein.

anytime burger soup

We work up big appetites on our farm, so I depend on recipes like this that are flavorful and fast. The soup is great served with corn bread.
GUYNELL BOYD JAYESS, MISSISSIPPI

1-1/2	pounds ground beef
1	medium onion, chopped
2	cans (15 ounces each) mixed vegetables
1	can (14-3/4 ounces) cream-style corn
1	can (14-1/2 ounces) stewed tomatoes
1	can (14-1/2 ounces) chicken broth
1	can (11-1/2 ounces) tomato juice
1	teaspoon salt
1/2	teaspoon pepper

☐ In a Dutch oven over medium heat, brown beef and onion; drain.

☐ Add remaining ingredients; bring to a boil. Reduce heat; cover and simmer for 10 minutes to allow flavors to blend.

Yield: 10 servings (about 2-1/2 quarts).

NUTRITION FACTS: 1 cup equals 164 calories, 6 g fat (3 g saturated fat), 33 mg cholesterol, 804 mg sodium, 13 g carbohydrate, 2 g fiber, 14 g protein.

pork-and-beans beef stew

My mom and dad, who are both wonderful cooks, instilled their love of cooking in me. I enjoy experimenting with different recipes and couldn't wait to try this unique stew. Sure enough, everyone loved it!
KELI LAMB COUPEVILLE, WASHINGTON

3	pounds ground beef
1	cup chopped onion
2	cans (10-3/4 ounces each) condensed tomato soup, undiluted
2-2/3	cups water
2	envelopes taco seasoning
2	cups each diced carrots and celery
2	cups cubed potatoes
1	can (28 ounces) pork and beans, undrained

Salt and pepper to taste

☐ In a skillet, cook beef and onion over medium heat until no longer pink.

☐ Meanwhile, in a Dutch oven, bring the soup, water and taco seasoning to a boil. Add vegetables and return to a boil.

☐ Reduce heat; cover and simmer for 20 minutes or until vegetables are tender. Drain beef; add to stew. Simmer, uncovered, for 5 minutes. Stir in pork and beans; heat through. Add salt and pepper.

Yield: 12 servings (3 quarts).

NUTRITION FACTS: 1 cup equals 309 calories, 11 g fat (5 g saturated fat), 56 mg cholesterol, 999 mg sodium, 29 g carbohydrate, 5 g fiber, 24 g protein.

ground beef and barley soup

I came across this recipe years ago at a recipe exchange through a church group. The contributor didn't sign her name, so I don't know whom to thank. But my husband and son always thank me for preparing it by helping themselves to seconds and thirds!
ELLEN MCCLEARY SCOTLAND, ONTARIO

1-1/2	pounds ground beef
3	celery ribs, sliced
1	medium onion, chopped
3	cans (10-1/2 ounces each) condensed beef consomme, undiluted
1	can (28 ounces) diced tomatoes, undrained
4	medium carrots, sliced
2	cups water
1	can (10-3/4 ounces) condensed tomato soup, undiluted
1/2	cup medium pearl barley
1	bay leaf

☐ In a Dutch oven, cook the beef, celery and onion over medium heat until the meat is no longer pink; drain. Add the remaining ingredients; bring to a boil. Reduce heat; simmer, uncovered, for 45-50 minutes or until barley is tender. Discard bay leaf.

Yield: 12 servings (3 quarts).

NUTRITION FACTS: 1 cup equals 168 calories, 5 g fat (2 g saturated fat), 29 mg cholesterol, 452 mg sodium, 17 g carbohydrate, 4 g fiber, 13 g protein.

potluck pasta soup

Friends and family are willing dinner guests when this Italian restaurant-inspired soup is on the menu.
MARILYN FOSS BEAVERTOWN, OHIO

1-1/2	pounds ground beef
8	cups water
2	cans (14-1/2 ounces each) Italian stewed tomatoes
2	cups diced carrots
1-1/2	cups diced celery
1	cup chopped onion
1/2	cup chopped green pepper
1	can (8 ounces) tomato sauce
1	envelope onion soup mix
1	tablespoon sugar
1	teaspoon Italian seasoning
2	garlic cloves, minced
2	bay leaves
1/2	teaspoon pepper
3	cups cooked elbow macaroni
1	can (15 ounces) garbanzo beans or chickpeas, rinsed and drained

▨ In a stockpot, cook beef over medium heat until no longer pink; drain. Add the water, tomatoes, carrots, celery, onion, green pepper, tomato sauce, soup mix, sugar and seasonings; bring to a boil. Reduce heat; simmer, uncovered, for 1 hour.

▨ Stir in macaroni and beans; heat through. Discard the bay leaves.

Yield: 20 servings (5 quarts).

NUTRITION FACTS: 1 cup equals 136 calories, 5 g fat (2 g saturated fat), 21 mg cholesterol, 376 mg sodium, 15 g carbohydrate, 3 g fiber, 9 g protein. **DIABETIC EXCHANGES:** 1 medium-fat meat, 1 vegetable, 1/2 starch.

from-the-freezer beef barley soup

Prepare this inexpensive soup ahead of time, and you'll have a nutritious meal waiting for days when you're too busy to cook.
LISA OTIS DRAIN, OREGON

2	pounds ground beef
2	medium onions, chopped
1/2	cup chopped celery
3	cups water
2	cans (14-1/2 ounces each) beef broth
1	cup quick-cooking barley
2	cans (14-1/2 ounces each) diced tomatoes with garlic and onion, undrained
2	teaspoons Worcestershire sauce
1	teaspoon salt
1	teaspoon dried basil

▨ In a Dutch oven, cook the beef, onions and celery over medium heat until meat is no longer pink; drain. Stir in the water and broth; bring to a boil. Reduce heat. Add barley; cover and simmer for 10-20 minutes or until barley is tender.

▨ Stir in the remaining ingredients; heat through. Transfer to three 1-qt. freezer containers; cool. Cover and freeze for up to 3 months.

TO USE FROZEN SOUP: Thaw in the refrigerator. Place in a saucepan and heat through.

Yield: 3 batches (4 servings each).

NUTRITION FACTS: 1 cup equals 198 calories, 8 g fat (3 g saturated fat), 37 mg cholesterol, 548 mg sodium, 16 g carbohydrate, 4 g fiber, 16 g protein.

chicken & turkey

lentil & chicken sausage stew
(pictured above)

This hearty soup will warm your family right down to their toes! It's packed with veggies and the rich tastes of autumn.
JAN VALDEZ CHICAGO, ILLINOIS

1	carton (32 ounces) reduced-sodium chicken broth
1	can (28 ounces) diced tomatoes, undrained
3	fully cooked spicy chicken sausage links (3 ounces each), cut into 1/2-inch slices
1	cup dried lentils, rinsed
1	medium onion, chopped
1	medium carrot, chopped
1	celery rib, chopped
2	garlic cloves, minced
1/2	teaspoon dried thyme

▢ In a 4- or 5-qt. slow cooker, combine all ingredients. Cover and cook on low for 8-10 hours or until lentils are tender.

Yield: 6 servings (2-1/4 quarts).

NUTRITION FACTS: 1-1/2 cups equals 231 calories, 4 g fat (1 g saturated fat), 33 mg cholesterol, 803 mg sodium, 31 g carbohydrate, 13 g fiber, 19 g protein. **DIABETIC EXCHANGES:** 2 lean meat, 2 vegetable, 1 starch.

mary's rich chicken soup

When the weather starts turning cooler, we like to sit down to dinner with this colorful and satisfying soup. Add hot rolls and a salad, and you have a hearty meal.
MARY WAGNER WOODBURN, OREGON

2	quarts chicken broth
2	cups cubed cooked chicken
1	jar (4 ounces) diced pimientos, undrained
1/4	cup chopped green onions
1	teaspoon dried tarragon
1/2	teaspoon salt
1/2	teaspoon pepper
2	chicken bouillon cubes
1/2	cup butter, cubed
1	cup all-purpose flour

▢ In a Dutch oven, combine the first eight ingredients; bring to a gentle boil. In a small saucepan, melt butter. Stir in flour; cook and stir for 2 minutes. Gradually add to boiling soup, stirring constantly until smooth. Return the soup to a boil. Reduce heat; simmer, uncovered, for 15 minutes.

Yield: 10 servings (2-1/2 quarts).

NUTRITION FACTS: 1 cup equals 198 calories, 12 g fat (6 g saturated fat), 50 mg cholesterol, 1,204 mg sodium, 11 g carbohydrate, 1 g fiber, 12 g protein.

terrific turkey chili

This chili is full of traditional flavor. I like to keep it light with toppings of cilantro, green onions and reduced-fat cheese.
KIM SEEGER BROOKLYN PARK, MINNESOTA

- 1 pound lean ground turkey
- 1 cup chopped onion
- 1 cup chopped green pepper
- 2 teaspoons minced garlic
- 1 can (28 ounces) crushed tomatoes
- 1 can (16 ounces) kidney beans, rinsed and drained
- 1 can (11-1/2 ounces) tomato juice
- 1 can (6 ounces) tomato paste
- 1 can (4 ounces) chopped green chilies
- 2 tablespoons brown sugar
- 1 tablespoon dried parsley flakes
- 1 tablespoon ground cumin
- 3 teaspoons chili powder
- 2 teaspoons dried oregano
- 1-1/2 teaspoons pepper

▢ In a large saucepan, cook the turkey, onion and green pepper over medium heat until meat is no longer pink. Add garlic; cook 1 minute longer. Drain.

▢ Stir in the remaining ingredients. Bring to a boil. Reduce heat; cover and simmer for 25 minutes or until heated through.

Yield: 6 servings (about 2 quarts).

NUTRITION FACTS: 1-1/3 cups equals 315 calories, 8 g fat (2 g saturated fat), 60 mg cholesterol, 706 mg sodium, 43 g carbohydrate, 11 g fiber, 23 g protein. **DIABETIC EXCHANGES:** 3 starch, 2 lean meat.

tomato chicken rice soup

When friends come for lunch, I warm up garlic toast to turn this satisfying soup into a complete meal. It's a great way to cut back on calories and fat.
GWEN SHAWLEY EL MIRAGE, ARIZONA

- 1/4 cup all-purpose flour
- 1 large onion, chopped
- 1 large green pepper, chopped
- 2 celery ribs, chopped
- 3 green onions, chopped
- 2 teaspoons canola oil
- 3 garlic cloves, minced
- 2 cups water
- 2 cans (14-1/2 ounces each) reduced-sodium chicken broth
- 2 cups cooked brown rice
- 2 cups cubed cooked chicken breast
- 1 can (14-1/2 ounces) diced tomatoes
- 1 teaspoon dried oregano
- 1 teaspoon dried thyme
- 1 bay leaf
- 3/4 teaspoon salt

▢ In a small nonstick skillet, brown flour over medium-high heat; set aside. In a Dutch oven, saute the onion, green pepper, celery and green onions in oil until tender. Add garlic; cook 1 minute longer. Stir in flour until blended. Stir in the remaining ingredients; bring to a boil. Reduce heat; simmer, uncovered, for 15 minutes. Discard bay leaf.

Yield: 7 servings (about 2-1/2 quarts).

NUTRITION FACTS: 1-1/2 cups equals 197 calories, 3 g fat (1 g saturated fat), 34 mg cholesterol, 682 mg sodium, 25 g carbohydrate, 3 g fiber, 17 g protein. **DIABETIC EXCHANGES:** 2 lean meat, 2 vegetable, 1 starch.

turkey & cannellini bean soup

(pictured at left)

This hearty meal-in-one will stick to your ribs on a cold autumn night. Slow cooking makes it so convenient.
AMY MARTELL CANTON, PENNSYLVANIA

1	pound bulk pork sausage
4	cups cubed cooked turkey
2	cans (14-1/2 ounces each) beef broth
1	can (15 ounces) white kidney or cannellini beans, rinsed and drained
1	can (14-1/2 ounces) diced tomatoes, undrained
4	medium carrots, chopped
1	medium onion, chopped
1	medium green pepper, chopped
1	celery rib, chopped
2	teaspoons Italian seasoning
1/4	teaspoon cayenne pepper

☐ Crumble sausage into a large skillet; cook and stir until no longer pink. Drain. Transfer to a 5- or 6-qt. slow cooker. Stir in the remaining ingredients. Cover and cook on low for 5-6 hours or until vegetables are tender.

Yield: 8 servings (3 quarts).

NUTRITION FACTS: 1-1/2 cups equals 318 calories, 15 g fat (5 g saturated fat), 74 mg cholesterol, 902 mg sodium, 16 g carbohydrate, 5 g fiber, 29 g protein.

turkey bean chili

Here's a quick recipe that tastes great. It won a ribbon at the Nebraska State Fair. Once you try it, you'll want to make it again and again. It's that easy.
LARITA LANG LINCOLN, NEBRASKA

2	cups cubed cooked turkey breast
2	cans (14-1/2 ounces each) diced tomatoes, undrained
1	can (15 ounces) black beans, rinsed and drained
1	can (15 ounces) great northern beans, rinsed and drained
1	cup barbecue sauce
1	medium onion, chopped
1	teaspoon chili powder
1	teaspoon ground cumin

☐ In a large saucepan, combine all ingredients. Bring to a boil. Reduce heat; simmer, uncovered, for 10-15 minutes to allow flavors to blend.

Yield: 6 servings.

NUTRITION FACTS: 1 cup equals 236 calories, 2 g fat (trace saturated fat), 40 mg cholesterol, 757 mg sodium, 32 g carbohydrate, 9 g fiber, 23 g protein.

vegetable chicken soup

This satisfying veggie soup hits the spot at lunch or dinner. Add a side salad and some whole grain bread for a filling and nutritious meal.
AMY CHEATHAM SANDUSKY, OHIO

1	large sweet onion, chopped
1	cup sliced baby portobello mushrooms
1/2	cup chopped green pepper
1/2	cup chopped sweet red pepper
1	tablespoon butter
1	tablespoon olive oil
5	garlic cloves, minced
3/4	pound boneless skinless chicken breasts, cut into 1/2-inch cubes
1	can (49-1/2 ounces) chicken broth
1	can (28 ounces) crushed tomatoes, undrained
2	medium carrots, cut into 1/4-inch slices
1/2	cup medium pearl barley
1-3/4	teaspoons Italian seasoning
1-1/2	teaspoons pepper
1/2	teaspoon salt

☐ In a large skillet, saute the onion, mushrooms and peppers in butter and oil until tender. Add garlic; cook 1 minute longer.

☐ Transfer to a 5-qt. slow cooker. Add the remaining ingredients. Cover and cook on low for 5-6 hours or until chicken and barley are tender.

Yield: 7 servings (2-3/4 quarts).

NUTRITION FACTS: 1-1/2 cups equals 212 calories, 6 g fat (2 g saturated fat), 36 mg cholesterol, 1,236 mg sodium, 27 g carbohydrate, 6 g fiber, 15 g protein.

chunky chicken noodle soup
(pictured above)

When winter holds me in its icy grip, I rely on this hearty, old-fashioned chicken soup to warm me up. It's just like Grandma used to make.
SHARON SKILDUM MAPLE GROVE, MINNESOTA

1/4	cup diced carrot
2	tablespoons diced celery
2	tablespoons chopped onion
1	teaspoon butter
2-1/2	cups reduced-sodium chicken broth
2/3	cup diced cooked chicken
1/4	teaspoon salt
1/4	teaspoon dried marjoram
1/4	teaspoon dried thyme

Dash pepper

1/2	cup uncooked medium egg noodles
1	teaspoon minced fresh parsley

▢ In a large saucepan, saute the carrot, celery and onion in butter until tender. Stir in the broth, chicken and seasonings; bring to a boil. Reduce heat. Add noodles; cook for 10 minutes or until tender. Sprinkle with parsley.

Yield: 2 servings.

NUTRITION FACTS: 1-3/4 cups equals 173 calories, 6 g fat (2 g saturated fat), 56 mg cholesterol, 1,144 mg sodium, 11 g carbohydrate, 1 g fiber, 19 g protein.

turkey barley soup

I originally created this recipe as a way to use leftover Thanksgiving turkey. I think you'll agree it's too good to serve only once a year! It makes a hearty meal with homemade bread.
JODI JEUDE CARBONDALE, COLORADO

1-1/2	cups sliced carrots
1-1/2	cups sliced fresh mushrooms
1	cup thinly sliced celery
1	cup chopped onion
2	tablespoons vegetable oil
9	cups turkey broth
2	cups cubed cooked turkey
1/2	cup medium pearl barley
2	bay leaves
1/4	teaspoon pepper

▢ In a 3-qt. saucepan, saute carrots, mushrooms, celery and onion in oil for 20 minutes or until tender. Add remaining ingredients; bring to a boil. Reduce heat; cover and simmer for 50-60 minutes or until barley is tender. Discard bay leaves before serving.

Yield: 8 servings (2 quarts).

NUTRITION FACTS: 1 cup equals 174 calories, 6 g fat (1 g saturated fat), 27 mg cholesterol, 1,094 mg sodium, 16 g carbohydrate, 3 g fiber, 15 g protein.

easy turkey meatball soup

We combined ready-made turkey meatballs with lots of vegetables to come up with this easy soup. Sprinkle servings with Parmesan cheese just before serving. This freezes well.

TASTE OF HOME TEST KITCHEN

3	cups cut fresh green beans
2	cups fresh baby carrots
2	cups chicken broth
1	teaspoon dried oregano
1	teaspoon dried basil
1	teaspoon minced garlic
2	cans (14-1/2 ounces each) Italian stewed tomatoes
1	package (12 ounces) refrigerated fully cooked Italian turkey meatballs
2	cups frozen corn

☐ In a large saucepan, combine the first six ingredients. Bring to a boil. Reduce heat; cover and simmer for 10 minutes.

☐ Add the tomatoes, meatballs and corn. Cover and cook over medium-low heat for 10 minutes or until meatballs are heated through.

TO USE FROZEN SOUP: Thaw in the refrigerator overnight. Transfer to a saucepan; cover and heat through.

Yield: 6 servings (2 quarts).

NUTRITION FACTS: 1-1/3 cups equals 232 calories, 7 g fat (2 g saturated fat), 43 mg cholesterol, 981 mg sodium, 28 g carbohydrate, 6 g fiber, 16 g protein.

presto chicken chili

My aunt gave me the recipe for this practically instant chili. It's a great way to use up your leftover chicken or turkey. Try sprinkling some crunchy corn chips over the top of each serving for added fun!

YVONNE MORGAN GRAND RAPIDS, MICHIGAN

2	cans (15 ounces each) great northern beans, rinsed and drained
2	jars (16 ounces each) picante sauce
4	cups cubed cooked chicken
1	to 2 teaspoons ground cumin

Shredded Monterey Jack cheese

☐ In a large saucepan, combine the beans, picante sauce, chicken and cumin.

☐ Bring to a boil. Reduce heat; cover and simmer the chili for 20 minutes to allow flavors to blend. Sprinkle each serving with cheese.

Yield: 6 servings.

NUTRITION FACTS: 1 cup (calculated without cheese) equals 261 calories, 7 g fat (2 g saturated fat), 83 mg cholesterol, 573 mg sodium, 15 g carbohydrate, 4 g fiber, 30 g protein.

Sprinkle chicken with lemon-pepper and salt; broil for 5-6 minutes on each side or until a thermometer reads 170°. Cut one tortilla into 1/4-in. strips; coarsely chop remaining tortilla.

In a saucepan, heat remaining oil. Fry tortilla strips until crisp and browned; remove with a slotted spoon.

In the same pan, cook the zucchini, carrot, cilantro, cumin, chili powder and chopped tortilla over medium heat for 4 minutes. Stir in the tomato mixture, broth, V8 juice, corn, tomato puree, jalapeno and bay leaf. Bring to a boil. Reduce heat; simmer, uncovered, for 20 minutes.

Cut chicken into strips and add to soup; heat through. Discard bay leaf. Garnish with the avocado, cheese and tortilla strips.

Yield: 3-1/2 cups.

NUTRITION FACTS: 1 cup equals 284 calories, 14 g fat (3 g saturated fat), 40 mg cholesterol, 617 mg sodium, 24 g carbohydrate, 5 g fiber, 18 g protein.

EDITOR'S NOTE: Wear disposable gloves when cutting hot peppers; the oils can burn skin. Avoid touching your face.

tortilla chicken soup

Grilled chicken and veggies add rich flavor to a soup perfect for using up fall's garden-fresh bounty.
KATHY AVERBECK DOUSMAN, WISCONSIN

2	medium tomatoes
1	small onion, cut into wedges
1	garlic clove, peeled
4	teaspoons canola oil, divided
1	boneless skinless chicken breast half (6 ounces)
1/4	teaspoon lemon-pepper seasoning
1/8	teaspoon salt
2	corn tortillas (6 inches)
1/2	cup diced zucchini
2	tablespoons chopped carrot
1	tablespoon minced fresh cilantro
3/4	teaspoon ground cumin
1/2	teaspoon chili powder
1	cup reduced-sodium chicken broth
1/2	cup spicy hot V8 juice
1/3	cup frozen corn
2	tablespoons tomato puree
1-1/2	teaspoons chopped seeded jalapeno pepper
1	bay leaf
1/4	cup cubed or sliced avocado
1/4	cup shredded Mexican cheese blend

Brush tomatoes, onion and garlic with 1 teaspoon oil. Broil 4 in. from the heat for 6-8 minutes or until tender, turning once. Peel and discard charred skins from tomatoes; place tomatoes in a blender. Add onion and garlic; cover and process 1-2 minutes or until smooth.

chicken bean soup

This easy soup is tasty and nutritious, too. I like to top individual bowls with a few sprigs of fresh parsley. Home-baked rolls—I use frozen bread dough—are an added treat.
PHYLLIS SHAUGHNESSY LIVONIA, NEW YORK

1	pound boneless skinless chicken breasts, cubed
2	cans (14-1/2 ounces each) chicken broth
2	cans (14-1/2 ounces each) Italian diced tomatoes, undrained
1	can (16 ounces) kidney beans, rinsed and drained
1	can (15-1/4 ounces) whole kernel corn, drained or 1-1/2 cups frozen corn
1	can (15 ounces) lima beans, rinsed and drained or 1-1/2 cups frozen lima beans
1	cup frozen peas and pearl onions
1	tablespoon snipped fresh dill or 1 teaspoon dill weed
1/2	teaspoon ground ginger, optional

In a 5-qt. slow cooker, combine all ingredients. Cover and cook on low for 4-5 hours or until chicken is no longer pink.

Yield: 12 servings (3 quarts).

NUTRITION FACTS: 1 cup equals 159 calories, 1 g fat (trace saturated fat), 22 mg cholesterol, 624 mg sodium, 22 g carbohydrate, 5 g fiber, 13 g protein. **DIABETIC EXCHANGES:** 1 starch, 1 lean meat, 1 vegetable.

chicken soup base

I keep plenty of this delicious soup base on hand for my father. He can serve it as is, or dress it up with some easy variations.
MARTHA TAYLOR CALIFORNIA, MISSOURI

1	broiler/fryer chicken (3-1/2 to 4 pounds)
3	quarts water
1	cup frozen chopped broccoli
1	cup shredded carrots
1	cup frozen peas
1	small onion, chopped
1/2	cup chopped celery
1/4	cup chicken bouillon granules
1	tablespoon chopped fresh parsley

▢ Place chicken and water in a Dutch oven; bring to a boil. Skim fat. Reduce heat; cover and simmer for 2 hours or until chicken is tender. Remove chicken; cool. Add enough water to broth to measure 3 quarts.

▢ Remove chicken from bones; cut into bite-size pieces and return to pan. Add remaining ingredients; cover and simmer for 10 minutes or until vegetables are tender. If desired, pour cooled soup into 1-pint freezer containers and freeze for future use.

FOR CHICKEN POTATO SOUP: In a saucepan, combine 1 pint thawed soup base, 1/2 cup cubed peeled potatoes, and salt and pepper to taste. Cover and cook over medium heat until potatoes are tender.

FOR CREAM OF CHICKEN SOUP: In a saucepan, combine 1/4 cup all-purpose flour and 1 cup milk; mix until smooth. Stir in 1 pint thawed soup base. Bring to a boil; boil for 2 minutes, stirring constantly. Add 1/2 teaspoon chicken bouillon granules and salt and pepper to taste.

Yield: 14 servings (6-1/2 pints soup base).

NUTRITION FACTS: 1 cup equals 145 calories, 7 g fat (2 g saturated fat), 44 mg cholesterol, 779 mg sodium, 4 g carbohydrate, 1 g fiber, 15 g protein.

chicken minestrone

A packaged minestrone soup mix is jazzed up with cubed chicken, fresh zucchini, portobello mushrooms and crunchy croutons for this satisfying main course. It's easy to prepare.
TASTE OF HOME TEST KITCHEN

1	package (9.3 ounces) minestrone soup mix
1	medium zucchini, quartered lengthwise and sliced
1	cup chopped baby portobello mushrooms
1	pound boneless skinless chicken breasts, cubed
1	tablespoon olive oil
1/4	cup butter, melted
1	teaspoon dried parsley flakes
6	slices day-old French bread (1-inch thick), cubed
2	tablespoons grated Parmesan cheese

▢ Prepare soup mix according to package directions, adding zucchini and mushrooms. Meanwhile, in a large skillet, cook chicken in oil for 10-12 minutes or until no longer pink. Stir into soup.

▢ For croutons, in a large bowl, combine butter and parsley. Add bread cubes and toss to coat. Arrange in a single layer on an ungreased baking sheet. Sprinkle with cheese.

▢ Bake at 400° for 7-8 minutes or until golden brown, stirring occasionally. Serve with soup.

Yield: 5 servings.

NUTRITION FACTS: 1-1/2 cups equals 588 calories, 19 g fat (9 g saturated fat), 95 mg cholesterol, 2,164 mg sodium, 64 g carbohydrate, 6 g fiber, 36 g protein.

creamy chicken gnocchi soup

Warm up on a snowy eve by enjoying a bowl of this chicken and pasta soup. It's quick to fix and loved by all who try it.
JACLYNN ROBINSON SHINGLETOWN, CALIFORNIA

1	pound boneless skinless chicken breasts, cut into 1/2-inch pieces
1/3	cup butter, divided
1	small onion, chopped
1	medium carrot, shredded
1	celery rib, chopped
2	garlic cloves, minced
1/3	cup all-purpose flour
3-1/2	cups 2% milk
1-1/2	cups heavy whipping cream
1	tablespoon reduced-sodium chicken bouillon granules
1/4	teaspoon coarsely ground pepper
1	package (16 ounces) potato gnocchi
1/2	cup chopped fresh spinach

◻ In a Dutch oven, brown chicken in 2 tablespoons butter. Remove and keep warm. In the same pan, saute the onion, carrot, celery and garlic in remaining butter until tender.

◻ Whisk in flour until blended; gradually stir in the milk, cream, bouillon and pepper. Bring to a boil. Reduce heat; cook and stir for 2 minutes or until thickened.

◻ Add the gnocchi and spinach; cook for 3-4 minutes or until spinach is wilted. Add the chicken. Cover and simmer for 10 minutes or until heated through (do not boil).

Yield: 8 servings (2 quarts).

NUTRITION FACTS: 1 cup equals 482 calories, 28 g fat (17 g saturated fat), 125 mg cholesterol, 527 mg sodium, 36 g carbohydrate, 2 g fiber, 21 g protein.

EDITOR'S NOTE: Look for potato gnocchi in the pasta or frozen foods section.

southwestern chicken soup

Here's the perfect recipe for a busy week because the slow cooker does most of the work for you!
HAROLD TARTAR WEST PALM BEACH, FLORIDA

1-1/4	pounds boneless skinless chicken breasts, cut into thin strips
1	tablespoon canola oil
2	cans (14-1/2 ounces each) reduced-sodium chicken broth
1	package (16 ounces) frozen corn, thawed
1	can (14-1/2 ounces) diced tomatoes, undrained
1	medium onion, chopped
1	medium green pepper, chopped
1	medium sweet red pepper, chopped
1	can (4 ounces) chopped green chilies
1-1/2	teaspoons seasoned salt, optional
1	teaspoon ground cumin
1/2	teaspoon garlic powder

◻ In a large skillet, saute the chicken in oil until lightly browned. Transfer to a 5-qt. slow cooker. Stir in the remaining ingredients. Cover and cook on low for 7-8 hours or until chicken and vegetables are tender. Stir before serving.

Yield: 10 servings.

NUTRITION FACTS: 1 cup equals 143 calories, 3 g fat (1 g saturated fat), 31 mg cholesterol, 364 mg sodium, 15 g carbohydrate, 3 g fiber, 15 g protein. **DIABETIC EXCHANGES:** 2 lean meat, 1 starch.

turkey-white bean soup

Packed with nutrition, this marvelous soup will satisfy any appetite. For an extra-special touch, top each serving with shredded Parmesan cheese.
MARY RELYEA CANASTOTA, NEW YORK

2	garlic cloves, minced
2	teaspoons olive oil
1/2	teaspoon dried rosemary, crushed
1/4	teaspoon crushed red pepper flakes
1	can (28 ounces) whole tomatoes in puree, cut up
1	can (14-1/2 ounces) reduced-sodium chicken broth
2	cups shredded carrots
2	cans (15 ounces each) white kidney or cannellini beans, rinsed and drained
1	package (6 ounces) fresh baby spinach, chopped
1-1/2	cups cubed cooked turkey breast
	Shredded Parmesan cheese, optional

◻ In a large saucepan over medium heat, cook garlic in oil for 1 minute. Add rosemary and pepper flakes; cook 1 minute longer.

◻ Stir in the tomatoes, broth and carrots. Bring to a boil. Reduce heat; cover and simmer for 15 minutes. Stir in the beans, spinach and turkey; return to a boil. Reduce heat; cover and simmer 10 minutes longer. Serve with cheese if desired.

Yield: 6 servings (2 quarts).

NUTRITION FACTS: 1-1/3 cups (calculated without cheese) equals 233 calories, 3 g fat (trace saturated fat), 30 mg cholesterol, 893 mg sodium, 32 g carbohydrate, 9 g fiber, 20 g protein.

turkey & dumpling soup
(pictured at left)

My husband has come to expect this soup on chilly evenings as it not only warms the body, but the heart as well.
KAREN SUE GARBACK-PRISTERA ALBANY, NEW YORK

1	leftover turkey carcass (from a 12- to 14-pound turkey)
9	cups water
3	teaspoons chicken bouillon granules
1	bay leaf
1	can (14-1/2 ounces) stewed tomatoes, cut up
1	medium turnip, peeled and diced
2	celery ribs, chopped
1	medium onion, chopped
1	medium carrot, chopped
1/4	cup minced fresh parsley
1	teaspoon salt

DUMPLINGS:

1/2	cup water
1/4	cup butter, cubed
1/2	cup all-purpose flour
1	teaspoon baking powder
1/8	teaspoon salt
2	eggs
1	tablespoon minced fresh parsley

▢ Place carcass, water, bouillon and bay leaf in a stockpot. Bring to a boil. Reduce heat; cover and simmer for 1-1/2 hours.

▢ Remove turkey carcass. Strain broth and skim fat; discard bay leaf. Return broth to the pan. Add the tomatoes, vegetables, parsley and salt. Remove turkey from bones and cut into bite-size pieces; add to soup. Discard bones. Bring the soup to a boil. Reduce heat; cover and simmer for 25-30 minutes or until the vegetables are crisp-tender.

▢ For dumplings, in a large saucepan, bring water and butter to a boil. Combine the flour, baking powder and salt; add all at once to pan and stir until a smooth ball forms. Remove from heat; let stand for 5 minutes. Add eggs, one at a time, beating well after each addition. Continue beating until mixture is smooth and shiny. Stir in parsley.

▢ Drop batter in 12 mounds into simmering soup. Cover and simmer for 20 minutes or until a toothpick inserted in a dumpling comes out clean (do not lift cover while simmering).

Yield: 6 servings (about 2 quarts).

NUTRITION FACTS: 1-1/2 cups equals 202 calories, 10 g fat (5 g saturated fat), 92 mg cholesterol, 1,238 mg sodium, 24 g carbohydrate, 3 g fiber, 6 g protein.

homemade turkey stock

I remember my mother making this homemade stock after every Thanksgiving. It's wonderful in soup, and it freezes well to use at any time.
ANGELA GOODMAN KANEOHE, HAWAII

1	leftover turkey carcass (from a 12- to 14-pound turkey)
4	quarts water
2	medium carrots, sliced
2	celery ribs, sliced
1	medium onion, sliced
3	fresh thyme sprigs
2	teaspoons minced fresh basil
1	sprig fresh parsley
1	bay leaf
1	garlic clove, minced

▢ Place all ingredients in a stockpot. Bring to a boil. Reduce heat; cover and simmer for 1-1/2 hours.

▢ Discard turkey carcass. Cool broth for 1 hour. Strain through a cheesecloth-lined colander; discard vegetables and herbs. If using immediately, skim fat from broth; or refrigerate for 8 hours or overnight, then remove fat from surface. Broth can be frozen for up to 2-3 months.

Yield: 14 servings (3-1/2 quarts).

NUTRITION FACTS: 1 cup equals 29 calories, 1 g fat (trace saturated fat), 13 mg cholesterol, 17 mg sodium, 2 g carbohydrate, 1 g fiber, 3 g protein.

barley chicken chili

(pictured above)

I was looking for a new chicken recipe when I discovered a dish I thought my husband might like. After making a few changes to fit our preferences, I had this zesty chili simmering on the stovetop. It was great! Leftovers freeze well, too.
KAYLEEN GREW ESSEXVILLE, MICHIGAN

1	cup chopped onion
1/2	cup chopped green pepper
1	teaspoon olive oil
2-1/4	cups water
1	can (15 ounces) tomato sauce
1	can (14-1/2 ounces) chicken broth
1	can (10 ounces) diced tomatoes and green chilies, undrained
1	cup quick-cooking barley
1	tablespoon chili powder
1/2	teaspoon ground cumin
1/4	teaspoon garlic powder
3	cups cubed cooked chicken

◻ In a large saucepan, saute onion and green pepper in oil until tender. Add the water, tomato sauce, broth, tomatoes, barley, chili powder, cumin and garlic powder; bring to a boil. Reduce heat; cover and simmer for 10 minutes. Add chicken. Cover and simmer for 5 minutes longer or until barley is tender.

Yield: 9 servings (about 2 quarts).

NUTRITION FACTS: 1 cup equals 197 calories, 5 g fat (1 g saturated fat), 42 mg cholesterol, 576 mg sodium, 21 g carbohydrate, 5 g fiber, 18 g protein.

chicken broth

Whether you're making a chicken soup or just a broth to use in other dishes, this recipe makes a tasty base for most anything.
NILA GRAHL GURNEE, ILLINOIS

1	broiler/fryer chicken (3 to 4 pounds), cut up
10	cups water
1	large carrot, sliced
1	large onion, sliced
1	celery rib, sliced
1	garlic clove, minced
1	bay leaf
1	teaspoon dried thyme
1	teaspoon salt
1/4	teaspoon pepper

◻ In a stockpot, combine all the ingredients. Slowly bring to a boil over low heat. Cover and simmer for 45-60 minutes or until the meat is tender, skimming the surface as foam rises.

◻ Remove chicken and set aside until cool enough to handle. Discard skin and bones. Chop chicken; set aside for soup or another use.

◻ Strain broth through a cheesecloth-lined colander, discarding vegetables and bay leaf. Skim fat. Broth can be covered and refrigerated for up to 3 days or frozen for 4 to 6 months.

Yield: 8 servings (2 quarts).

NUTRITION FACTS: 1 cup equals 33 calories, 1 g fat (trace saturated fat), 1 mg cholesterol, 296 mg sodium, 1 g carbohydrate, 0 fiber, 2 g protein.

carl's chicken noodle soup

I like lots of vegetables in my chicken noodle soup. Feel free to make substitutions with whatever you have on hand. Add a crusty loaf of warm bread for a satisfying meal!
CARL BATES PLEASANTON, CALIFORNIA

- 1 pound boneless skinless chicken breast halves, cut into 1/2-inch pieces
- 1 medium onion, chopped
- 2 teaspoons olive oil
- 2 garlic cloves, minced
- 2 cans (49-1/2 ounces each) chicken broth
- 2 cups frozen sliced okra, thawed
- 3 celery ribs, sliced
- 1-1/2 cups cut fresh green beans
- 3 medium carrots, sliced
- 1 can (8-3/4 ounces) whole kernel corn, drained
- 2 tablespoons dried parsley flakes
- 2 teaspoons Italian seasoning
- 2 bay leaves
- 1/2 teaspoon salt
- 1/2 teaspoon pepper
- 3-1/2 cups uncooked egg noodles

☐ In a Dutch oven, saute chicken and onion in oil until chicken is no longer pink. Add garlic; cook 1 minute longer. Add the broth, okra, celery, beans, carrots, corn and seasonings. Bring to a boil. Reduce heat; cover and simmer for 30 minutes or until vegetables are tender.

☐ Stir in noodles; cook 5-7 minutes longer or until tender. Discard bay leaves.

Yield: 10 servings (about 4 quarts).

NUTRITION FACTS: 1-1/2 cups equals 174 calories, 4 g fat (1 g saturated fat), 42 mg cholesterol, 1,449 mg sodium, 20 g carbohydrate, 3 g fiber, 14 g protein.

easy alphabet soup

I'm a teenager and love to make this fun chicken soup for my family. It makes me so happy when they tell me how much they like it!
SARAH MACKEY NEW SMYRNA BEACH, FLORIDA

- 3 medium carrots, chopped
- 2 celery ribs, chopped
- 3/4 cup chopped sweet onion
- 1 tablespoon olive oil
- 2 quarts chicken broth
- 3 cups cubed cooked chicken breast
- 1/4 teaspoon dried thyme
- 1-1/2 cups uncooked alphabet pasta
- 3 tablespoons minced fresh parsley

☐ In a Dutch oven, saute the carrots, celery and onion in oil until tender. Stir in the broth, chicken and thyme. Bring to a boil. Stir in pasta. Reduce heat; simmer, uncovered, for 10 minutes or until pasta is tender. Stir in parsley.

Yield: 10 servings (2-1/2 quarts).

NUTRITION FACTS: 1 cup equals 163 calories, 4 g fat (1 g saturated fat), 26 mg cholesterol, 828 mg sodium, 20 g carbohydrate, 2 g fiber, 12 g protein.

southwestern turkey dumpling soup

Here's a regional twist on traditional turkey dumpling soup. I especially like this recipe because it's fast, easy and makes the most of leftover turkey or chicken.
LISA WILLIAMS STEAMBOAT SPRINGS, COLORADO

1	can (15 ounces) tomato sauce
1	can (14-1/2 ounces) diced tomatoes, undrained
1-3/4	cups water
1	envelope chili seasoning
3	cups diced cooked turkey or chicken
1	can (16 ounces) kidney beans, rinsed and drained
1	can (15 ounces) black beans, rinsed and drained
1	can (15-1/4 ounces) whole kernel corn, drained

DUMPLINGS:

1-1/2	cups biscuit/baking mix
1/2	cup cornmeal
3/4	cup shredded cheddar cheese, divided
2/3	cup milk

▨ In a Dutch oven, combine the first five ingredients; bring to a boil. Reduce heat; cover and simmer for 10 minutes, stirring occasionally. Add beans and corn.

▨ In a large bowl, combine biscuit mix, cornmeal and 1/2 cup of cheese; stir in milk. Drop by heaping tablespoonfuls onto the simmering soup. Cover and cook for 12-15 minutes or until dumplings are firm. Sprinkle with remaining cheese; cover and cook 1 minute longer or until the cheese is melted.

Yield: 6-8 servings (2-1/2 quarts).

NUTRITION FACTS: 1 cup equals 424 calories, 11 g fat (4 g saturated fat), 54 mg cholesterol, 1,358 mg sodium, 51 g carbohydrate, 8 g fiber, 29 g protein.

curried turkey vegetable soup

Chock-full of veggies, my aromatic soup has just the right hint of curry. It's a delicious way to use your leftover holiday turkey.
VIRGINIA ANTHONY JACKSONVILLE, FLORIDA

2	medium onions, chopped
2	tablespoons canola oil
2	to 3 tablespoons all-purpose flour
1	teaspoon curry powder
3	cups reduced-sodium chicken broth
1	cup diced red potatoes
1	celery rib, sliced
1/2	cup thinly sliced fresh carrots
2	tablespoons minced fresh parsley
1-1/2	teaspoons minced fresh sage
2	cups cubed cooked turkey breast
1-1/2	cups fat-free half-and-half
1	package (9 ounces) fresh baby spinach, coarsely chopped
1/4	teaspoon salt
1/4	teaspoon pepper

▨ In a Dutch oven, saute onions in oil until tender. Stir in flour and curry until blended. Gradually stir in broth. Add the potatoes, celery, carrots, parsley and sage. Bring to a boil. Reduce heat; cover and simmer for 10-12 minutes or until vegetables are tender.

▨ Stir in the turkey, half-and-half, spinach, salt and pepper. Cook and stir until spinach is wilted and soup is heated through.

Yield: 6 servings (2 quarts).

NUTRITION FACTS: 1-1/3 cups equals 219 calories, 6 g fat (1 g saturated fat), 40 mg cholesterol, 534 mg sodium, 20 g carbohydrate, 3 g fiber, 20 g protein. **DIABETIC EXCHANGES:** 2 lean meat, 1 starch, 1 vegetable, 1 fat.

slow-cooked chicken noodle soup

This satisfying homemade soup with a hint of cayenne is brimming with vegetables, chicken and noodles. The recipe came from my father-in-law, but I made some adjustments to give it my own spin.
NORMA REYNOLDS OVERLAND PARK, KANSAS

12	fresh baby carrots, cut into 1/2-inch pieces
4	celery ribs, cut into 1/2-inch pieces
3/4	cup finely chopped onion
1	tablespoon minced fresh parsley
1/2	teaspoon pepper
1/4	teaspoon cayenne pepper
1-1/2	teaspoons mustard seed
2	garlic cloves, peeled and halved
1-1/4	pounds boneless skinless chicken breast halves
1-1/4	pounds boneless skinless chicken thighs
4	cans (14-1/2 ounces each) chicken broth
1	package (9 ounces) refrigerated linguine

▢ In a 5-qt. slow cooker, combine the first six ingredients. Place mustard seed and garlic on a double thickness of cheesecloth; bring up corners of cloth and tie with kitchen string to form a bag. Place in slow cooker. Add chicken and broth. Cover and cook on low for 5-6 hours or until meat is tender.

▢ Discard spice bag. Remove chicken; cool slightly. Stir linguine into soup; cover and cook on high for 30 minutes or until tender. Cut chicken into pieces and return to soup; heat through.

Yield: 12 servings (3 quarts).

NUTRITION FACTS: 1 cup equals 193 calories, 5 g fat (1 g saturated fat), 58 mg cholesterol, 244 mg sodium, 14 g carbohydrate, 1 g fiber, 21 g protein.

spinach tortellini soup

I'm always looking for easy recipes I can prepare on busy days, and this soup perfectly fits the bill. Try it with fresh bread.
JACQUELINE DINTINO WESTMINSTER, MARYLAND

3	small red potatoes, peeled and cubed
2	medium carrots, sliced
1	celery rib, chopped
1	small onion, chopped
2	tablespoons plus 1-1/2 teaspoons chicken bouillon granules
2	quarts water
3	cups cubed cooked chicken
1	package (10 ounces) frozen chopped spinach, thawed and squeezed dry
1	teaspoon dried parsley flakes
1/2	teaspoon garlic powder
1/2	teaspoon dried oregano
1/2	teaspoon pepper
1/4	teaspoon salt
2	packages (9 ounces each) refrigerated cheese tortellini

▢ In a Dutch oven, combine the potatoes, carrots, celery, onion, bouillon and water. Bring to a boil. Reduce heat; cover and simmer for 10 minutes.

▢ Stir in the chicken, spinach, parsley, garlic powder, oregano and pepper and salt; return to a boil. Add tortellini; cook, uncovered, for 7-9 minutes or until tortellini is tender.

Yield: 10 servings (3-3/4 quarts).

NUTRITION FACTS: 1-1/2 cups equals 271 calories, 8 g fat (3 g saturated fat), 60 mg cholesterol, 974 mg sodium, 29 g carbohydrate, 2 g fiber, 20 g protein.

zippy chicken soup

(pictured at left)

This spicy soup is one of my husband's cold-weather favorites. It's quick to make but tastes like it simmered all day, and what a great way to use up those last tortilla chips in the bag.
LINDA LASHLEY REDGRANITE, WISCONSIN

1/2	pound boneless skinless chicken breasts, cut into 1-inch cubes
2	cans (14-1/2 ounces each) reduced-sodium chicken broth, divided
2	cups frozen corn
1	can (15 ounces) black beans, rinsed and drained
1	can (10 ounces) diced tomatoes and green chilies, undrained
1	jalapeno pepper, seeded and chopped
2	tablespoons minced fresh cilantro
3	teaspoons chili powder
1/2	teaspoon ground cumin
1	tablespoon cornstarch
18	tortilla chips

Shredded reduced-fat Mexican cheese blend, optional

▢ In a nonstick saucepan coated with cooking spray, cook chicken over medium heat for 4-6 minutes or until no longer pink. Set aside 2 tablespoons of broth; add remaining broth to pan. Stir in the corn, beans, tomatoes, jalapeno, cilantro, chili powder and cumin. Bring to a boil. Reduce heat; simmer, uncovered, for 15 minutes.

▢ Combine the cornstarch and reserved broth until smooth; gradually stir into soup. Bring to a boil; cook and stir for 2 minutes or until thickened. Top each serving with tortilla chips. Garnish with cheese if desired.

Yield: 6 servings (2 quarts).

NUTRITION FACTS: 1-1/3 cups with 3 tortilla chips (calculated without cheese) equals 194 calories, 2 g fat (trace saturated fat), 24 mg cholesterol, 752 mg sodium, 29 g carbohydrate, 5 g fiber, 17 g protein. **DIABETIC EXCHANGES:** 2 starch, 2 lean meat.

EDITOR'S NOTE: Wear disposable gloves when cutting hot peppers; the oils can burn skin. Avoid touching your face.

chicken sausage cannellini soup

Bursting with fabulous Italian flavors, this hearty soup is sure to chase away winter's chills. Serve with some crusty rolls for a satisfying dinner.
CHERYL RAVESI MILFORD, MASSACHUSETTS

3/4	pound fully cooked Italian chicken sausage links, halved lengthwise and sliced
1	medium onion, chopped
1	tablespoon olive oil
3	garlic cloves, minced
2	cans (15 ounces each) white kidney or cannellini beans, rinsed and drained
2	cans (14-1/2 ounces each) no-salt-added diced tomatoes
2	medium zucchini, quartered and sliced
1	can (14-1/2 ounces) reduced-sodium chicken broth
8	ounces whole fresh mushrooms, quartered
1	cup water
1/4	cup prepared pesto
1/4	cup dry red wine or additional reduced-sodium chicken broth
1	tablespoon balsamic vinegar
1	teaspoon minced fresh oregano or 1/4 teaspoon dried oregano
1/2	teaspoon pepper

Grated Parmesan cheese

▢ In a Dutch oven, cook sausage and onion in oil until sausage is browned. Add garlic; cook 1 minute longer.

▢ Stir in the beans, tomatoes, zucchini, broth, mushrooms, water, pesto, wine, vinegar, oregano and pepper. Bring to a boil. Reduce heat; simmer, uncovered, for 25-30 minutes or until vegetables are tender. Sprinkle with cheese.

Yield: 6 servings (2-1/2 quarts).

NUTRITION FACTS: 1-2/3 cups (calculated without cheese) equals 337 calories, 12 g fat (3 g saturated fat), 47 mg cholesterol, 838 mg sodium, 35 g carbohydrate, 10 g fiber, 22 g protein. **DIABETIC EXCHANGES:** 2 lean meat, 2 vegetable, 1-1/2 starch, 1-1/2 fat.

turkey meatball soup

(pictured above)

Every Italian-American family I know seems to have their own version of meatball soup. This recipe is my family's version.
CHRISTIE LADD MECHANICSBURG, PENNSYLVANIA

2	egg whites, lightly beaten
1/2	cup seasoned bread crumbs
1	tablespoon grated Parmesan cheese
4	teaspoons Italian seasoning, divided
1	pound lean ground turkey
3	medium carrots, sliced
3	celery ribs, finely chopped
1	tablespoon olive oil
4	garlic cloves, minced
3	cans (14-1/2 ounces each) reduced-sodium chicken broth
1/4	teaspoon pepper
1/2	cup ditalini or other small pasta

▨ In a small bowl, combine the egg whites, bread crumbs, cheese and 2 teaspoons Italian seasoning. Crumble turkey over mixture and mix well. Shape into 3/4-in. balls.

▨ Place in a 15-in. x 10-in. x 1-in. baking pan coated with cooking spray. Bake, uncovered, at 350° for 10-15 minutes or until no longer pink.

▨ Meanwhile, in a Dutch oven, saute carrots and celery in oil until tender. Add garlic; cook 1 minute longer. Add the broth, pepper and remaining Italian seasoning. Bring to a boil. Reduce heat; cover and simmer for 20 minutes.

▨ Stir in pasta; cook 10-12 minutes longer or until vegetables and pasta are tender. Add meatballs and heat through.

Yield: 6 servings.

NUTRITION FACTS: 1 cup equals 258 calories, 10 g fat (2 g saturated fat), 60 mg cholesterol, 783 mg sodium, 21 g carbohydrate, 2 g fiber, 21 g protein. **DIABETIC EXCHANGES:** 2 lean meat, 1-1/2 starch, 1/2 fat.

chicken rice soup

Our granddaughters have been making this easy soup for years. All of the kids love it—despite the chopped onion!
TRACY FISCHLER TALLAHASSEE, FLORIDA

8	cups chicken broth
3	celery ribs, sliced
1	small onion, chopped

Salt and pepper to taste

2	cups cubed cooked chicken
1	cup uncooked long grain rice

▨ In a large saucepan, combine broth, celery, onion, salt and pepper; bring to a boil. Reduce heat; cover and simmer for 10 minutes. Add chicken and rice; return to a boil. Reduce heat; cover and simmer for 20-25 minutes or until the rice is tender.

Yield: 10 servings (2-1/2 quarts).

NUTRITION FACTS: 1 cup equals 137 calories, 3 g fat (1 g saturated fat), 25 mg cholesterol, 780 mg sodium, 17 g carbohydrate, 1 g fiber, 11 g protein.

turkey wild rice soup

A dear friend brought me some of this soup when I was ill. I asked her for the recipe, and I've made it several times since. Now I like to take it to friends when they're not feeling well. It's filling and really warms you up on a wintry day!
DORIS COX NEW FREEDOM, PENNSYLVANIA

1	medium onion, chopped
1	can (4 ounces) sliced mushrooms, drained
2	tablespoons butter
3	cups water
2	cups chicken broth
1	package (6 ounces) long grain and wild rice mix
2	cups diced cooked turkey
1	cup heavy whipping cream

Minced fresh parsley

▢ In a large saucepan, saute onion and mushrooms in butter until onion is tender. Add water, broth and rice mix with seasoning; bring to a boil. Reduce heat; simmer for 20-25 minutes or until rice is tender. Stir in turkey and cream and heat through. Sprinkle with parsley.

Yield: 6 servings.

NUTRITION FACTS: 1 cup equals 364 calories, 21 g fat (12 g saturated fat), 100 mg cholesterol, 857 mg sodium, 25 g carbohydrate, 1 g fiber, 19 g protein.

chicken cacciatore soup

This quick cacciatore meets with my Italian husband's approval. Each brothy spoonful is brimming with vegetables and tender pieces of chicken.
NANCY ROTH SAINT JOSEPH, ILLINOIS

1/2	pound medium fresh mushrooms, quartered
2	medium leeks (white portion only), sliced
2	tablespoons olive oil
3	cans (14-1/2 ounces each) reduced-sodium chicken broth
3	cups cubed cooked chicken
1	can (14-1/2 ounces) diced tomatoes with basil, oregano and garlic, undrained
1	medium zucchini, quartered lengthwise and cut into 1/2-inch slices
1	each medium green, sweet red and yellow peppers, chopped
1	cup uncooked bow tie pasta
1/2	teaspoon dried thyme
1/4	teaspoon pepper
1/2	cup shredded Parmesan cheese
1/4	cup fresh basil leaves, thinly sliced

▢ In a Dutch oven, saute mushrooms and leeks in oil until tender. Stir in the broth, chicken, tomatoes, zucchini, peppers, pasta, thyme and pepper.

▢ Bring to a boil. Reduce heat; simmer, uncovered, for 15-20 minutes or until pasta and vegetables are tender. Top each serving with cheese and basil.

Yield: 7 servings (about 2-1/2 quarts).

NUTRITION FACTS: 1-1/2 cups equals 283 calories, 11 g fat (3 g saturated fat), 58 mg cholesterol, 951 mg sodium, 21 g carbohydrate, 3 g fiber, 27 g protein.

chicken 'n' dumpling soup

I had to marry into my husband's family in order to learn this recipe! It's our traditional Christmas Eve meal, served before going to church.
RACHEL HINZ ST. JAMES, MINNESOTA

1	broiler/fryer chicken (3 to 3-1/2 pounds)
3	quarts water
1/4	cup chicken bouillon granules
1	bay leaf
1	teaspoon whole peppercorns
1/8	teaspoon ground allspice
6	cups uncooked wide noodles
4	cups sliced carrots
1	package (10 ounces) frozen mixed vegetables
3/4	cup sliced celery
1/2	cup chopped onion
1/4	cup uncooked long grain rice
2	tablespoons minced fresh parsley

DUMPLINGS:

1-1/3	cups all-purpose flour
2	teaspoons baking powder
1	teaspoon dried thyme
1/2	teaspoon salt
2/3	cup milk
2	tablespoons canola oil

▢ In a stockpot, combine the first six ingredients; bring to a boil. Reduce heat; cover and simmer for 1-1/2 hours. Remove chicken; allow to cool. Strain broth; discard bay leaf and peppercorns.

▢ Remove chicken from bones; discard bones. Cut meat into bite-size pieces. Return broth to pan; skim fat. Add the chicken, noodles, vegetables, rice and parsley; bring to a simmer.

▢ For dumplings, combine the flour, baking powder, thyme and salt in a bowl. Combine milk and oil; stir into dry ingredients. Drop by teaspoonfuls onto simmering soup. Reduce heat; cover and simmer for 15 minutes (do not lift the cover).

Yield: 20 servings (5 quarts).

NUTRITION FACTS: 1 cup equals 198 calories, 7 g fat (2 g saturated fat), 39 mg cholesterol, 650 mg sodium, 22 g carbohydrate, 2 g fiber, 12 g protein.

hearty chicken noodle soup

These wonderful old-fashioned noodles give chicken soup a delightful down-home flavor. No one can resist this one!
CINDY RENFROW SUSSEX, NEW JERSEY

1	stewing chicken (about 6 pounds), cut up
8	cups water

1	large onion, quartered
1	cup chopped fresh parsley
1	celery rib, sliced
5	teaspoons chicken bouillon granules
5	whole peppercorns
4	whole cloves
1	bay leaf
2	teaspoons salt
1/2	teaspoon pepper

Dash dried thyme

2	medium carrots, thinly sliced

NOODLES:

1-1/4	cups all-purpose flour
1/2	teaspoon salt
1	egg
2	tablespoons milk

▢ In a stockpot, combine the first 12 ingredients; bring to a boil. Reduce heat; cover and simmer for 2-1/2 hours or until chicken is tender.

▢ Remove chicken from pot. When cool enough to handle, remove meat from bones; discard bones. Cut meat into bite-size pieces. Strain broth and skim fat; return to the pot. Add chicken and carrots.

▢ For noodles, in a small bowl, combine flour and salt. Make a well in the center. Beat egg and milk; pour into well. Stir together, forming a dough.

▢ Turn dough onto a floured surface; knead 8-10 times. Roll into a 12-in. x 9-in. rectangle. Cut into 1/2-in. strips; cut the strips into 1-in. pieces. Bring soup to a simmer; add noodles. Cover and cook for 12-15 minutes or until noodles are tender.

Yield: 12 servings (3 quarts).

NUTRITION FACTS: 1 cup equals 316 calories, 15 g fat (4 g saturated fat), 106 mg cholesterol, 937 mg sodium, 13 g carbohydrate, 1 g fiber, 30 g protein.

southwest turkey soup

Ground turkey and a handful of other ingredients are all that's required for this satisfying soup that's spiced with salsa, green chilies and chili powder.
GENISE KRAUSE STURGEON BAY, WISCONSIN

- 1 pound ground turkey
- 1 tablespoon olive oil
- 2 cans (16 ounces each) kidney beans, rinsed and drained
- 2 cans (14-1/2 ounces each) chicken broth
- 2 cups frozen corn
- 1 cup salsa
- 1 can (4 ounces) chopped green chilies
- 1 to 2 tablespoons chili powder
Sour cream and minced fresh cilantro

▫ In a Dutch oven, cook turkey in oil over medium heat until meat is no longer pink; drain.

▫ Add the beans, broth, corn, salsa, chilies and chili powder. Bring to a boil. Reduce heat; cover and simmer for 10-15 minutes to allow flavors to blend. Serve with sour cream and cilantro.

Yield: 6 servings (2-1/2 quarts).

NUTRITION FACTS: 1-1/2 cups (calculated without optional ingredients) equals 381 calories, 14 g fat (4 g saturated fat), 54 mg cholesterol, 1,163 mg sodium, 41 g carbohydrate, 9 g fiber, 24 g protein.

chicken barley soup

With chicken, barley and a host of delicious veggies, my soup is a tasty antidote to cold and flu chills.
PATRICIA RANDALL NEWTON, KANSAS

- 1 pound boneless skinless chicken breasts, cut into 3/4-inch pieces
- 2 tablespoons canola oil, divided
- 2 cups chopped leeks (white portion only)
- 1 celery rib, thinly sliced
- 1 carrot, thinly sliced
- 2 cups sliced fresh mushrooms
- 1 garlic clove, minced
- 2 cans (14-1/2 ounces each) reduced-sodium chicken broth
- 2-1/4 cups water
- 1 bay leaf
- 1/2 teaspoon dried thyme
- 1/4 teaspoon salt
- 1/4 teaspoon pepper
- 1/2 cup quick-cooking barley

▫ In a Dutch oven, cook chicken in 1 tablespoon oil until no longer pink. Remove and set aside.

▫ In the same pan, saute the leeks, celery and carrot in remaining oil for 4 minutes. Add mushrooms and garlic; cook 2 minutes longer. Stir in the broth, water, seasonings and chicken. Bring to a boil. Reduce heat; cover and simmer for 15 minutes.

▫ Stir in barley and return to a boil. Reduce heat; cover and simmer for 10-15 minutes or until barley and vegetables are tender. Discard bay leaf.

Yield: 6 servings.

NUTRITION FACTS: 1 cup equals 218 calories, 7 g fat (1 g saturated fat), 42 mg cholesterol, 550 mg sodium, 19 g carbohydrate, 4 g fiber, 21 g protein. **DIABETIC EXCHANGES:** 2 lean meat, 1 starch, 1 vegetable, 1 fat.

colorful chicken 'n' squash soup

(pictured at left)

When I turned 40, I decided to live a healthier lifestyle, which included cooking healthier for my family. I make this soup every week, and everyone loves it.
TRINA BIGHAM FAIRHAVEN, MASSACHUSETTS

- 1 broiler/fryer chicken (4 pounds), cut up
- 13 cups water
- 5 pounds butternut squash, peeled and cubed (about 10 cups)
- 1 bunch kale, trimmed and chopped
- 6 medium carrots, chopped
- 2 large onions, chopped
- 3 teaspoons salt

▢ Place chicken and water in a stockpot. Bring to a boil. Reduce heat; cover and simmer for 1 hour or until chicken is tender.

▢ Remove chicken from broth. Strain broth and skim fat. Return broth to the pan; add the squash, kale, carrots and onions. Bring to a boil. Reduce heat; cover and simmer for 25-30 minutes or until vegetables are tender.

▢ When chicken is cool enough to handle, remove meat from bones and cut into bite-size pieces. Discard bones and skin. Add chicken and salt to soup; heat through.

Yield: 14 servings (5-1/4 quarts).

NUTRITION FACTS: 1-1/2 cups equals 228 calories, 8 g fat (2 g saturated fat), 50 mg cholesterol, 579 mg sodium, 22 g carbohydrate, 6 g fiber, 18 g protein. **DIABETIC EXCHANGES:** 2 lean meat, 1 starch, 1 vegetable, 1/2 fat.

lightened-up pasta fagioli soup

After trying pasta fagioli at a popular restaurant, I was determined to make it at home, only healthier. Ground turkey and vegetables with no added salt helped me get it done!
CINDIE KITCHIN GRANTS PASS, OREGON

- 1 pound lean ground turkey
- 1 large onion, chopped
- 2 celery ribs, chopped
- 2 medium carrots, sliced
- 1 garlic clove, minced
- 3 cups water
- 1 can (16 ounces) kidney beans, rinsed and drained
- 2 cans (8 ounces each) no-salt-added tomato sauce
- 1 can (14-1/2 ounces) no-salt-added diced tomatoes, undrained
- 1 tablespoon dried parsley flakes
- 2 teaspoons reduced-sodium beef bouillon granules
- 1/2 teaspoon dried oregano
- 1/2 teaspoon dried basil
- 1/4 teaspoon pepper
- 2 cups shredded cabbage
- 1 cup fresh or frozen cut green beans (1-inch pieces)
- 1/2 cup uncooked elbow macaroni

▢ In a Dutch oven coated with cooking spray, cook the turkey, onion, celery and carrots over medium heat until meat is no longer pink. Add garlic; cook 1 minute longer. Add the water, beans, tomato sauce, tomatoes, parsley, bouillon, oregano, basil and pepper. Bring to a boil. Reduce heat; cover and simmer for 20 minutes.

▢ Add the cabbage, green beans and macaroni; cover and simmer 8-10 minutes longer or until the vegetables and macaroni are tender.

Yield: 6 servings (2-1/4 quarts).

NUTRITION FACTS: 1-1/2 cups equals 276 calories, 7 g fat (2 g saturated fat), 60 mg cholesterol, 379 mg sodium, 33 g carbohydrate, 8 g fiber, 21 g protein. **DIABETIC EXCHANGES:** 2 starch, 2 lean meat.

chicken dumpling soup

(pictured above)

This soup with light dumplings always brings positive comments. I like to fix it for my friends when they're sick.

TAMI CHRISTMAN SODA SPRINGS, IDAHO

12	green onions, chopped
1/2	cup butter
1/2	cup all-purpose flour
10	cups water
1	package (16 ounces) frozen peas and carrots
2	cans (10 ounces each) chunk white chicken, drained, divided
1/3	cup chicken bouillon granules
1/2	teaspoon pepper, divided
5	cups biscuit/baking mix
2	tablespoons dried parsley flakes
1-1/3	cups milk

▨ In a stockpot, saute onions in butter until tender. Stir in flour until blended. Gradually add water. Stir in the vegetables, one can of chicken, bouillon and 1/4 teaspoon pepper; bring to a boil.

▨ In a large bowl, combine the biscuit mix, parsley and remaining pepper. Stir in milk just until moistened. Fold in remaining chicken.

▨ Drop by rounded tablespoonfuls onto simmering soup. Cover and simmer for 15 minutes or until a toothpick inserted in a dumpling comes out clean (do not lift cover while simmering).

Yield: 20 servings (5 quarts).

NUTRITION FACTS: 1 cup equals 266 calories, 14 g fat (5 g saturated fat), 27 mg cholesterol, 1,091 mg sodium, 25 g carbohydrate, 2 g fiber, 10 g protein.

lightened-up slow cooker chili

The company I work for has an annual chili cook-off, and this unusual recipe of mine was a winner.

CAROLYN ETZLER THURMONT, MARYLAND

1	pound Italian turkey sausage links, casings removed
3/4	pound boneless skinless chicken thighs, cut into 3/4-inch pieces
1	medium onion, chopped
2	cans (14-1/2 ounces each) diced tomatoes with mild green chilies, undrained
2	cans (8 ounces each) tomato sauce
1	can (16 ounces) kidney beans, rinsed and drained
1	can (15 ounces) white kidney or cannellini beans, rinsed and drained
1	can (15 ounces) pinto beans, rinsed and drained
1	can (15 ounces) black beans, rinsed and drained
1	teaspoon chili powder
1/2	teaspoon garlic powder
1/8	teaspoon pepper

▨ Crumble sausage into a nonstick skillet coated with cooking spray. Add chicken and onion; cook and stir over medium heat until meat is no longer pink.

▨ Transfer to a 5-qt. slow cooker. Stir in the remaining ingredients. Cover and cook on low for 4-5 hours or until chicken is no longer pink.

Yield: 11 servings (2-3/4 quarts).

NUTRITION FACTS: 1 cup equals 272 calories, 6 g fat (1 g saturated fat), 45 mg cholesterol, 826 mg sodium, 32 g carbohydrate, 8 g fiber, 21 g protein.

turkey noodle soup

I usually try three new recipes a week. My wonderful husband willingly samples everything I make...even if it is a flop! This old-fashioned soup is one of his all-time favorites.
KAREN CHINIGO LISBON, CONNECTICUT

1	leftover turkey carcass (from a 12- to 14-pound turkey)
3-1/2	quarts water
4	chicken bouillon cubes
1	large onion, halved
4	whole peppercorns
2	bay leaves
1	teaspoon poultry seasoning
1	teaspoon seasoned salt
1/2	to 3/4 teaspoon pepper
1	cup chopped carrots
1	cup chopped celery
1	medium potato, peeled and diced
1/2	cup chopped onion
1	medium turnip, peeled and diced, optional
1	cup uncooked egg noodles

▢ Place the first nine ingredients in a stockpot; bring to a boil. Reduce heat; cover and simmer for 1 hour.

▢ Strain broth; discard onion, peppercorns and bay leaves. Remove carcass; allow to cool. Remove turkey from bones and cut into bite-size pieces; set aside.

▢ Add vegetables to broth; bring to a boil. Reduce heat; cover and simmer for 20 minutes or until tender. Add noodles and reserved turkey. Return to a boil; cook, uncovered, for 10 minutes or until noodles are tender.

Yield: 14 servings (3-1/2 quarts).

NUTRITION FACTS: 1 cup equals 88 calories, 2 g fat (trace saturated fat), 15 mg cholesterol, 522 mg sodium, 8 g carbohydrate, 1 g fiber, 7 g protein.

chicken tortellini soup

Shredded rotisserie chicken is complemented by fresh green spinach and cheese tortellini in this quick-to-fix soup.
CHARLENE CHAMBERS ORMOND BEACH, FLORIDA

1-1/2	cups sliced fresh mushrooms
2	tablespoons butter
2	garlic cloves, minced
4	cans (14-1/2 ounces each) reduced-sodium chicken broth
1	package (9 ounces) refrigerated cheese tortellini
4	cups shredded rotisserie chicken
1	package (6 ounces) fresh baby spinach, coarsely chopped
1/2	teaspoon pepper
8	teaspoons grated Parmesan cheese

▢ In a Dutch oven, saute mushrooms in butter until tender. Add garlic; cook 1 minute longer.

▢ Add broth and bring to a boil. Stir in tortellini; return to a boil. Cook for 7-9 minutes or until tender, stirring occasionally. Add the chicken, spinach and pepper; cook until spinach is wilted. Sprinkle each serving with 1 teaspoon cheese.

Yield: 8 servings (2 quarts).

NUTRITION FACTS: 1 cup equals 287 calories, 12 g fat (5 g saturated fat), 90 mg cholesterol, 1,130 mg sodium, 17 g carbohydrate, 1 g fiber, 27 g protein.

italian dinner soup

(pictured at left)

My husband takes soup or stew to work every day for lunch. This hearty soup is his very favorite. Enjoy!
JOAN WINTERLE CENTER BARNSTEAD, NEW HAMPSHIRE

1	pound boneless skinless chicken breasts, cubed
1	medium green pepper, chopped
1	medium sweet red pepper, chopped
1	medium onion, chopped
1	celery rib, thinly sliced
1	small carrot, thinly sliced
1	garlic clove, minced
4	cups water
1	can (28 ounces) Italian crushed tomatoes
1	can (14-1/2 ounces) reduced-sodium chicken broth
3	tablespoons grated Parmesan cheese
1	teaspoon Italian seasoning
1/2	teaspoon crushed red pepper flakes
1/4	teaspoon salt
1/4	teaspoon pepper
1	cup uncooked elbow macaroni
7	tablespoons shredded part-skim mozzarella cheese

▨ In a nonstick Dutch oven coated with cooking spray, cook the chicken over medium heat until no longer pink. Remove and keep warm.

▨ Add peppers, onion, celery and carrot to pan; cook and stir until crisp-tender. Add the garlic; cook 1 minute longer. Add the chicken, water, tomatoes, broth, Parmesan cheese and seasonings. Bring to a boil. Reduce heat; simmer, uncovered, for 40 minutes.

▨ Stir in macaroni; cook 20 minutes longer or until tender. Top each serving with mozzarella cheese.

Yield: 7 servings (about 2-1/2 quarts).

NUTRITION FACTS: 1-1/2 cups equals 203 calories, 4 g fat (2 g saturated fat), 42 mg cholesterol, 707 mg sodium, 22 g carbohydrate, 3 g fiber, 20 g protein. **DIABETIC EXCHANGES:** 2 lean meat, 1-1/2 starch.

spice it up soup

Turkey Italian sausage and jalapeno peppers add kick to this chunky soup. I make plenty and freeze what's left over in individual servings.
GUYLA COOPER ENVILLE, TENNESSEE

1	pound uncooked hot turkey Italian sausage links, sliced
1/2	pound lean ground beef (90% lean)
1	large onion, chopped
1	medium green pepper, chopped
3	garlic cloves, minced
2	cans (14-1/2 ounces each) beef broth
2	cups water
2	cups fresh or frozen corn
1	can (14-1/2 ounces) diced tomatoes with green chilies, undrained
1	cup diced carrots
1/3	cup minced fresh cilantro
2	jalapeno peppers, seeded and chopped
1/2	teaspoon salt
1/2	teaspoon ground cumin

▨ In a Dutch oven, cook the sausage, beef, onion and green pepper over medium heat until meat is no longer pink. Add garlic; cook 1 minute longer. Drain.

▨ Stir in the remaining ingredients. Bring to a boil. Reduce heat; cover and simmer for 30-40 minutes to allow flavors to blend.

Yield: 8 servings (about 2-1/2 quarts).

NUTRITION FACTS: 1-1/3 cups equals 222 calories, 9 g fat (3 g saturated fat), 41 mg cholesterol, 1,153 mg sodium, 18 g carbohydrate, 2 g fiber, 18 g protein. **DIABETIC EXCHANGES:** 2 lean meat, 1 starch, 1/2 vegetable, 1/2 fat.

EDITOR'S NOTE: Wear disposable gloves when cutting hot peppers; the oils can burn skin. Avoid touching your face.

low-fat chicken dumpling soup

A savory broth, hearty chunks of chicken and rich dumplings provide plenty of comforting flavor in this wholesome soup.
BRENDA WHITE MORRISON, ILLINOIS

1	pound boneless skinless chicken breasts, cut into 1-1/2-inch cubes
3	cans (14-1/2 ounces each) reduced-sodium chicken broth
3	cups water
4	medium carrots, chopped
1	medium onion, chopped
1	celery rib, chopped
1	teaspoon minced fresh parsley
1/2	teaspoon salt
1/4	teaspoon garlic powder
1/4	teaspoon poultry seasoning
1/4	teaspoon pepper

DUMPLINGS:

3	egg whites
1/2	cup 1% cottage cheese
2	tablespoons water
1/4	teaspoon salt
1	cup all-purpose flour

☐ In a large nonstick skillet coated with cooking spray, cook chicken until no longer pink. Add the broth, water, vegetables and seasonings. Bring to a boil. Reduce heat; simmer, uncovered, for 30 minutes or until vegetables are tender.

☐ Meanwhile, for dumplings, in a large bowl, beat the egg whites and cottage cheese until blended. Add water and salt. Stir in the flour and mix well.

☐ Bring soup to a boil. Drop dumplings by tablespoonfuls onto the boiling soup. Reduce heat; cover and simmer for 15 minutes or until a toothpick inserted in dumplings comes out clean (do not lift cover while simmering).

Yield: 4 servings.

NUTRITION FACTS: 1-1/2 cups equals 363 calories, 4 g fat (2 g saturated fat), 73 mg cholesterol, 900 mg sodium, 39 g carbohydrate, 4 g fiber, 42 g protein. **DIABETIC EXCHANGES:** 4 lean meat, 2-1/2 starch.

rustic tortellini soup

This soup is quick to fix on a busy night and full of healthy, tasty ingredients. The recipe originally called for spicy sausage links, but I've found that turkey sausage is just as good.
TRACY FASNACHT IRWIN, PENNSYLVANIA

3	Italian turkey sausage links (4 ounces each), casings removed
1	medium onion, chopped
6	garlic cloves, minced
2	cans (14-1/2 ounces each) reduced-sodium chicken broth
1-3/4	cups water
1	can (14-1/2 ounces) diced tomatoes, undrained
1	package (9 ounces) refrigerated cheese tortellini
1	package (6 ounces) fresh baby spinach, coarsely chopped
2-1/4	teaspoons minced fresh basil or 3/4 teaspoon dried basil
1/4	teaspoon pepper

Dash crushed red pepper flakes

▨ Crumble sausage into a Dutch oven; add onion. Cook and stir over medium heat until meat is no longer pink. Add garlic; cook 1 minute longer. Stir in the broth, water and tomatoes. Bring to a boil.

▨ Add tortellini; return to a boil. Cook for 7-9 minutes or until tender, stirring occasionally. Reduce heat; add the spinach, basil, pepper and pepper flakes. Cook 2-3 minutes longer or until spinach is wilted.

Yield: 6 servings (2 quarts).

NUTRITION FACTS: 1-1/3 cups equals 203 calories, 8 g fat (2 g saturated fat), 40 mg cholesterol, 878 mg sodium, 18 g carbohydrate, 3 g fiber, 16 g protein.

southwestern turkey soup

This spicy soup is loaded with turkey, beans, corn and tomatoes. We like it really hot, so we tend to use all three tablespoons of jalapenos...and then some. It's so good on a wintry Midwestern day.
BRENDA KRUSE AMES, IOWA

1	medium onion, chopped
1	tablespoon olive oil
1	can (14-1/2 ounces) chicken broth
2	to 3 tablespoons diced jalapeno pepper
3	teaspoons ground cumin
1-1/2	teaspoons chili powder
1/4	teaspoon salt
1/4	teaspoon cayenne pepper
3	cups cubed cooked turkey
1	can (15 ounces) black beans, rinsed and drained
1	can (10 ounces) diced tomatoes and green chilies, undrained
1-1/2	cups frozen corn

Sour cream, coarsely crushed tortilla chips, shredded cheddar cheese and sliced ripe olives, optional

▨ In a large saucepan, saute onion in oil until tender. Stir in the broth, jalapeno, cumin, chili powder, salt and cayenne. Add the turkey, beans, tomatoes and corn.

▨ Bring to a boil. Reduce heat; cover and simmer for 20-30 minutes to allow flavors to blend. Garnish with sour cream, chips, cheese and olives if desired.

Yield: 7 servings.

NUTRITION FACTS: 1 cup (calculated without optional ingredients) equals 223 calories, 6 g fat (1 g saturated fat), 47 mg cholesterol, 680 mg sodium, 20 g carbohydrate, 5 g fiber, 23 g protein.

EDITOR'S NOTE: Wear disposable gloves when cutting hot peppers; the oils can burn skin. Avoid touching your face.

mom's chicken noodle soup

My mother was a pastor's wife, and she did a lot of cooking for potlucks. This recipe is one that she created herself. Now I frequently serve it to my own family.
MARLENE DOOLITTLE STORY CITY, IOWA

2 to 3	pounds bone-in chicken breasts and thighs
2	quarts water
1	medium onion, chopped
2	teaspoons chicken bouillon granules
2	celery ribs, diced
2	medium carrots, diced
2	medium potatoes, peeled and cubed
1-1/2	cups fresh or frozen cut green beans
1	teaspoon salt
1/4	teaspoon pepper

NOODLES:

1	cup all-purpose flour
1	egg, lightly beaten
1/2	teaspoon salt
1	teaspoon butter, softened
1/4	teaspoon baking powder
2	to 3 tablespoons milk

◻ In a Dutch oven, cook chicken in water until tender; cool slightly. Remove chicken from bones; discard bones. Skim fat from broth. Cut chicken into bite-size pieces; add to broth with the remaining ingredients except noodles.

◻ Bring to a boil. Reduce heat and simmer, uncovered, for 50-60 minutes or until vegetables are tender.

◻ Meanwhile, for noodles, place flour in a small bowl and make a well in the center. Stir together the remaining ingredients; pour into well. Working the mixture with your hands, form a dough. Knead dough for 5-6 minutes.

◻ Cover and let rest for 10 minutes. On a floured surface, roll dough out to a square, 1/16- to 1/8-in. thick, and cut into 1/4-in.-wide strips.

◻ Cook noodles in boiling salted water for 2-3 minutes or until tender. Drain noodles and add to soup just before serving.

Yield: 6 servings.

NUTRITION FACTS: 1 cup equals 352 calories, 12 g fat (4 g saturated fat), 96 mg cholesterol, 1,074 mg sodium, 36 g carbohydrate, 4 g fiber, 25 g protein.

mexican chicken chili

Corn and black beans give this satisfying chili a Mexican flair the whole family will love. Adjust the cayenne if you have small children or are looking for a little less zip.
STEPHANIE RABBITT-SCHAPP CINCINNATI, OHIO

1	pound boneless skinless chicken breasts, cubed
1	tablespoon canola oil
2	cans (14-1/2 ounces each) diced tomatoes, undrained
2	cups frozen corn
1	can (15 ounces) black beans, rinsed and drained
1	can (14-1/2 ounces) reduced-sodium chicken broth
1	can (4 ounces) chopped green chilies
2	tablespoons chili powder
1	tablespoon ground cumin
1/2	teaspoon salt
1/4	teaspoon cayenne pepper

◻ In a small skillet, brown the chicken in oil over medium heat.

◻ Transfer to a 5-qt. slow cooker. Stir in the remaining ingredients. Cover and cook on low for 5-6 hours or until chicken is tender.

Yield: 6 servings.

NUTRITION FACTS: 1-1/3 cups equals 254 calories, 5 g fat (1 g saturated fat), 42 mg cholesterol, 843 mg sodium, 31 g carbohydrate, 8 g fiber, 23 g protein.

pork, ham & sausage

green chili pork stew

Anyone living in or visiting the Southwest knows that green chilies are a staple. I grew up on this delicacy and would like everyone to discover how delicious it is.

CARRIE BURTON SIERRA VISTA, ARIZONA

1	boneless pork shoulder butt roast (2-1/2 to 3 pounds), cut into 1-inch cubes
1	tablespoon canola oil
1	cup chopped onion
3	garlic cloves, minced
2	cups water
1	can (28 ounces) stewed tomatoes
1	to 2 cans (4 ounces each) chopped green chilies
2	cups cubed peeled potatoes
1	tablespoon chopped fresh cilantro
2	teaspoons ground cumin
2	teaspoons dried oregano
2	teaspoons fennel seed
1	teaspoon salt
1/4	teaspoon pepper
1	can (15 ounces) pinto beans, rinsed and drained

In a soup kettle or Dutch oven, brown pork in oil over medium heat on all sides. Add onion and garlic; saute for 3-5 minutes. Drain. Add the water, tomatoes, chilies, potatoes and seasonings; bring to a boil. Reduce heat; cover and simmer for 45 minutes.

Add beans; cover and simmer for 20-30 minutes or until the meat and vegetables are tender.

Yield: 10 servings (2-1/2 quarts).

NUTRITION FACTS: 1 cup equals 232 calories, 9 g fat (3 g saturated fat), 47 mg cholesterol, 523 mg sodium, 22 g carbohydrate, 4 g fiber, 17 g protein.

spaghetti soup for 2

You'll enjoy how convenient it is to make this small-batch soup recipe. I like to serve mine with biscuits, breadsticks or corn bread.

SHIRLEY TAYLOR RUSSIAVILLE, INDIANA

1	Italian sausage link, casing removed
1	can (14-1/2 ounces) chicken broth
1/2	cup water
1/2	cup cubed peeled potatoes
1/4	cup chopped carrot
1/4	cup chopped onion
1/4	cup canned sliced mushrooms
1/4	teaspoon dried basil
1/8	teaspoon Italian seasoning
1/8	to 1/4 teaspoon hot pepper sauce

Dash celery seed
Dash garlic salt

1/3	cup broken uncooked spaghetti (2-inch pieces)

▨ Crumble sausage into a large saucepan; cook over medium heat until no longer pink. Drain. Add the broth, water, vegetables and seasonings; bring to a boil. Reduce heat; cover and simmer for 30 minutes.

▨ Add spaghetti. Cover and simmer 8-10 minutes longer or until spaghetti and vegetables are tender.

Yield: 2 servings.

NUTRITION FACTS: 1-1/2 cups equals 339 calories, 16 g fat (6 g saturated fat), 45 mg cholesterol, 1,519 mg sodium, 34 g carbohydrate, 3 g fiber, 16 g protein.

sweet potato pork stew

I'm an avid recipe collector and have fun trying new dishes. Fortunately, my family doesn't mind experimenting with new tastes. Everyone loves the rich and bold blend of flavors in this perfect-for-fall stew.

SUSAN SCHLENVOGT WAUKESHA, WISCONSIN

2	pounds boneless pork, trimmed and cut into 1-inch cubes
3	tablespoons Dijon mustard
1/2	cup all-purpose flour
3	tablespoons brown sugar
3	tablespoons canola oil
2	garlic cloves, minced
2-1/3	cups chicken broth
4	to 5 small onions, quartered
2	medium sweet potatoes, peeled and cubed
1/2	teaspoon salt
1/4	teaspoon pepper
1/4	cup minced fresh parsley

▨ In a large bowl, toss pork with mustard until lightly coated. In a large resealable plastic bag, combine flour and brown sugar; add pork and shake to coat.

▨ In a Dutch oven over medium-high heat, brown pork in oil. Add garlic; cook 1 minute longer. Add broth; bring to a boil. Scrape bottom of skillet to loosen any browned bits. Reduce heat; cover and simmer for 30 minutes or until pork is no longer pink.

▨ Add the onions, sweet potatoes, salt and pepper; cover and simmer 30 minutes more or until the pork and potatoes are tender. Stir in parsley.

Yield: 8 servings (2 quarts).

NUTRITION FACTS: 1 cup equals 308 calories, 12 g fat (3 g saturated fat), 68 mg cholesterol, 624 mg sodium, 23 g carbohydrate, 2 g fiber, 25 g protein.

hearty minestrone

(pictured at left)

Here is my all-time favorite soup. It reminds me of spaghetti and sauce in soup form! I love to make big batches and freeze some for later.
KATIE KOZIOLEK HARTLAND, MINNESOTA

1	pound ground pork
1/2	cup chopped celery
1/2	cup chopped onion
1/2	teaspoon minced garlic
1	can (28 ounces) crushed tomatoes
1	can (16 ounces) kidney beans, rinsed and drained
1	can (15 ounces) garbanzo beans or chickpeas, rinsed and drained
2	cups tomato juice
1	can (15 ounces) tomato sauce
1	can (14-1/2 ounces) beef broth
3	medium carrots, chopped
1	medium zucchini, halved lengthwise and thinly sliced
1	tablespoon Italian seasoning
1	to 1-1/2 teaspoons salt
1/2	teaspoon sugar, optional
1/8	teaspoon pepper

ADDITIONAL INGREDIENTS (FOR EACH BATCH):

1/2	cup water
1	cup uncooked ziti or small tube pasta

▧ In a Dutch oven, cook the pork, celery and onion over medium heat until meat is no longer pink. Add garlic; cook 1 minute longer. Drain.

▧ Stir in the tomatoes, beans, tomato juice, tomato sauce, broth, carrots, zucchini, Italian seasoning, salt, sugar if desired and pepper. Bring to a boil. Reduce heat; cover and simmer for 30-35 minutes or until carrots are tender.

▧ Transfer 6 cups of soup to a freezer container; cool. Freeze for up to 3 months. Add water and pasta to remaining soup; bring to a boil. Cover and cook until pasta is tender.

TO USE FROZEN SOUP: Thaw in the refrigerator; transfer to a large saucepan. Stir in water. Bring to a boil; reduce heat. Add pasta; cover and cook until tender.

Yield: 2 batches (6 servings each).

NUTRITION FACTS: 1 cup equals 242 calories, 7 g fat (2 g saturated fat), 25 mg cholesterol, 853 mg sodium, 32 g carbohydrate, 6 g fiber, 15 g protein.

hominy sausage soup

I serve my soup with cheese nachos as a starter to a Southwest-style lunch, following it up with chicken or beef taco salad.
JESSIE GUNN STEPHENS SHERMAN, TEXAS

1/4	pound bulk pork sausage
1	teaspoon cumin seeds
1/8	teaspoon ground coriander
1/8	teaspoon cayenne pepper
2	cups reduced-sodium chicken broth
3/4	cup canned hominy, rinsed and drained
1	to 2 tablespoons chopped jalapeno pepper
1/4	teaspoon pepper
1	tablespoon minced fresh cilantro

▧ Crumble sausage into a small skillet. Cook over medium heat for 3-4 minutes or until no longer pink; drain. In a small saucepan, toast cumin seeds over medium heat for 2-3 minutes or until browned. Add coriander and cayenne; cook and stir for 30 seconds.

▧ Add the broth, hominy, jalapeno, pepper and sausage. Bring to a boil. Reduce heat; simmer, uncovered, for 12-15 minutes to allow flavors to blend. Stir in cilantro.

Yield: 2 servings.

NUTRITION FACTS: 1-1/4 cups equals 276 calories, 18 g fat (6 g saturated fat), 47 mg cholesterol, 1,768 mg sodium, 12 g carbohydrate, 3 g fiber, 15 g protein.

EDITOR'S NOTE: Wear disposable gloves when cutting hot peppers; the oils can burn skin. Avoid touching your face.

bow tie sausage soup

You'll find that the flavor of this wonderful soup is even better the next day. It is so satisfying!
ALICE RABE BEEMER, NEBRASKA

1-1/2	pounds hot or sweet Italian sausage links
1	medium onion, chopped
1	medium green pepper, cut into strips
1	garlic clove, minced
1	can (28 ounces) diced tomatoes, undrained
6	cups water
2	to 2-1/2 cups uncooked bow tie pasta
1	tablespoon sugar
1	tablespoon Worcestershire sauce
2	teaspoons chicken bouillon granules
1	teaspoon salt
1	teaspoon dried basil
1	teaspoon dried thyme

▢ Remove casings from sausage; cut into 1-in. pieces. In a Dutch oven, brown sausage over medium heat. Remove sausage with a slotted spoon; drain, reserving 2 tablespoons drippings. Saute onion and green pepper in drippings until tender. Add garlic; cook 1 minute longer.

▢ Return sausage to the pan; stir in the remaining ingredients. Bring to a boil. Reduce heat. Simmer, uncovered, for 15-20 minutes or until pasta is tender, stirring occasionally.

Yield: 12 servings (3 quarts).

NUTRITION FACTS: 1 cup equals 165 calories, 8 g fat (3 g saturated fat), 23 mg cholesterol, 703 mg sodium, 16 g carbohydrate, 2 g fiber, 8 g protein.

sausage macaroni soup

Macaroni and Italian sausage make this tomato-veggie soup thick and hearty. It offers a nice change of pace on busy nights.
ROBIN SABROWSKY PLYMOUTH, WISCONSIN

1	Italian sausage link, cut into 1/2-inch pieces
1	small onion, chopped
1/2	medium green pepper, chopped
1	can (14-1/2 ounces) Italian diced tomatoes, undrained
1-1/2	cups water
1	can (8 ounces) tomato sauce
1	teaspoon sugar
1	teaspoon chicken bouillon granules
1/4	teaspoon garlic powder
1/3	cup uncooked elbow macaroni
2	tablespoons shredded part-skim mozzarella cheese

▢ In a large saucepan, cook the sausage, onion and green pepper until sausage is browned; drain. Stir in the tomatoes, water, tomato sauce, sugar, bouillon and garlic powder. Bring to a boil. Reduce heat; cover and simmer for 15 minutes, stirring occasionally.

▢ Stir in macaroni. Cover and simmer 10-15 minutes longer or until macaroni is tender. Sprinkle with cheese.

Yield: 4 servings.

NUTRITION FACTS: 1 cup equals 122 calories, 3 g fat (1 g saturated fat), 7 mg cholesterol, 943 mg sodium, 20 g carbohydrate, 2 g fiber, 5 g protein.

meaty mushroom chili

Since our two daughters did not like beans in their chili, I adapted a recipe to suit our whole family's tastes. We all agree that mushrooms are an appealing alternative.
MARJOL BURR CATAWBA, OHIO

1	pound bulk Italian sausage
1	pound ground beef
1	cup chopped onion
1	pound fresh mushrooms, sliced
1	can (46 ounces) V8 juice
1	can (6 ounces) tomato paste
1	teaspoon sugar
1	teaspoon Worcestershire sauce
1	teaspoon salt
1	teaspoon garlic powder
1	teaspoon dried oregano
1/2	teaspoon dried basil
1/2	teaspoon pepper

Sour cream, optional

◩ In a Dutch oven, cook sausage, beef and onion over medium heat until the meat is no longer pink; drain.

◩ Stir in the mushrooms, V8 juice, tomato paste, sugar, Worcestershire sauce and seasonings. Bring to a boil. Reduce heat; cover and simmer for 1 hour. Garnish with sour cream if desired.

Yield: 8 servings (2 quarts).

NUTRITION FACTS: 1 cup equals 364 calories, 23 g fat (9 g saturated fat), 71 mg cholesterol, 1,189 mg sodium, 17 g carbohydrate, 3 g fiber, 21 g protein.

turnip sausage stew

Here's a rich and delicious stew that makes a perfect little batch. Serve it with a rustic artisan bread.
CARMA BLOSSER LIVERMORE, COLORADO

1/2	pound bulk pork sausage
2	medium potatoes, peeled and cubed
2	medium carrots, sliced lengthwise and cut into 2-inch pieces
1	medium turnip, peeled and cubed
1/2	medium onion, chopped
3-1/2	cups water
1/4	teaspoon salt
1/8	teaspoon pepper
1	cup stewed tomatoes

◩ In a large saucepan, cook sausage over medium heat until no longer pink; drain.

◩ Add the potatoes, carrots, turnip, onion, water, salt and pepper. Bring to a boil. Reduce heat; cover and simmer for 15-20 minutes or until vegetables are tender. Stir in tomatoes; heat through.

Yield: 2 servings.

NUTRITION FACTS: 1-3/4 cups equals 445 calories, 21 g fat (8 g saturated fat), 41 mg cholesterol, 1,069 mg sodium, 53 g carbohydrate, 7 g fiber, 13 g protein.

presto tortellini soup

Bring a little Italian flair to your table with a restaurant-style tortellini soup. You won't believe how easy this one is.
KAREN SHIVELEY SPRINGFIELD, MINNESOTA

- 2 packages (7 ounces each) pork breakfast sausage links
- 2 cans (14-1/2 ounces each) Italian stewed tomatoes
- 2 cups water
- 1 cup chopped onion
- 1/2 cup chopped celery
- 1 garlic clove, minced
- 1 teaspoon dried oregano
- 1/8 to 1/4 teaspoon cayenne pepper
- 1/8 to 1/4 teaspoon hot pepper sauce
- 1 bay leaf
- 3/4 cup refrigerated tortellini

▨ In a large saucepan, brown sausage; drain and cut into bite-size pieces. Return to pan; stir in the next nine ingredients.

▨ Bring to a boil. Reduce heat; simmer, uncovered, for 15 minutes. Add tortellini. Bring to a boil. Reduce heat; simmer, uncovered, for 5 minutes or until pasta is tender. Discard bay leaf.

Yield: 8 servings (2 quarts).

NUTRITION FACTS: 1 cup equals 117 calories, 6 g fat (2 g saturated fat), 18 mg cholesterol, 449 mg sodium, 11 g carbohydrate, 2 g fiber, 5 g protein.

kale and sausage soup

Several years ago, I had a dish in a local restaurant that was so good I was determined to duplicate it at home. I played with the recipe until I finally got it just right.
JOHN CROCE JR. YARMOUTH, MASSACHUSETTS

1	pound bulk pork sausage
2	medium onions, chopped
2	tablespoons olive oil
2	garlic cloves, minced
3	cans (14-1/2 ounces each) chicken broth
2	cups water
3	teaspoons chicken bouillon granules
10	cups chopped fresh kale
3	medium potatoes, peeled and cubed
2	cans (15-1/2 ounces each) kidney beans, rinsed and drained

▨ In a Dutch oven over medium heat, cook sausage and onions in oil for 5 minutes or until sausage is browned; drain. Add garlic; cook for 1 minute longer. Add broth, water, bouillon and kale; bring to a boil. Reduce heat; leaving the cover ajar, simmer for 1 hour.

▨ Add potatoes and cook for 10-15 minutes or until tender. Add beans; heat through.

Yield: 12 servings (3 quarts).

NUTRITION FACTS: 1 cup equals 185 calories, 10 g fat (3 g saturated fat), 14 mg cholesterol, 643 mg sodium, 18 g carbohydrate, 3 g fiber, 7 g protein.

favorite italian sausage stew

Here's your answer to what's for dinner on those cold winter nights. We created a quick and flavorful stew that will warm you from head to toe!
TASTE OF HOME TEST KITCHEN

1/2	pound bulk Italian sausage
2	garlic cloves, minced
1	tablespoon cornstarch
1	can (14-1/2 ounces) reduced-sodium beef broth
1	can (14-1/2 ounces) Italian diced tomatoes
4	small red potatoes, quartered
1/4	cup sliced fresh carrots
1	tablespoon minced fresh basil
1/2	cup sliced zucchini
1/4	cup shredded Parmesan cheese, optional

▨ In a large saucepan, cook sausage over medium heat until meat is no longer pink. Add garlic; cook 1 minute longer. Drain. Combine the cornstarch and broth until smooth; stir into sausage mixture. Add the tomatoes, potatoes, carrots and basil. Bring to a boil. Reduce heat; add zucchini.

▨ Cover and simmer for about 15 minutes or until vegetables are tender. Sprinkle with cheese if desired.

Yield: 4 servings.

NUTRITION FACTS: 1-1/4 cups equals 187 calories, 8 g fat (3 g saturated fat), 25 mg cholesterol, 868 mg sodium, 20 g carbohydrate, 2 g fiber, 9 g protein.

spicy pork chili

(pictured at left)

For a pleasant change from traditional beef chili recipes, try my chili that uses pork. This is especially satisfying on a chilly Canadian winter day.
CHRISTINE HARTRY EMO, ONTARIO

1	pound ground pork
2	large onions, chopped
1	medium sweet red pepper, chopped
1	medium green pepper, chopped
1	cup chopped celery
4	garlic cloves, minced
2	cans (14-1/2 ounces each) diced tomatoes, undrained
1	can (16 ounces) kidney beans, rinsed and drained
1	can (6 ounces) tomato paste
3/4	cup water
2	teaspoons brown sugar
1	teaspoon dried oregano
1	teaspoon chili powder
1/4	teaspoon crushed red pepper flakes
1/4	teaspoon cayenne pepper

Dash hot pepper sauce

In a Dutch oven over medium heat, cook pork and onions until pork is no longer pink; drain. Stir in peppers and celery; cook for 5 minutes. Add garlic; cook 1 minute longer. Add remaining ingredients; bring to a boil. Reduce heat; cover and simmer for 45 minutes.

Yield: 6-8 servings (2-1/2 quarts).

NUTRITION FACTS: 1-1/4 cups equals 227 calories, 9 g fat (3 g saturated fat), 38 mg cholesterol, 221 mg sodium, 23 g carbohydrate, 6 g fiber, 16 g protein.

root vegetable soup with sausage

I had a similar soup at a restaurant and re-created it at home. To my surprise, it came out even better than the original! This soup actually won top honors in our town's annual cook-off.
DONNA CLASS KEYSER, WEST VIRGINIA

1/2	pound bulk Italian sausage
1	medium butternut squash (about 3 pounds), peeled and cubed
4	large potatoes, peeled and cubed
3	large sweet potatoes, peeled and cubed
1	large rutabaga, peeled and cubed
1	pound fresh baby carrots
1	medium turnip, peeled and diced
10	cups water

2	cans (14-1/2 ounces each) vegetable broth
2	tablespoons sugar
1-1/2	teaspoons salt
1	teaspoon ground ginger
1/8	teaspoon pepper
1/4	cup heavy whipping cream

Crumble sausage into a stockpot. Cook over medium heat until no longer pink; drain.

Stir in the vegetables, water, broth, sugar and seasonings; bring to a boil. Reduce heat; cover and simmer for 35-40 minutes or until vegetables are tender. Cool slightly.

In a blender, process the soup in batches until smooth. Return to the pan; whisk in cream. Heat through (do not boil).

Yield: 20 servings (5 quarts).

NUTRITION FACTS: 1 cup equals 168 calories, 2 g fat (1 g saturated fat), 6 mg cholesterol, 439 mg sodium, 35 g carbohydrate, 6 g fiber, 4 g protein. **DIABETIC EXCHANGES:** 2 starch, 1/2 fat.

harvest butternut & pork stew

Cure your craving for something different with this savory autumn stew that's so tasty with warm bread.
ERIN CHILCOAT SMITHTOWN, NEW YORK

1/3	cup plus 1 tablespoon all-purpose flour, divided
1	tablespoon paprika
1	teaspoon salt
1	teaspoon ground coriander
1-1/2	pounds boneless pork shoulder butt roast, cut into 1-inch cubes
1	tablespoon canola oil
2-3/4	cups cubed peeled butternut squash
1	can (14-1/2 ounces) diced tomatoes, undrained
1	cup frozen corn, thawed
1	medium onion, chopped
2	tablespoons cider vinegar
1	bay leaf
2-1/2	cups reduced-sodium chicken broth
1-2/3	cups frozen shelled edamame, thawed

▢ In a large resealable plastic bag, combine 1/3 cup flour, paprika, salt and coriander. Add pork, a few pieces at a time, and shake to coat.

▢ In a large skillet, brown pork in oil in batches; drain. Transfer to a 5-qt. slow cooker. Add the squash, tomatoes, corn, onion, vinegar and bay leaf. In a small bowl, combine broth and remaining flour until smooth; stir into slow cooker.

▢ Cover and cook on low for 8-10 hours or until pork and vegetables are tender. Stir in edamame; cover and cook 30 minutes longer. Discard bay leaf.

Yield: 6 servings (2 quarts).

NUTRITION FACTS: 1-1/3 cups equals 371 calories, 16 g fat (5 g saturated fat), 67 mg cholesterol, 635 mg sodium, 30 g carbohydrate, 5 g fiber, 28 g protein. **DIABETIC EXCHANGES:** 3 medium-fat meat, 1-1/2 starch, 1 vegetable, 1/2 fat.

kielbasa-black bean soup

I know you'll come to rely on this nutritious soup like I have. It's loaded with beans and sausage for a real stick-to-the-ribs meal.
JOY RACKHAM CHIMACUM, WASHINGTON

- 4 cups (2 pounds) dried black beans
- 2 celery ribs, chopped
- 1 medium onion, chopped
- 1/2 cup chopped green pepper
- 1 tablespoon canola oil
- 3 garlic cloves, minced
- 2 smoked ham hocks
- 7 cups water
- 2 cans (4 ounces each) chopped green chilies
- 2 teaspoons chicken bouillon granules
- 1/2 teaspoon sugar
- 3 bay leaves
- 1 teaspoon chili powder
- 1 teaspoon ground cumin
  Pinch pepper
- 1 pound fresh kielbasa or Polish sausage links
- 1 can (14-1/2 ounces) diced tomatoes, undrained

▢ Soak beans according to package directions. Drain and rinse beans, discarding liquid. In a Dutch oven, saute the celery, onion and green pepper in oil until tender. Add garlic; cook 1 minute longer. Add the beans, ham hocks, water, chilies, bouillon, sugar and seasonings. Bring to a boil. Reduce heat; cover and simmer for 1-1/2 hours or until beans are tender.

▢ Meanwhile, in a large skillet, cook kielbasa until a thermometer reads 160°. Cut in half lengthwise; slice into 1/4-inch pieces. Add kielbasa and tomatoes to soup.

▢ Remove ham hocks; cool slightly. Remove meat from bones; cut into cubes. Return to soup and heat through. Discard bay leaves.

Yield: 12 servings (3 quarts).

NUTRITION FACTS: 1 cup equals 434 calories, 15 g fat (5 g saturated fat), 35 mg cholesterol, 648 mg sodium, 53 g carbohydrate, 13 g fiber, 24 g protein.

hot italian sausage soup

(pictured at right)

Loaded with zesty sausage and an array of veggies, this soup will hit the spot! I'm part owner of a small tavern, and on Saturdays, we provide soups and deli sandwiches free of charge. Our patrons love this one.
DAN BUTE OTTAWA, ILLINOIS

- 1 pound bulk hot Italian sausage
- 1 can (14-1/2 ounces) Italian stewed tomatoes
- 1 can (8 ounces) tomato sauce
- 1 cup frozen Italian vegetables
- 3/4 cup julienned green, sweet red and/or yellow pepper
- 1/4 cup chopped onion
- 1/4 cup white wine or chicken broth
- 1 teaspoon brown sugar
- 1 teaspoon minced fresh parsley
- 1/2 teaspoon Italian seasoning
- 1/8 teaspoon salt
- 1/8 teaspoon pepper

▢ In a large skillet, cook sausage over medium heat until no longer pink.

▢ Meanwhile, in a large saucepan, combine the remaining ingredients. Bring to a boil. Reduce heat; cover and simmer for 10 minutes or until vegetables are tender.

▢ Drain sausage; add to soup and heat through.

Yield: 4 servings.

NUTRITION FACTS: 1 cup equals 262 calories, 15 g fat (5 g saturated fat), 45 mg cholesterol, 1,224 mg sodium, 16 g carbohydrate, 3 g fiber, 14 g protein.

country italian soup

My mom gave me this recipe a few years back, and it quickly became a family favorite. It's loaded with veggies.
KIM L'HOTE VIOLA, WISCONSIN

1	pound bulk Italian sausage
1	large onion, sliced
2	celery ribs, sliced
2	garlic cloves, minced
5	cups water
2	medium potatoes, peeled and chopped
1	can (14-1/2 ounces) diced tomatoes, undrained
2	medium carrots, sliced
2	teaspoons salt
1	teaspoon dried basil
1	teaspoon dried thyme
1/2	teaspoon dried oregano
1/2	teaspoon pepper
1/4	teaspoon cayenne pepper, optional
1	bay leaf
2	medium zucchini, sliced

◻ In a Dutch oven over medium heat, cook the sausage, onion and celery until meat is no longer pink; drain. Add garlic; cook 1 minute longer.

◻ Add the water, potatoes, tomatoes, carrots and seasonings. Bring to a boil. Reduce heat; cover and simmer for 15 minutes. Stir in zucchini; simmer 8-10 minutes longer or until vegetables are tender. Discard bay leaf.

Yield: 10 servings (2-1/2 quarts).

NUTRITION FACTS: 1 cup equals 211 calories, 14 g fat (5 g saturated fat), 34 mg cholesterol, 876 mg sodium, 13 g carbohydrate, 2 g fiber, 8 g protein.

dublin dumpling stew

I've become a better cook over the years...thanks in part to many wonderful recipes, like this one, from my sister.
ANNETTE FISHER MARION, OHIO

1	pound boneless pork, trimmed and cut into 1-inch cubes
2	tablespoons butter
1/2	cup chopped onion
1/2	cup chopped celery
1	garlic clove, minced
5	medium carrots
3	cups water
1	tablespoon beef bouillon granules
1	teaspoon salt
1/4	cup all-purpose flour
1/2	cup cold water
1	package (10 ounces) frozen mixed vegetables

DUMPLINGS:

1-1/2	cups all-purpose flour
1	tablespoon sugar
2	teaspoons baking powder
1	teaspoon caraway seeds
1/2	teaspoon salt
1/4	teaspoon ground mustard
1	egg
2/3	cup milk
2	tablespoons canola oil

◻ In a Dutch oven, brown pork in butter over medium heat. Add the onion, celery and garlic; cook until vegetables are tender.

◻ Quarter carrots lengthwise, then cut into 2-in. pieces; add to pork mixture. Add the water, bouillon and salt. Bring to a boil. Reduce heat; cover and simmer for 45 minutes or until the meat and vegetables are tender.

◻ Combine flour and cold water until smooth; stir into stew. Bring to a boil; cook and stir for 2 minutes or until thickened. Add mixed vegetables; reduce heat to low.

◻ For dumplings, in a small bowl, combine the flour, sugar, baking powder, caraway seeds, salt and mustard. Beat the egg, milk and oil; add to dry ingredients all at once. Stir just until moistened.

◻ Drop by tablespoonfuls over stew. Cover and simmer for 25 minutes or until a toothpick inserted into a dumpling comes out clean (do not lift the lid while simmering).

Yield: 6 servings.

NUTRITION FACTS: 1-2/3 cups equals 411 calories, 15 g fat (5 g saturated fat), 94 mg cholesterol, 1,256 mg sodium, 45 g carbohydrate, 5 g fiber, 24 g protein.

creamed cabbage and ham soup

Here's a delicious pairing of ham and cabbage in a thick and hearty soup. It's a favorite on our table during the winter months.
LAURIE HARMS GRINNELL, IOWA

2	cups chicken broth
1	medium onion, diced
1	cup diced celery
1	medium head cabbage, shredded
1	carrot, diced
1/4	cup butter, cubed
3	tablespoons all-purpose flour
1	cup milk
2	cups half-and-half cream
2	cups cubed fully cooked ham
1-1/2	teaspoons salt
1/4	teaspoon pepper
1/2	teaspoon dried thyme

Chopped fresh parsley

◻ In a Dutch oven, combine broth and vegetables. Cover and simmer until vegetables are tender, about 20 minutes.

◻ In a large saucepan, melt butter; stir in flour. Gradually add milk and cream; cook and stir until thickened. Stir into vegetable mixture. Add ham, salt, pepper and thyme; heat through. Garnish with parsley.

Yield: 8 servings (2 quarts).

NUTRITION FACTS: 1 cup equals 262 calories, 16 g fat (9 g saturated fat), 68 mg cholesterol, 1,262 mg sodium, 16 g carbohydrate, 4 g fiber, 12 g protein.

ham 'n' veggie soup

(pictured at left)

When I added some ham to this flavorful broth chock-full of vegetables, the soup became a complete meal.
BARBARA THOMPSON LANSDALE, PENNSYLVANIA

1	medium onion, thinly sliced and separated into rings
1	medium zucchini, cubed
1	tablespoon olive oil
1	pound sliced fresh mushrooms
3	cups fresh or frozen corn
3	cups cubed fully cooked ham
6	medium tomatoes, peeled, seeded and chopped
1/2	cup chicken broth
1-1/2	teaspoons salt
1/2	teaspoon garlic powder
1/2	teaspoon pepper

Shredded part-skim mozzarella cheese

▢ In a large saucepan, saute onion and zucchini in oil for 5 minutes or until onion is tender. Add the mushrooms, corn and ham; cook and stir for 5 minutes.

▢ Stir in the tomatoes, broth, salt, garlic powder and pepper. Bring to a boil. Reduce heat; cover and simmer for 5 minutes. Uncover; simmer 5-8 minutes longer. Garnish with mozzarella cheese.

Yield: 10 servings (2-1/2 quarts).

NUTRITION FACTS: 1 cup equals 160 calories, 6 g fat (1 g saturated fat), 22 mg cholesterol, 955 mg sodium, 18 g carbohydrate, 3 g fiber, 12 g protein.

sweet 'n' snappy chili

Folks are pleasantly surprised to see my chili brimming with ground pork instead of beef.
JOANNE WITHERS OSAKIS, MINNESOTA

2	pounds ground pork
2	celery ribs, chopped
1	medium onion, chopped
1	small green pepper, chopped
2	garlic cloves, minced
2	cans (16 ounces each) chili beans, undrained
1	can (28 ounces) diced tomatoes, undrained
1	can (4 ounces) chopped green chilies
3	cups water
1/4	cup packed brown sugar
3	tablespoons chili powder
2	teaspoon ground cumin
3/4	teaspoon ground ginger

▢ In a Dutch oven, cook pork over medium heat until no longer pink; drain. Remove and set aside.

▢ In the same pan, saute the celery, onion and green pepper until vegetables are tender. Add garlic; cook 1 minute longer. Drain. Add pork and remaining ingredients; bring to boil. Reduce heat; cover and simmer for 45 minutes to allow flavors to blend.

Yield: 8 servings (2 quarts).

NUTRITION FACTS: 1 cup equals 320 calories, 16 g fat (6 g saturated fat), 67 mg cholesterol, 392 mg sodium, 24 g carbohydrate, 6 g fiber, 23 g protein.

hot pot stew

This full-bodied stew is ideal for blustery rainy days in autumn or spring. It's a comforting meal served with crusty bread.
SANDRA ALLEN LEADVILLE, COLORADO

1	cup cubed lean boneless pork (1/2-inch pieces)
1	cup cubed fully cooked ham
1	cup coarsely chopped green pepper
1/2	cup chopped onion
1/2	cup chopped celery
1	garlic clove, minced
3	cups cubed red potatoes
3	cups water
1	can (15 ounces) pinto beans, rinsed and drained
1	can (15.8 ounces) great northern beans, rinsed and drained
1-1/4	teaspoons sugar
1	teaspoon chicken bouillon granules
1	teaspoon beef bouillon granules
1/4	teaspoon ground nutmeg
1/4	teaspoon coarsely ground pepper
1	package (10 ounces) frozen chopped spinach or turnip greens or 1 can (14-1/2 ounces) spinach or turnip greens, drained

▢ In a Dutch oven coated with cooking spray, brown pork over medium-high heat. Add ham, green pepper, onion, celery and garlic. Reduce heat to medium; cook for 8-10 minutes or until vegetables are just tender, stirring occasionally. Add the next nine ingredients. Reduce heat; cover and simmer for 20 minutes or until meat is tender. Add spinach and cook until heated through.

Yield: 10 servings (2-1/2 quarts).

NUTRITION FACTS: 1 cup equals 161 calories, 2 g fat (1 g saturated fat), 17 mg cholesterol, 486 mg sodium, 24 g carbohydrate, 6 g fiber, 12 g protein. **DIABETIC EXCHANGES:** 1-1/2 starch, 1 lean meat.

☐ Saute celery and onion in drippings until tender. Add sugar; cook and stir for 1 minute or until sugar is dissolved. Gradually stir in flour; cook and stir for 1 minute or until blended. Add the broth, picante sauce, tomato sauce and pepper; bring to a boil. Cook and stir for 2 minutes or until thickened.

☐ Just before serving, add lettuce and heat through. Sprinkle with croutons and bacon.

Yield: 8 servings (2 quarts).

NUTRITION FACTS: 1 cup equals 268 calories, 14 g fat (5 g saturated fat), 35 mg cholesterol, 1,689 mg sodium, 24 g carbohydrate, 2 g fiber, 10 g protein.

sage 'n' rosemary pork stew

This stew satisfies the appetites of both my husband and son, who are real meat-and-potatoes men. It's easy on the family budget, yet is special enough to serve to guests.
GAIL DVORCHAK SMOCK, PENNSYLVANIA

1	boneless pork shoulder butt roast (3 to 4 pounds), cut into 3/4-inch cubes
1	tablespoon canola oil
1	can (49-1/2 ounces) chicken broth
1-1/2	cups water
3/4	cup chopped onion
1-1/4	teaspoons dried rosemary, crushed
3/4	teaspoon salt
1/2	teaspoon dried sage
1/2	teaspoon pepper
4	cups cubed red potatoes
1	package (9 ounces) frozen cut green beans
1-1/2	cups frozen lima beans
1	teaspoon Dijon mustard
1/3	cup all-purpose flour
1/2	cup half-and-half cream

☐ In a Dutch oven over medium heat, brown pork in oil; drain. Add the broth, water, onion, rosemary, salt, sage and pepper; bring to a boil. Reduce heat and simmer, uncovered, for 40-45 minutes or until pork is almost tender.

☐ Stir in the potatoes, beans and mustard. Return to a boil; reduce heat and simmer, uncovered, for 40-45 minutes or until vegetables and pork are tender.

☐ In a small bowl, combine flour and cream; stir until smooth. Add to stew. Bring to a boil; cook and stir for 2 minutes or until thickened.

Yield: 12 servings (3 quarts).

NUTRITION FACTS: 1 cup equals 299 calories, 14 g fat (5 g saturated fat), 75 mg cholesterol, 772 mg sodium, 18 g carbohydrate, 3 g fiber, 23 g protein. **DIABETIC EXCHANGES:** 3 medium-fat meat, 1 starch.

b.l.t. soup

The B.L.T. is a family favorite, so I came up with a soup that has all the fabulous flavor of the sandwich. But I gave it a little extra zip by adding picante sauce.
SHARON RICHARDSON DALLAS, TEXAS

3	tablespoons butter
2	teaspoons canola oil
3	cups cubed French bread
1	pound bacon strips, diced
2	cups finely chopped celery
1	medium onion, finely chopped
2	tablespoons sugar
6	tablespoons all-purpose flour
5	cups chicken broth
1	jar (16 ounces) picante sauce
1	can (8 ounces) tomato sauce
1/8	teaspoon pepper
3	cups shredded lettuce

☐ In a Dutch oven, heat butter and oil over medium heat. Add bread cubes; stir until crisp and golden brown. Remove and set aside. In the same pan, cook bacon until crisp. Drain, reserving 1/4 cup drippings; set bacon aside.

bisques, chowders & cheese soups

cheeseburger paradise soup

I've never met a person who didn't enjoy this creamy soup, and it's hearty enough to serve as a main course with your favorite bread or rolls.

NADINA IADIMARCO BURTON, OHIO

6	medium potatoes, peeled and cubed
1	small carrot, grated
1	small onion, chopped
1/2	cup chopped green pepper
2	tablespoons chopped seeded jalapeno pepper
3	cups water
2	tablespoons plus 2 teaspoons beef bouillon granules
2	garlic cloves, minced
1/8	teaspoon pepper
2	pounds ground beef
1/2	pound sliced fresh mushrooms
2	tablespoons butter
5	cups 2% milk, divided
6	tablespoons all-purpose flour
1	package (16 ounces) process cheese (Velveeta), cubed

Crumbled cooked bacon

▢ In a Dutch oven, combine the first nine ingredients; bring to a boil. Reduce heat; cover and simmer for 10-15 minutes or until potatoes are tender.

▢ Meanwhile, in a large skillet, cook beef and mushrooms in butter over medium heat until meat is no longer pink; drain. Add to soup. Stir in 4 cups milk; heat through.

▢ In a small bowl, combine flour and remaining milk until smooth; gradually stir into soup. Bring to a boil; cook and stir for 2 minutes or until thickened. Reduce heat; stir in cheese until melted. Garnish with bacon.

Yield: 14 servings (about 3-1/2 quarts).

NUTRITION FACTS: 1 cup (calculated without bacon) equals 370 calories, 20 g fat (10 g saturated fat), 79 mg cholesterol, 947 mg sodium, 24 g carbohydrate, 1 g fiber, 23 g protein.

EDITOR'S NOTE: Wear disposable gloves when cutting hot peppers; the oils can burn skin. Avoid touching your face.

cheddar seafood chowder

Flavored with crab, shrimp and cheddar cheese, this chowder is so good that I make it weekly. Sometimes I substitute chicken or ham for the seafood and leave out the Clamato juice. Either way, this pretty soup is a winner!

AMI PATON WACONIA, MINNESOTA

1/2	cup finely chopped onion
1/4	cup butter
1	can (14-1/2 ounces) chicken broth
1	cup cubed peeled potato
2	celery ribs, chopped
2	medium carrots, chopped
1/4	cup Clamato juice
1/4	teaspoon lemon-pepper seasoning
1/4	cup all-purpose flour
2	cups 2% milk
2	cups (8 ounces) shredded sharp cheddar cheese
1	can (6 ounces) crabmeat, drained, flaked and cartilage removed
1	cup cooked shrimp

In a saucepan, saute onion in butter until tender. Stir in the broth, potato, celery, carrots, Clamato juice and lemon-pepper. Bring to a boil. Reduce heat; cover and simmer for 15-20 minutes or until vegetables are tender.

In a small bowl, whisk flour and milk until smooth; add to soup. Bring to a boil; cook and stir for 2 minutes or until thickened. Reduce heat. Add the cheese, crab and shrimp; cook and stir until cheese is melted.

Yield: 4 servings.

NUTRITION FACTS: 1-1/2 cups equals 550 calories, 33 g fat (22 g saturated fat), 198 mg cholesterol, 1,233 mg sodium, 28 g carbohydrate, 2 g fiber, 35 g protein.

cheesy tortilla soup

My daughter came up with this dish when trying to duplicate a soup she sampled at a restaurant. I always pass along to her the rave reviews I get whenever I serve it.

LAVONDA OWEN MARLOW, OKLAHOMA

1	envelope chicken fajita seasoning mix
1	pound boneless skinless chicken breasts, diced
2	tablespoons canola oil
1/2	cup chopped onion
1/4	cup butter, cubed
1/3	cup all-purpose flour
2	cans (14-1/2 ounces each) chicken broth
1/3	cup canned diced tomatoes with chilies
1	cup cubed process cheese (Velveeta)
1-1/2	cups (6 ounces) shredded Monterey Jack cheese, divided
1-1/2	cups half-and-half cream
1/2	cup shredded cheddar cheese

Guacamole and tortilla chips

Prepare fajita mix according to package directions; add chicken and marinate as directed. In a large skillet, cook chicken in oil until no longer pink; set aside.

In a large saucepan, saute onion in butter until tender. Stir in flour until blended. Gradually stir in broth. Bring to a boil. Cook and stir for 2 minutes or until thickened and bubbly. Add the tomatoes, process cheese and 1 cup Monterey Jack; cook and stir until cheese is melted.

Stir in cream and reserved chicken; heat through (do not boil). Sprinkle with cheddar and remaining Monterey Jack cheese; top with guacamole and chips.

Yield: 8 servings (2 quarts).

NUTRITION FACTS: 1 cup (calculated without guacamole and chips) equals 395 calories, 27 g fat (15 g saturated fat), 109 mg cholesterol, 1,273 mg sodium, 11 g carbohydrate, trace fiber, 23 g protein.

au gratin chicken chowder

Everyone will want more of this quick and rich chowder. The flavor is unbeatable! Canned corn and packaged potatoes make it a snap to prepare.
ELLA EBERLY ENGLEWOOD, OHIO

6	bacon strips, diced
1	small onion, chopped
1	package (4.9 ounces) au gratin potatoes
2	cups water
1-1/2	cups 2% milk
1-1/4	cups chicken broth
1	can (15-1/4 ounces) whole kernel corn, drained
1	bay leaf
3	cups cubed cooked chicken
2/3	cup evaporated milk

☐ In a large saucepan, cook bacon over medium heat until crisp. Remove to paper towels with a slotted spoon; drain, reserving 2 tablespoons drippings.

☐ Saute onion in drippings until tender. Add the potatoes with contents of sauce mix, water, milk, broth, corn and bay leaf. Cook, uncovered, over medium heat for 15-20 minutes or until potatoes are tender, stirring occasionally.

☐ Reduce heat. Stir in the chicken, evaporated milk and bacon; heat through. Discard bay leaf.

Yield: 6 servings (about 2 quarts).

NUTRITION FACTS: 1-1/3 cups equals 451 calories, 20 g fat (7 g saturated fat), 92 mg cholesterol, 1,162 mg sodium, 33 g carbohydrate, 2 g fiber, 30 g protein.

chilled corn and shrimp soup

Hot days call for cool foods, like this refreshing, delicately spiced soup. It's so pretty and unique, your guests are sure to remember it.
MARY MARLOWE LEVERETTE COLUMBIA, SOUTH CAROLINA

1/2	cup chopped sweet onion
3	tablespoons olive oil
1-1/2	pounds uncooked small shrimp, peeled and deveined
2	garlic cloves, minced
1	teaspoon curry powder
2	cups buttermilk
1	package (16 ounces) frozen shoepeg corn, thawed, divided
1	cup (8 ounces) reduced-fat sour cream
1	teaspoon hot pepper sauce
1	teaspoon salt
1/2	teaspoon coarsely ground pepper
2	tablespoons minced chives

☐ In a skillet, saute onion in oil until tender. Add the shrimp, garlic and curry; cook 4-6 minutes longer or until shrimp turn pink. Remove from the heat and set aside.

☐ In a blender, combine the buttermilk, 2 cups corn, sour cream, pepper sauce, salt and pepper. Cover and process until smooth; transfer to a large bowl. Add remaining corn and shrimp mixture. Cover and refrigerate for at least 3 hours. Garnish servings with chives.

Yield: 4 servings.

NUTRITION FACTS: 1 cup equals 317 calories, 13 g fat (4 g saturated fat), 153 mg cholesterol, 689 mg sodium, 23 g carbohydrate, 2 g fiber, 26 g protein.

seafood bisque

We live on the Gulf Coast, where fresh seafood is plentiful. I combined several recipes to come up with my bisque. It's great as a first course or an entree, and it can be made with just shrimp or just crab if you prefer.

PAT EDWARDS DAUPHIN ISLAND, ALABAMA

2	cans (10-3/4 ounces each) condensed cream of mushroom soup, undiluted
1	can (10-3/4 ounces) condensed cream of celery soup, undiluted
2-2/3	cups 2% milk
4	green onions, chopped
1/2	cup finely chopped celery
1	garlic clove, minced
1	teaspoon Worcestershire sauce
1/4	teaspoon hot pepper sauce
1-1/2	pounds uncooked medium shrimp, peeled and deveined
1	can (6 ounces) crabmeat, drained, flaked and cartilage removed
1	jar (4-1/2 ounces) whole mushrooms, drained
3	tablespoons Madeira wine or chicken broth
1/2	teaspoon salt
1/2	teaspoon pepper

▨ In a Dutch oven, combine the first eight ingredients. Bring to a boil. Reduce heat; add the shrimp, crab and mushrooms. Simmer, uncovered, for 10 minutes. Stir in the wine, salt and pepper; cook 2-3 minutes longer.

Yield: 10 servings (2-1/2 quarts).

NUTRITION FACTS: 1 cup equals 169 calories, 6 g fat (3 g saturated fat), 127 mg cholesterol, 817 mg sodium, 10 g carbohydrate, 1 g fiber, 18 g protein.

zucchini garden chowder

Years ago, when my husband and I put in our first garden, a neighbor suggested zucchini since it's easy to grow. Our kids were reluctant to try new things, so I used our squash in this cheesy chowder—it met with solid approval from all of us!

NANETTE JORDAN FLINT, MICHIGAN

2	medium zucchini, chopped
1	medium onion, chopped
2	tablespoons minced fresh parsley
1	teaspoon dried basil
1/3	cup butter, cubed
1/3	cup all-purpose flour
1	teaspoon salt
1/4	teaspoon pepper
3	cups water
3	teaspoons chicken bouillon granules
1	teaspoon lemon juice
1	can (14-1/2 ounces) diced tomatoes, undrained
1	can (12 ounces) evaporated milk
1	package (10 ounces) frozen corn
1/4	cup grated Parmesan cheese
2	cups (8 ounces) shredded cheddar cheese

Pinch sugar, optional

▨ In a Dutch oven, saute the zucchini, onion, parsley and basil in butter until vegetables are tender. Stir in the flour, salt and pepper. Gradually stir in water. Add the bouillon and lemon juice. Bring to a boil; cook and stir for 2 minutes or until thickened.

▨ Add the tomatoes, milk and corn; bring to a boil. Reduce heat; cover and simmer for 5 minutes or until corn is tender. Stir in cheeses and sugar if desired.

Yield: 8-10 servings (about 2-1/2 quarts).

NUTRITION FACTS: 1 cup equals 258 calories, 16 g fat (11 g saturated fat), 55 mg cholesterol, 905 mg sodium, 18 g carbohydrate, 2 g fiber, 11 g protein.

southwestern bean chowder

(pictured at left)

I'm really fortunate that my young children are great eaters, and my husband loves this nutritious soup, too.
JULIANNE MEYERS HINESVILLE, GEORGIA

- 2 cans (15 ounces each) white kidney or cannellini beans, rinsed and drained, divided
- 1 medium onion, chopped
- 1/4 cup chopped celery
- 1/4 cup chopped green pepper
- 1 tablespoon olive oil
- 2 garlic cloves, minced
- 3 cups vegetable broth
- 1-1/2 cups frozen corn, thawed
- 1 medium carrot, shredded
- 1 can (4 ounces) chopped green chilies
- 1 tablespoon ground cumin
- 1/2 teaspoon chili powder
- 4-1/2 teaspoons cornstarch
- 2 cups 2% milk
- 1 cup (4 ounces) shredded cheddar cheese

Minced fresh cilantro and additional shredded cheddar cheese, optional

In a bowl, mash one can beans with a fork; set aside.

In a Dutch oven, saute the onion, celery and pepper in oil until tender. Add garlic; cook 1 minute longer. Stir in the mashed beans, broth, corn, carrot, chilies, cumin, chili powder and remaining beans. Bring to a boil. Reduce heat; simmer, uncovered, for 20 minutes.

Combine cornstarch and milk until smooth. Stir into bean mixture. Bring to a boil; cook and stir for 2 minutes or until thickened. Stir in cheese until melted. Serve with cilantro and additional cheese if desired.

Yield: 8 servings (2 quarts).

NUTRITION FACTS: 1 cup (calculated without additional cheese) equals 236 calories, 8 g fat (4 g saturated fat), 20 mg cholesterol, 670 mg sodium, 31 g carbohydrate, 6 g fiber, 11 g protein. **DIABETIC EXCHANGES:** 2 starch, 1 lean meat, 1/2 fat.

cheddar ham soup

I knew this recipe was a keeper when my mother-in-law asked for it. And although the recipe makes enough to feed a crowd, don't expect leftovers!
MARTY MATTHEWS CLARKSVILLE, TENNESSEE

- 2 cups diced peeled potatoes
- 2 cups water
- 1/2 cup sliced carrot
- 1/4 cup chopped onion
- 1/4 cup butter, cubed
- 1/4 cup all-purpose flour
- 2 cups 2% milk
- 1/4 to 1/2 teaspoon salt
- 1/4 teaspoon pepper
- 2 cups (8 ounces) shredded cheddar cheese
- 1-1/2 cups cubed fully cooked ham
- 1 cup frozen peas

In a large saucepan, combine the potatoes, water, carrot and onion. Bring to a boil. Reduce heat; cover and cook for 10-15 minutes or until tender.

Meanwhile, in another saucepan, melt butter. Stir in flour until smooth. Gradually add the milk, salt and pepper. Bring to a boil; cook and stir for 2 minutes or until thickened. Stir in cheese until melted. Stir into undrained potato mixture. Add ham and peas; heat through.

Yield: 7 servings.

NUTRITION FACTS: 1 cup equals 303 calories, 17 g fat (11 g saturated fat), 64 mg cholesterol, 763 mg sodium, 20 g carbohydrate, 2 g fiber, 17 g protein.

makeover mom's clam chowder

When we lived in Michigan, this was a perfect comforting soup when blustery winds blew into town. The steaming bowls of soup warmed us right down to our toes! The Taste of Home Test Kitchen created this lightened-up version.

CHRISTINE SCHENHER SAN CLEMENTE, CALIFORNIA

3/4	cup each chopped onion, celery and carrots
1/2	cup chopped green pepper
1/4	cup butter
1	carton (32 ounces) reduced-sodium chicken broth
1	bottle (8 ounces) clam juice
2	teaspoons reduced-sodium chicken bouillon granules
1	bay leaf
1/2	teaspoon dried parsley flakes
1/2	teaspoon salt
1/4	teaspoon curry powder
1/4	teaspoon pepper
1	medium potato, peeled and cubed
2/3	cup all-purpose flour
2	cups 2% milk, divided
4	cans (6-1/2 ounces each) minced clams, undrained
1	cup half-and-half cream

In a Dutch oven over medium heat, cook the onion, celery, carrots and green pepper in butter until tender. Stir in the broth, clam juice, bouillon and seasonings. Add potato. Bring to a boil. Reduce heat; simmer, uncovered, for 15-20 minutes or until potato is tender.

In a small bowl, combine flour and 1 cup milk until smooth. Gradually stir into soup. Bring to a boil; cook and stir for 1-2 minutes or until thickened. Stir in the clams, cream and remaining milk; heat through (do not boil). Discard bay leaf.

Yield: 12 servings (3 quarts).

NUTRITION FACTS: 1 cup equals 155 calories, 7 g fat (4 g saturated fat), 34 mg cholesterol, 726 mg sodium, 15 g carbohydrate, 1 g fiber, 8 g protein. **DIABETIC EXCHANGES:** 1 starch, 1 lean meat, 1 fat.

DELICIOUS CHOWDER

Though chowders take many forms, they typically share three common ingredients: dairy products like milk or cream; pork, such as bacon or ham; and potatoes. There are almost as many tempting variations on chowder as there are cooks!

cheesy cauliflower soup

If you prefer chunky soup, skip the blender step and stir the cheese and cream into the slow cooker mixture, then heat on high until the cheese is melted.
SHERYL PUNTER WOODSTOCK, ONTARIO

1	large head cauliflower, broken into florets
2	celery ribs
2	large carrots
1	large green pepper
1	small sweet red pepper
1	medium red onion
4	cups chicken broth
1/2	teaspoon Worcestershire sauce
1/4	teaspoon salt
1/8	teaspoon pepper
2	cups (8 ounces) shredded cheddar cheese
2	cups half-and-half cream

▢ Place cauliflower in a 4-qt. slow cooker. Chop the celery, carrots, peppers and onion; add to slow cooker. Stir in the broth, Worcestershire sauce, salt and pepper. Cover and cook on low for 5-6 hours or until vegetables are tender.

▢ In a blender, process soup in batches until smooth. Return all to slow cooker; stir in cheese and cream. Cover and cook on high for 30 minutes or until cheese is melted.

Yield: 9 servings (2-1/4 quarts).

NUTRITION FACTS: 1 cup equals 209 calories, 13 g fat (9 g saturated fat), 56 mg cholesterol, 730 mg sodium, 12 g carbohydrate, 4 g fiber, 10 g protein.

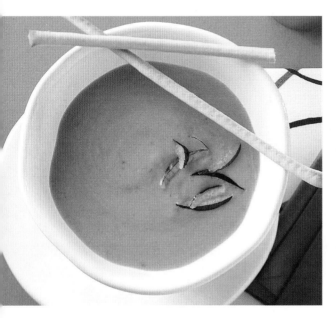

fish chowder

It's actually quite easy to make chowder loaded with big, traditional flavors in a little batch that's perfect for two! This recipe is even more special to me because it was my mother's.
PAT GONET WENHAM, MASSACHUSETTS

1	bacon strip, diced
2	tablespoons chopped onion
1/2	cup water
1	medium potato, cubed
1/4	teaspoon seafood seasoning

Dash salt and pepper

1	haddock, halibut or cod fillet (6 ounces)
1	cup 2% milk
2	teaspoons butter

▢ In a small saucepan, saute bacon and onion until tender. Add the water, potato, seafood seasoning, salt and pepper. Bring to a boil. Reduce heat; place fillet on top.

▢ Cover and cook for 15-20 minutes or until fish flakes easily with a fork. Stir in milk and butter; heat through. Flake fish into pieces before serving.

Yield: 2 servings.

NUTRITION FACTS: 1-1/4 cups equals 320 calories, 13 g fat (6 g saturated fat), 76 mg cholesterol, 403 mg sodium, 26 g carbohydrate, 2 g fiber, 24 g protein. **DIABETIC EXCHANGES:** 2 lean meat, 1 starch, 1 vegetable, 1/2 fat-free milk.

easy shrimp chowder

My family's favorite chowder is a joy to make with handy pantry ingredients. The rich flavor will have you hooked.
E. TWITCHELL TURNER, MAINE

  3 medium potatoes, peeled and diced
  2 medium onions, sliced
  2 cups water
3/4 teaspoon salt
Dash seafood seasoning, optional
1-1/2 cups milk
  1 can (5 ounces) evaporated milk
  4 ounces process cheese (Velveeta), cubed
  1 can (6 ounces) small shrimp, drained
  2 tablespoons butter
  1 tablespoon minced fresh parsley

◻ In a large saucepan, combine the potatoes, onions, water, salt and seafood seasoning if desired; bring to a boil. Reduce heat; cover and simmer until the potatoes are tender.

◻ Stir in the milk, evaporated milk and cheese; heat until cheese is melted. Add the shrimp, butter and parsley; heat through.

Yield: 6 servings.

NUTRITION FACTS: 1 cup equals 268 calories, 12 g fat (7 g saturated fat), 98 mg cholesterol, 947 mg sodium, 26 g carbohydrate, 2 g fiber, 14 g protein.

chicken wild rice chowder

This tasty soup is comfort food at its finest—perfect to help you power through a cold day. You'll love the fact that it's table-ready in just 25 minutes.
TASTE OF HOME TEST KITCHEN

  2 cups sliced fresh carrots
1/2 cup chopped onion
1/2 cup chopped celery
  2 tablespoons butter
  3 tablespoons all-purpose flour
  2 cans (14-1/2 ounces each) chicken broth
2-2/3 cups cubed cooked chicken breasts
  1 package (8.8 ounces) ready-to-serve long grain and wild rice
1/4 cup half-and-half cream
1/8 teaspoon pepper

◻ In a large saucepan, saute the carrots, onion and celery in butter until tender. Stir in flour until blended; gradually add broth. Bring to a boil; cook and stir for 2 minutes or until thickened. Stir in the chicken, rice, cream and pepper; heat through.

Yield: 4 servings.

NUTRITION FACTS: 1-1/3 cups equals 371 calories, 12 g fat (5 g saturated fat), 99 mg cholesterol, 1,369 mg sodium, 32 g carbohydrate, 3 g fiber, 32 g protein.

farmhouse ham chowder

Leftover ham and veggies add body to this hearty chowder, but ranch dressing is the secret that gives it zest. A little smoked Gouda brings a nice touch.
LISA RENSHAW KANSAS CITY, MISSOURI

1/2	cup finely chopped onion
1/2	cup finely chopped celery
1/2	cup chopped sweet red pepper
2	tablespoons butter
1/4	cup all-purpose flour
1	envelope ranch salad dressing mix
4-1/4	cups milk
2	cups frozen cubed hash brown potatoes, thawed
2	cups frozen corn, thawed
2	cups cubed fully cooked ham
1	teaspoon minced fresh thyme or 1/4 teaspoon dried thyme
1/2	cup shredded smoked Gouda cheese

In a large saucepan, saute the onion, celery and red pepper in butter until crisp-tender. Stir in flour and dressing mix until blended; gradually stir in milk. Bring to a boil; cook and stir for 2 minutes or until thickened.

Add the potatoes, corn, ham and thyme. Bring to a boil. Reduce heat; simmer, uncovered, for 8-10 minutes to allow flavors to blend. Stir in cheese until blended.

Yield: 8 servings (2 quarts).

NUTRITION FACTS: 1 cup equals 267 calories, 11 g fat (6 g saturated fat), 48 mg cholesterol, 1,288 mg sodium, 29 g carbohydrate, 2 g fiber, 14 g protein.

golden potato soup

I have requests for this soup for lots of family events, especially deer camp. If you're in the mood for comfort food, this is the recipe for you!
SHELLY WOODS BLISSFIELD, MICHIGAN

6	cups cubed Yukon Gold potatoes
2	cups water
1	cup sliced celery
1	cup sliced carrots
1/2	cup chopped onion
2	teaspoons dried parsley flakes
2	teaspoons chicken bouillon granules
1	teaspoon salt
1/2	teaspoon pepper
1/4	cup all-purpose flour
2	cups milk, divided
1	package (16 ounces) process cheese (Velveeta), cubed
1	cup cubed fully cooked ham
1/3	cup real bacon bits

In a Dutch oven, combine the first nine ingredients. Bring to a boil over medium heat. Reduce heat; cover and simmer for 12-14 minutes or until the potatoes are tender.

Meanwhile, in a small bowl, combine flour and 1/4 cup milk until smooth; add to soup. Bring to a boil; cook and stir for 2 minutes or until thickened. Stir in cheese and remaining milk until cheese is melted. Add ham and bacon; heat through.

Yield: 8 servings (2-3/4 quarts).

NUTRITION FACTS: 1-1/3 cups equals 401 calories, 19 g fat (11 g saturated fat), 57 mg cholesterol, 1,666 mg sodium, 36 g carbohydrate, 3 g fiber, 22 g protein.

salmon bisque

(pictured at left)

This soup is a tempting way to prepare heart-healthy salmon. Even though it uses 2% milk, it has a rich mouthfeel. Serve with a green salad and crusty whole-grain bread.
BARBARA PARKS RENTON, WASHINGTON

1	small sweet red pepper
1	salmon fillet (8 ounces)
1/2	cup finely chopped carrot
1	tablespoon chopped shallot
1	tablespoon canola oil
2	garlic cloves, minced
3	tablespoons all-purpose flour
1	can (14-1/2 ounces) chicken broth
2	cups 2% milk
1	teaspoon seafood seasoning
1/4	teaspoon Liquid Smoke, optional

▢ Broil red pepper 4 in. from the heat until skin blisters, about 5 minutes. With tongs, rotate pepper a quarter turn. Broil and rotate until all sides are blistered and blackened. Immediately place pepper in a bowl; cover and let stand for 15-20 minutes. Peel off and discard charred skin. Remove stems and seeds. Set roasted pepper aside.

▢ Broil salmon 4 in. from the heat for 8-12 minutes or until fish flakes easily with a fork. Break salmon into small pieces; set aside.

▢ In a large saucepan, saute carrot and shallot in oil until tender. Add garlic; saute 1 minute longer. Stir in flour until blended. Gradually add broth. Bring to a boil; cook and stir for 1-2 minutes or until thickened.

▢ Transfer to a blender; add roasted pepper. Cover and puree until smooth. Return to the pan. Stir in the milk, seafood seasoning, Liquid Smoke if desired and salmon; heat through.

Yield: 4 servings.

NUTRITION FACTS: 1 cup equals 239 calories, 12 g fat (3 g saturated fat), 43 mg cholesterol, 674 mg sodium, 14 g carbohydrate, 1 g fiber, 17 g protein. **DIABETIC EXCHANGES:** 2 lean meat, 1 starch, 1 fat.

ham & corn chowder

Generous amounts of corn, ham and potato turn this into a fast favorite. No one will know it came together in 25 minutes, especially if you add the pretty garnishes I recommend.
MARION ST. JEAN HOMOSASSA, FLORIDA

1	can (10-3/4 ounces) reduced-fat reduced-sodium condensed cream of celery soup, undiluted
1-1/2	cups fat-free milk
1	can (15-1/4 ounces) whole kernel corn, drained
1	can (14-3/4 ounces) cream-style corn
1/2	cup cubed fully cooked ham
2	tablespoons dried minced onion
2	tablespoons minced fresh parsley
1	can (14-1/2 ounces) diced potatoes, drained

Sour cream, shredded cheddar cheese and/or paprika, optional

▢ In a large saucepan, combine soup and milk. Heat through, stirring frequently. Stir in the corn, ham, onion and parsley. Bring to a boil. Reduce heat; cover and simmer for 5 minutes. Add potatoes; heat through. Garnish each serving with sour cream, cheese and/or paprika if desired.

Yield: 6 servings.

NUTRITION FACTS: 1 cup (calculated without garnishes) equals 202 calories, 3 g fat (1 g saturated fat), 9 mg cholesterol, 909 mg sodium, 35 g carbohydrate, 3 g fiber, 8 g protein.

classic broccoli cheese soup

(pictured above)

Basic ingredients have never tasted or looked so good. The green broccoli florets and the brilliant orange carrots make this rich soup a colorful addition to any table.
EVELYN MASSNER OAKVILLE, IOWA

2	cups sliced fresh carrots
2	cups broccoli florets
1	cup sliced celery
1-1/2	cups chopped onion
1/2	cup butter
3/4	cup all-purpose flour
1	can (10-1/2 ounces) condensed chicken broth, undiluted
4	cups whole milk
1/2	pound process cheese (Velveeta), cubed

▨ In a large saucepan, bring 2 quarts water to a boil. Add carrots, broccoli and celery; cover and boil for 5 minutes. Drain and set aside.

▨ In the same saucepan, saute onion in butter. Add flour and stir to make smooth paste. Gradually add chicken broth and milk. Cook until mixture thickens, about 8-10 minutes. Add vegetables; heat until tender. Stir in cheese until melted.

Yield: 6-8 servings (2 quarts).

NUTRITION FACTS: 1 cup equals 472 calories, 31 g fat (19 g saturated fat), 88 mg cholesterol, 1,033 mg sodium, 32 g carbohydrate, 3 g fiber, 18 g protein.

cheeseburger chowder

On blustery days, my family craves this rich and creamy soup. Serve it with oven-fresh corn bread or biscuits for a meal that will stick to your ribs!
REBECCA MCCABE EKALAKA, MONTANA

1	pound ground beef
1/4	cup chopped onion
1-1/2	cups water
3	teaspoons beef bouillon granules
1/2	teaspoon salt
2	cups cubed red potatoes
1	celery rib, thinly sliced
3	tablespoons all-purpose flour
2-1/2	cups milk, divided
1	cup (4 ounces) shredded cheddar cheese

▨ In a large saucepan, cook beef and onion over medium heat until meat is no longer pink; drain. Stir in the water, bouillon and salt. Add potatoes and celery. Bring to a boil. Reduce heat; cover and simmer for 15-20 minutes or until potatoes are tender.

▨ Combine flour and 1/2 cup milk until smooth; gradually stir into beef mixture. Bring to a boil; cook and stir for 2 minutes or until thickened and bubbly. Stir in the remaining milk; heat through. Stir in cheese until melted.

Yield: 7 servings.

NUTRITION FACTS: 1 cup equals 261 calories, 14 g fat (8 g saturated fat), 61 mg cholesterol, 696 mg sodium, 15 g carbohydrate, 1 g fiber, 19 g protein.

golden clam chowder

My recipe makes it easy to enjoy delicious homemade clam chowder any night. Bits of crispy bacon are not only traditional, they make the chowder feel rich and indulgent.
AMANDA BOWYER CALDWELL, IDAHO

2	celery ribs
2	medium carrots
1	medium onion
2	teaspoons olive oil
4	garlic cloves, minced
4	medium potatoes, peeled and diced
2	cans (6-1/2 ounces each) minced clams, undrained
1	bottle (8 ounces) clam juice
1	cup plus 1 tablespoon water, divided
1	teaspoon dried thyme
1/2	teaspoon salt
1/2	teaspoon pepper
1	can (12 ounces) evaporated milk
2	teaspoons cornstarch
2	bacon strips, cooked and crumbled

☐ Finely chop the celery, carrots and onion. In a Dutch oven, saute vegetables in oil until tender. Add garlic; cook 1 minute longer. Stir in the potatoes, clams, clam juice, 1 cup water, thyme, salt and pepper. Bring to a boil. Reduce heat; cover and simmer for 12-15 minutes or until potatoes are tender.

☐ Gradually stir in milk; heat through. Combine cornstarch and remaining water until smooth; stir into chowder. Bring to a boil; cook and stir for 2 minutes or until thickened. Stir in bacon.

Yield: 7 servings.

NUTRITION FACTS: 1 cup equals 195 calories, 5 g fat (3 g saturated fat), 27 mg cholesterol, 574 mg sodium, 28 g carbohydrate, 2 g fiber, 10 g protein. **DIABETIC EXCHANGES:** 1 starch, 1 lean meat, 1 vegetable, 1 fat.

red pepper shrimp bisque

Here's a soup that goes nicely with a steak and salad. It's great for special dinners because it feels festive, yet it's surprisingly easy to make.
STEPHANIE BUTTARS PHOENIX, ARIZONA

1	cup chicken broth
1	jar (7 ounces) roasted sweet red peppers, drained
1/2	teaspoon sugar
1/2	teaspoon paprika
1	cup coarsely chopped cooked shrimp (6 ounces)
1/2	cup heavy whipping cream
1/4	cup grated Romano cheese, divided
1/4	teaspoon salt
1/8	teaspoon pepper

Dash hot pepper sauce

☐ In a small saucepan, bring broth and roasted peppers to a boil. Reduce heat; cover and simmer for 5 minutes. Remove from the heat and cool slightly.

☐ Transfer to a blender; cover and process until pureed. Return to the saucepan. Add sugar and paprika; bring to a boil. Reduce heat; simmer, uncovered, for 5 minutes. Add the shrimp, cream, 2 tablespoons cheese, salt, pepper and hot pepper sauce. Cook and stir for 2 minutes or until heated through. Garnish with remaining cheese.

Yield: 2 servings.

NUTRITION FACTS: 1-1/4 cups equals 400 calories, 28 g fat (16 g saturated fat), 224 mg cholesterol, 1,284 mg sodium, 15 g carbohydrate, trace fiber, 24 g protein.

In a large saucepan, bring the potatoes, broth, celery, onions and red pepper to a boil. Reduce heat; cover and simmer for 13-15 minutes or until vegetables are tender. Stir in milk. Gently mash vegetables with a potato masher, leaving some chunks of potatoes.

Combine flour and evaporated milk until smooth; gradually stir into potato mixture. Bring to a boil; cook and stir for 2 minutes or until thickened. Stir in the remaining ingredients. Return to a boil. Cook and stir for 2-3 minutes or until shrimp turn pink.

Yield: 8 servings.

NUTRITION FACTS: 1 cup equals 192 calories, 2 g fat (trace saturated fat), 130 mg cholesterol, 334 mg sodium, 21 g carbohydrate, 2 g fiber, 23 g protein. **DIABETIC EXCHANGES:** 2-1/2 lean meat, 1 starch, 1 vegetable.

broccoli crab bisque

For a casual company meal, I like to serve this creamy soup along with miniature ham sandwiches.
KAREN BALISTRIERI OCONOMOWOC, WISCONSIN

1	cup sliced leeks (white portion only)
1	cup sliced fresh mushrooms
1	cup chopped fresh broccoli florets
1/4	cup butter
1	garlic clove, minced
1/4	cup all-purpose flour
1/4	to 1/2 teaspoon dried thyme
1/8	teaspoon pepper
1	bay leaf
3	cups chicken broth
1	cup half-and-half cream
1	cup (4 ounces) shredded Swiss cheese
1	can (6 ounces) crabmeat, drained

In a large saucepan, saute the leeks, mushrooms and broccoli in butter until tender. Add garlic; cook 1 minute longer. Add the flour, thyme, pepper and bay leaf; mix well. Stir in broth and cream. Bring to a boil; cook and stir for 2 minutes or until thickened.

Add the cheese and crab; stir until cheese is melted and soup is heated through. Discard bay leaf.

Yield: 8 servings (2 quarts).

NUTRITION FACTS: 1 cup equals 191 calories, 13 g fat (8 g saturated fat), 62 mg cholesterol, 532 mg sodium, 7 g carbohydrate, 1 g fiber, 11 g protein.

low-fat shrimp chowder

This yummy chowder is chock-full of shrimp and vegetables. The skim milk and reduced-sodium broth help keep it on the surprisingly healthy side. It tastes even better the next day, after the flavors have melded overnight.
MICHELLE CONLEY EVANSTON, WYOMING

1	pound red potatoes, peeled and cubed
2-1/2	cups reduced-sodium chicken broth
3	celery ribs, chopped
8	green onions, chopped
1/2	cup chopped sweet red pepper
1-1/2	cups fat-free milk
1/4	cup all-purpose flour
1/2	cup fat-free evaporated milk
1-1/2	pounds uncooked medium shrimp, peeled and deveined
2	tablespoons minced fresh parsley
1/2	teaspoon paprika
1/2	teaspoon Worcestershire sauce
1/8	teaspoon cayenne pepper
1/8	teaspoon pepper

new england clam chowder

I left a cruise ship with a great souvenir...the recipe for this splendid chowder! It's a traditional soup that stands the test of time.
AGNES WARD STRATFORD, ONTARIO

12	fresh cherrystone clams
3	cups cold water
2	bacon strips, diced
1	small onion, chopped
2	medium potatoes, peeled and finely chopped
1/4	teaspoon salt
1/4	teaspoon pepper
2	tablespoons all-purpose flour
1	cup milk
1/2	cup half-and-half cream

▢ Tap clams; discard any that do not close. Place clams and water in a large saucepan. Bring to a boil. Reduce heat; cover and simmer for 5-6 minutes or until clams open.

▢ Remove meat from clams; chop meat and set aside. Strain liquid through a cheesecloth-lined colander; set aside.

▢ In a large saucepan, cook bacon over medium heat until crisp. Using a slotted spoon, remove to paper towels. Saute onion in drippings until tender.

▢ Return bacon to the pan; add clam meat and reserved liquid. Stir in the potatoes, salt and pepper. Bring to a boil. Reduce heat; cover and simmer for 10-12 minutes or until potatoes are tender.

▢ Combine flour and milk until smooth; gradually stir into soup. Bring to a boil; cook and stir for 2 minutes or until thickened. Gradually stir in cream; heat through (do not boil).

Yield: 7 servings.

NUTRITION FACTS: 1 cup equals 138 calories, 6 g fat (3 g saturated fat), 24 mg cholesterol, 175 mg sodium, 14 g carbohydrate, 1 g fiber, 6 g protein. **DIABETIC EXCHANGES:** 1 starch, 1 lean meat, 1/2 fat.

potato cheese soup

This satisfying potato soup has a velvety texture that's neither too thick nor too thin. The subtle flavors of the beer and cheese balance each other nicely, creating a soup that's sure to warm you head to toe!
PATTI LAVELL ISLAMORADA, FLORIDA

2	pounds potatoes (about 6 medium), peeled and cubed
1	small onion, chopped
2	cups water
1-1/2	cups 2% milk
1	cup beer or chicken broth
2	tablespoons Worcestershire sauce
2	chicken bouillon cubes
3/4	teaspoon salt
1/2	teaspoon ground mustard
1/2	teaspoon white pepper
2	cups (8 ounces) shredded cheddar cheese

Salad croutons and/or crumbled cooked bacon, optional

▢ Place the potatoes, onion and water in a large saucepan. Bring to a boil. Reduce heat; cover and cook for 15-20 minutes or until tender. Remove from the heat; cool slightly (do not drain). In a blender, cover and process mixture in batches until smooth. Return all to the pan and heat through.

▢ Stir in the milk, beer, Worcestershire sauce, bouillon, salt, mustard and white pepper; heat through. Stir in cheese just until melted. Top with croutons and/or bacon if desired.

Yield: 8 servings (2 quarts).

NUTRITION FACTS: 1 cup (calculated without optional ingredients) equals 211 calories, 9 g fat (7 g saturated fat), 34 mg cholesterol, 738 mg sodium, 21 g carbohydrate, 1 g fiber, 9 g protein.

anything goes sausage soup

(pictured at left)

I call this recipe "anything goes" because you can add or take out a variety of ingredients, and the soup still turns out absolutely delicious. It's impossible to have just one bowl, unless, of course, your first bowl is huge and filled to the brim!
SHEENA WELLARD NAMPA, IDAHO

1	pound bulk pork sausage
4	cups water
1	can (10-3/4 ounces) condensed cream of mushroom soup, undiluted
1	can (10-3/4 ounces) condensed cheddar cheese soup, undiluted
5	medium red potatoes, cubed
4	cups chopped cabbage
3	large carrots, thinly sliced
4	celery ribs, chopped
1	medium zucchini, chopped
1	large onion, chopped
5	chicken bouillon cubes
1	tablespoon dried parsley flakes
3/4	teaspoon pepper
1	can (12 ounces) evaporated milk

▨ In a large skillet, cook sausage over medium heat until no longer pink; drain. Transfer to a 6-qt. slow cooker. Stir in the water and soups until blended. Add the vegetables, bouillon, parsley and pepper.

▨ Cover and cook on low for 9-10 hours or until vegetables are tender. Stir in milk; cover and cook 30 minutes longer.

Yield: 15 servings (about 4 quarts).

NUTRITION FACTS: 1 cup equals 174 calories, 9 g fat (4 g saturated fat), 21 mg cholesterol, 847 mg sodium, 17 g carbohydrate, 2 g fiber, 6 g protein.

school day chowder

This hearty soup is a nice change of pace for brown-baggers. It's a full meal when you add fresh fruit and a cookie.
KAREN ANN BLAND GOVE, KANSAS

1/2	pound hot dogs, halved lengthwise and sliced
1	cup sliced celery
1/2	cup sliced carrot
1/2	cup chopped green pepper
1/4	cup chopped onion
1/4	cup butter, cubed
1/4	cup all-purpose flour
1/8	teaspoon pepper
2-1/2	to 3 cups milk
2	cups (8 ounces) shredded cheddar cheese

▨ In a large saucepan, combine the hot dogs, celery, carrot, green pepper, onion and butter. Cook and stir over medium heat until vegetables are tender. Stir in flour and pepper until blended. Gradually add milk. Bring to a boil; cook and stir for 2 minutes or until thickened. Add cheese; stir until melted.

Yield: 5 servings.

NUTRITION FACTS: 1 serving equals 503 calories, 40 g fat (23 g saturated fat), 115 mg cholesterol, 915 mg sodium, 17 g carbohydrate, 1 g fiber, 20 g protein.

makeover hash brown soup

This lightened-up soup has all the rich and creamy goodness you'd expect, but with less fat, sodium and calories. It's the perfect recipe to chase away chills on a cool autumn day.
JUDITH WEBB BLUE SPRINGS, MISSOURI

2	green onions, chopped
2	teaspoons canola oil
1	package (28 ounces) frozen O'Brien potatoes, thawed
2	cups 2% milk
1	can (10-3/4 ounces) reduced-fat reduced-sodium condensed cream of chicken soup, undiluted
6	turkey bacon strips, diced and cooked
1/2	cup shredded cheddar cheese

▨ In a small skillet, saute onions in oil until tender. In a 5-qt. slow cooker, combine the potatoes, milk, soup and onions.

▨ Cover and cook on low for 6-7 hours or until heated through. Top each serving with 2 tablespoons bacon and 1 tablespoon cheese.

Yield: 8 servings.

NUTRITION FACTS: 3/4 cup equals 206 calories, 9 g fat (4 g saturated fat), 26 mg cholesterol, 520 mg sodium, 24 g carbohydrate, 2 g fiber, 8 g protein.

creamy vegetable chowder

This rich, comforting soup has it all. It's easy to lower the fat content by using turkey bacon, vegetable broth and skim milk. Either way, it's delicious!

SUZANNA VANDEBRAKE PEYTON, COLORADO

3/4	pound sliced bacon, chopped
2	large onions
2	medium carrots
2	celery ribs
2	medium parsnips
2	small turnips
3/4	cup all-purpose flour
1/2	teaspoon salt
1/2	teaspoon cayenne pepper
2	cartons (32 ounces each) chicken broth
1	medium sweet potato, peeled and chopped
3	small red potatoes, chopped
2	bay leaves
1	tablespoon Worcestershire sauce
1/4	teaspoon hot pepper sauce
1	cup half-and-half cream
1/2	cup minced fresh parsley

☐ In a Dutch oven, cook bacon over medium heat until crisp. Remove to paper towels; drain, reserving 3 tablespoons drippings. Chop the onions, carrots, celery, parsnips and turnips; add to the pan. Cook and stir for 6-8 minutes or until fragrant.

☐ Sprinkle vegetables with flour, salt and cayenne; stir until blended. Gradually add broth. Bring to a boil; cook and stir for 2 minutes or until thickened. Stir in the sweet potato, potatoes, bay leaves, Worcestershire sauce and pepper sauce.

☐ Reduce heat; cover and simmer for 15-20 minutes or until potatoes are tender. Stir in cream and parsley; heat through. Discard bay leaves.

Yield: 12 servings (3 quarts).

NUTRITION FACTS: 1 cup equals 205 calories, 10 g fat (4 g saturated fat), 24 mg cholesterol, 956 mg sodium, 21 g carbohydrate, 3 g fiber, 6 g protein.

slow-cooked halibut chowder

Here's a great way to mix up your dinnertime repertoire. Mashed potato flakes are a great hands-free way to thicken the chowder as it simmers in the slow cooker. We're spoiled in Alaska with abundant fresh halibut, but feel free to substitute whatever fish you like.
DONNA GOUTERMONT JUNEAU, ALASKA

2	cups water
2	cups 2% milk
2	medium potatoes, cubed
1	large onion, chopped
1	cup mashed potato flakes
1	can (8 ounces) tomato sauce
2	garlic cloves, minced
1	teaspoon celery salt
1	teaspoon dried parsley flakes
1/2	teaspoon ground mustard
1/4	teaspoon chili powder
1/4	teaspoon cayenne pepper
1	pound halibut fillets, cut into chunks
1	tablespoon butter

In a 3-qt. slow cooker, combine the first 12 ingredients. Cover and cook on low for 5 hours or until potatoes are tender.

Add halibut and butter. Cover and cook 30-45 minutes longer or until fish flakes easily with a fork.

Yield: 6 servings (2 quarts).

NUTRITION FACTS: 1-1/4 cups equals 254 calories, 6 g fat (3 g saturated fat), 37 mg cholesterol, 534 mg sodium, 27 g carbohydrate, 2 g fiber, 21 g protein. **DIABETIC EXCHANGES:** 2 lean meat, 2 starch.

cheddar corn chowder

My children absolutely love this rich and flavorful soup. They have just one complaint—it seems I never make a big enough batch to suit them!
MARLENE LESCHINSKY WINNIPEG, MANITOBA

1	medium onion, chopped
1	cup diced sweet red pepper
2	tablespoons butter
1/4	cup all-purpose flour
2	cups chicken or vegetable broth
2	large potatoes, diced
1	can (11 ounces) whole kernel corn, drained or 1-1/2 cups frozen corn
1/2	teaspoon ground mustard
1/2	teaspoon paprika
1/4	teaspoon salt
1/4	teaspoon crushed red pepper flakes
1/8	teaspoon pepper
2	cups milk
1-1/2	cups (6 ounces) shredded cheddar cheese
4	green onions, thinly sliced

In a large saucepan, saute onion and red pepper in butter until tender. Stir in flour until blended; gradually add broth. Bring to a boil; cook and stir for 1 minute or until thickened.

Add the potatoes, corn, mustard, paprika, salt, pepper flakes and pepper; return to a boil. Reduce heat; cover and simmer for 15-20 minutes or until potatoes are tender.

Add milk; cook and stir until soup comes to a boil. Remove from the heat; stir in cheese until melted. Sprinkle with green onions.

Yield: 8 servings (2 quarts).

NUTRITION FACTS: 1 cup equals 272 calories, 12 g fat (7 g saturated fat), 37 mg cholesterol, 605 mg sodium, 31 g carbohydrate, 3 g fiber, 10 g protein.

macaroni and cheese soup

I've worked as a cook for too many years to count and have made this one-of-a-kind soup at many different jobs. It's always been a big hit.
EMMA HEAD SUNRISE BEACH, MISSOURI

3	quarts water
5	teaspoons chicken bouillon granules
1-1/2	cups sliced celery
2	large carrots, shredded
1	large onion, chopped
1	medium green pepper, chopped
2-1/2	cups uncooked elbow macaroni
1	cup butter, cubed
3/4	cup all-purpose flour
6	cups milk
1	pound process cheese (Velveeta), cubed

▢ In a stockpot, bring water and bouillon to a boil. Add celery, carrots, onion and green pepper; cook for 4 minutes or until tender. Add macaroni. Cover and return to a boil; boil 2 minutes. Remove from the heat; let stand for 8-10 minutes or just until macaroni is tender.

▢ Meanwhile, melt butter in a large saucepan. Add flour, stirring until smooth. Gradually add milk, stirring constantly. Bring to a boil; cook and stir for 2 minutes. Stir in cheese until melted; add to undrained macaroni mixture.

Yield: 20 servings (5 quarts).

NUTRITION FACTS: 1 cup equals 261 calories, 17 g fat (11 g saturated fat), 49 mg cholesterol, 619 mg sodium, 18 g carbohydrate, 1 g fiber, 9 g protein.

confetti chowder

Grandma's philosophy was, "Add a little color to your food, and folks will eat up a storm!" This delightful golden chowder was one of her favorite recipes, and the broccoli, carrots and zucchini in it add flavor as well as color.
ROSE BOMBA LISBON, NEW HAMPSHIRE

3	tablespoons butter
1	cup chopped carrots
1	cup diced zucchini
1	cup broccoli florets
1/2	cup chopped onion
1/2	cup chopped celery
1/4	cup all-purpose flour
1/2	teaspoon salt
1/2	teaspoon pepper
1/4	teaspoon sugar
3	cups milk
1	cup chicken broth
1	cup whole kernel corn
1	cup diced fully cooked ham
1/2	cup peas
1	jar (2 ounces) sliced pimiento, drained
1	cup (4 ounces) shredded cheddar cheese

▢ Melt butter in a Dutch oven. Add the carrots, zucchini, broccoli, onion and celery; cook and stir for 5 minutes or until crisp-tender. Sprinkle flour, salt, pepper and sugar over vegetables; mix well.

▢ Stir in milk and chicken broth; cook and stir until thickened and bubbly. Add corn, ham, peas and pimiento; cook and stir until heated through. Remove from the heat; stir in cheese until melted.

Yield: 8 servings (2 quarts).

NUTRITION FACTS: 1 cup equals 237 calories, 13 g fat (8 g saturated fat), 48 mg cholesterol, 762 mg sodium, 17 g carbohydrate, 2 g fiber, 12 g protein.

lightened-up crab bisque

I decided to try making a light seafood soup after tasting one while dining out. I came up with this low-fat bisque and everyone loved it. It was even featured on a local TV show!
CORNEY WELSH BATON ROUGE, LOUISIANA

2	cups chopped onions
1	cup chopped celery
1	cup chopped green pepper
1/4	cup reduced-fat margarine
4	garlic cloves, minced
4	cups diced peeled potatoes
2	cups fat-free milk
4	cups fat-free half-and-half
10	ounces reduced-fat process cheese (Velveeta), cubed
3	cans (6 ounces each) lump crabmeat, drained
3/4	teaspoon salt
1/4	teaspoon white pepper

☐ In a Dutch oven, saute the onions, celery and green pepper in margarine until tender. Add garlic; cook 1 minute longer. Reduce heat to medium; add the potatoes and milk. Cook, uncovered, for 20 minutes or until potatoes are just tender, stirring occasionally.

☐ Remove 1-1/2 cups of the potato mixture; mash and return to the pan. Reduce heat to low. Stir in half-and-half and process cheese. Cook and stir until cheese is melted. Add the crab, salt and pepper; heat through.

Yield: 12 servings (3 quarts).

NUTRITION FACTS: 1 cup equals 237 calories, 5 g fat (2 g saturated fat), 44 mg cholesterol, 802 mg sodium, 27 g carbohydrate, 2 g fiber, 18 g protein. **DIABETIC EXCHANGES:** 1 fat-free milk, 1 lean meat, 1 vegetable, 1/2 starch, 1/2 fat.

hot dog soup

We can always count on our pastor for good advice and good recipes, like this thick and hearty soup. Chock-full of hot dogs and veggies, it quickly became my children's favorite.
KIM HOLLIDAY BELLEFONTE, PENNSYLVANIA

4	medium carrots, cut into thin strips
2	medium potatoes, peeled and cubed
2	medium parsnips, peeled and chopped
1	medium onion, chopped
1/4	cup butter
2	tablespoons all-purpose flour
1	package (1 pound) hot dogs, halved lengthwise and cut into bite-size pieces
1	can (12 ounces) evaporated milk
1	can (10-3/4 ounces) condensed cream of mushroom soup, undiluted
1	cup water
1	teaspoon dried basil
1/2	teaspoon pepper

☐ In a large saucepan, saute the carrots, potatoes, parsnips and onion in butter for 5 minutes. Stir in flour until blended. Add the hot dogs, milk, soup, water, basil and pepper; bring to a boil. Reduce heat; cover and simmer for 25-30 minutes or until vegetables are tender, stirring occasionally.

Yield: 8 servings (2 quarts).

NUTRITION FACTS: 1 cup equals 418 calories, 28 g fat (14 g saturated fat), 64 mg cholesterol, 968 mg sodium, 30 g carbohydrate, 4 g fiber, 12 g protein.

bacon & swiss mushroom soup

(pictured at left)

I've always enjoyed cooking and recently created this satisfying soup. In addition to bacon, you can also garnish it with chopped green onion tops or shredded Swiss cheese.
TOBY MERCER INMAN, SOUTH CAROLINA

10	bacon strips, diced
1	pound sliced fresh mushrooms
1	medium onion, chopped
3	garlic cloves, minced
1	quart heavy whipping cream
1	can (14-1/2 ounces) chicken broth
1-1/4	cups shredded Swiss cheese
3	tablespoons cornstarch
1/2	teaspoon salt
1/2	teaspoon pepper
3	tablespoons cold water

▢ In a large saucepan, cook bacon over medium heat until crisp. Using a slotted spoon, remove to paper towels; drain, reserving 2 tablespoons drippings. In the drippings, saute mushrooms and onion until tender. Add garlic; cook 1 minute longer. Stir in cream and broth. Gradually stir in cheese until melted.

▢ In a small bowl, combine the cornstarch, salt, pepper and water until smooth. Stir into soup. Bring to a boil; cook and stir for 2 minutes or until thickened. Garnish with bacon.

Yield: 8 servings (2 quarts).

NUTRITION FACTS: 1 cup equals 592 calories, 56 g fat (33 g saturated fat), 193 mg cholesterol, 649 mg sodium, 12 g carbohydrate, 1 g fiber, 13 g protein.

creamy crab bisque

I've enjoyed cooking and baking ever since my 4-H days in rural Iowa. The seasonings in this bisque nicely bring out the delicate flavor of crab.
KATHY WALKER FORT COLLINS, COLORADO

1/2	cup chopped celery
2	tablespoons chopped onion
1/4	cup butter
1/4	cup all-purpose flour
2-1/2	cups milk
2	beef bouillon cubes
1	cup half-and-half cream
1	can (6 ounces) crabmeat, drained
1/2	cup sliced fresh mushrooms
1/2	teaspoon dried basil
1/4	teaspoon garlic powder
1/4	to 1/2 teaspoon Creole seasoning
1/8	to 1/4 teaspoon pepper

▢ In a large saucepan over medium heat, cook celery and onion in butter until tender. Stir in flour until blended; gradually add milk. Bring to a boil; cook and stir for 2 minutes or until thickened.

▢ Stir in the bouillon, cream, crab, mushrooms, basil, garlic powder, 1/4 teaspoon Creole seasoning and 1/8 teaspoon pepper. Bring to a boil. Reduce heat; cover and simmer for 20 minutes, stirring frequently. Season to taste with remaining Creole seasoning and pepper if desired.

Yield: 4 servings.

NUTRITION FACTS: 1 cup equals 355 calories, 23 g fat (14 g saturated fat), 119 mg cholesterol, 849 mg sodium, 17 g carbohydrate, 1 g fiber, 17 g protein.

EDITOR'S NOTE: The following spices may be substituted for 1 teaspoon Creole seasoning: 1/4 teaspoon each salt, garlic powder and paprika; and a pinch each of dried thyme, ground cumin and cayenne pepper.

fresh corn chowder

Fresh sweet corn shines in this simple recipe. Try it with Vidalia or other sweet onions for a seasonal treat.
MARGARET OLIEN NEW RICHMOND, WISCONSIN

4	large ears sweet corn, husks removed
1	large onion, chopped
1	celery rib, chopped
1	tablespoon butter
1-1/2	cups diced peeled potatoes
1	cup water
2	teaspoons chicken bouillon granules
1/4	teaspoon dried thyme
1/4	teaspoon pepper
6	tablespoons all-purpose flour
3	cups 2% milk

▢ Cut corn off the cobs; set aside. In a large saucepan, saute onion and celery in butter until tender. Add the potatoes, water, bouillon, thyme, pepper and corn. Bring to a boil.

▢ Reduce heat; cover and simmer for 15 minutes or until potatoes are tender.

▢ Combine flour and milk until smooth; gradually stir into soup. Bring to a boil; cook and stir for 2 minutes or until thickened.

Yield: 7 servings.

NUTRITION FACTS: 1 cup equals 204 calories, 5 g fat (3 g saturated fat), 13 mg cholesterol, 410 mg sodium, 35 g carbohydrate, 4 g fiber, 8 g protein. **DIABETIC EXCHANGES:** 2 starch, 1/2 reduced-fat milk.

fontina-vegetable crab soup

Cayenne pepper adds a little heat to rich, creamy soup loaded with vegetables and crab. Serve this as a first course or as a meal by itself.

CHARLENE CHAMBERS ORMOND BEACH, FLORIDA

1-1/2	cups frozen corn, thawed
1	large onion, chopped
1	cup roasted sweet red peppers, drained and chopped
1	celery rib, chopped
1	tablespoon canola oil
1	garlic clove, minced
2	cans (14-1/2 ounces each) chicken broth
1	teaspoon minced fresh thyme or 1/4 teaspoon dried thyme
1/4	teaspoon cayenne pepper
1/4	cup all-purpose flour
3/4	cup heavy whipping cream
4	ounces fontina cheese, cut into 1/4-inch cubes
1/2	cup canned lump crabmeat

▢ Pat corn dry; transfer to a greased 15-in. x 10-in. x 1-in. baking pan. Bake at 450° for 12-15 minutes or until lightly browned, stirring once.

▢ Meanwhile, in a Dutch oven, saute the onion, red peppers and celery in oil until tender. Add garlic; cook 1 minute longer. Stir in the broth, thyme, cayenne and corn. Bring to a boil. Reduce heat; simmer, uncovered, for 15 minutes.

▢ Combine flour and cream until smooth. Gradually stir into broth mixture; add cheese. Bring to a gentle boil; cook and stir for 2 minutes or until thickened and cheese is melted. Top servings with crab.

Yield: 5 servings.

NUTRITION FACTS: 1 cup soup with about 1 tablespoon crab equals 366 calories, 24 g fat (13 g saturated fat), 99 mg cholesterol, 1,169 mg sodium, 22 g carbohydrate, 2 g fiber, 14 g protein.

southwest chicken corn chowder

My family really enjoys my lightened-up take on chowder. Even my little grandson likes it! The fat-free evaporated milk stands in beautifully for calorie-laden cream.

EILEEN ROBITAILLE RIVERSIDE, CALIFORNIA

- 1 large onion, chopped
- 1 garlic clove, minced
- 1/2 teaspoon olive oil
- 1 can (14-1/2 ounces) reduced-sodium chicken broth
- 1 can (10-3/4 ounces) reduced-fat reduced-sodium condensed cream of chicken soup, undiluted
- 2 cups cubed cooked chicken breast
- 1 can (4 ounces) chopped green chilies, drained
- 2 cans (14-3/4 ounces each) cream-style corn
- 1 can (12 ounces) fat-free evaporated milk
- 1/2 teaspoon chili powder
- 1/2 teaspoon ground cumin
- 6 tablespoons shredded reduced-fat cheddar cheese
- 4-1/2 teaspoons chopped cilantro

◻ In a large nonstick saucepan, saute onion and garlic in oil until tender.

◻ Stir in the broth, soup, chicken and chilies until blended. Bring to a boil. Reduce heat; stir in the corn, milk, chili powder and cumin. Heat through (do not boil). Sprinkle each serving with cheese and cilantro.

Yield: 9 servings (2-1/4 quarts).

NUTRITION FACTS: 1 cup soup with 2 teaspoons cheese equals 206 calories, 5 g fat (2 g saturated fat), 35 mg cholesterol, 669 mg sodium, 27 g carbohydrate, 2 g fiber, 16 g protein. **DIABETIC EXCHANGES:** 2 starch, 2 lean meat.

scallop & shrimp chowder

Delicate seafood makes this rich and cheesy chowder feel extra-special. Crispy bacon makes a yummy classic garnish.

TASTE OF HOME TEST KITCHEN

- 6 bacon strips, chopped
- 2 celery ribs, finely chopped
- 1/2 cup chopped sweet orange pepper
- 1 small onion, finely chopped
- 2 garlic cloves, minced
- 1/4 cup all-purpose flour
- 1 can (14-1/2 ounces) chicken broth
- 2 cups 2% milk
- 2 medium red potatoes, cubed
- 1 teaspoon seafood seasoning
- 1/4 teaspoon salt
- 1/2 pound uncooked medium shrimp, peeled and deveined
- 1/2 pound bay scallops
- 1-1/2 cups (6 ounces) shredded cheddar cheese

◻ In a large saucepan, cook bacon over medium heat until crisp. Remove to paper towels with a slotted spoon; drain, reserving 2 tablespoons drippings.

◻ In the drippings, saute the celery, orange pepper and onion until crisp-tender. Add garlic; cook 1 minute longer. Stir in flour until blended; gradually add broth and milk. Bring to a boil; cook and stir for 1 minute or until thickened.

◻ Add the potatoes, seafood seasoning and salt; return to a boil. Reduce heat; cover and simmer for 10-15 minutes or until potatoes are tender.

◻ Add shrimp and scallops; cook and stir for 3-4 minutes or until shrimp turn pink and scallops are opaque. Stir in cheese until melted. Garnish each serving with bacon.

Yield: 6 servings.

NUTRITION FACTS: 1 cup equals 309 calories, 14 g fat (8 g saturated fat), 104 mg cholesterol, 981 mg sodium, 19 g carbohydrate, 1 g fiber, 26 g protein.

corn chowder with dumplings

Here's my spiced-up version of corn chowder. Dumplings give a familiar soup that extra-special surprise!
SHANNON KOHN SIMPSONVILLE, SOUTH CAROLINA

2	large onions, chopped
2	teaspoons canola oil
4	cups chicken broth
3	cups frozen corn
2	cups cubed peeled potatoes
1	cup heavy whipping cream
1	to 3 teaspoons minced chipotle pepper in adobo sauce
1/4	teaspoon salt

CHEDDAR CORNMEAL DUMPLINGS:

1/2	cup all-purpose flour
1/4	cup yellow cornmeal
1	teaspoon baking powder
1/4	teaspoon salt
1/2	cup milk
1/4	cup shredded cheddar cheese

☐ In a large saucepan, saute onions in oil until tender. Add the broth, corn, potatoes, cream, chipotle pepper and salt. Bring to a boil. Reduce heat; simmer, uncovered, for 3-5 minutes.

☐ For dumplings, in a small bowl, combine the flour, cornmeal, baking powder and salt. Stir in milk and cheese just until moistened. Drop by tablespoonfuls onto simmering chowder.

☐ Cover and simmer for 20 minutes or until a toothpick inserted near the center of a dumpling comes out clean (do not lift cover while simmering).

Yield: 4 servings.

NUTRITION FACTS: 1-1/4 cups equals 577 calories, 29 g fat (16 g saturated fat), 93 mg cholesterol, 1,424 mg sodium, 71 g carbohydrate, 7 g fiber, 14 g protein.

ethnic favorites

greek chicken soup

Here is my go-to soup when I'm under the weather. It always makes me feel better. It's delicious for lunch or dinner, even when you're feeling great.

ANGIE PITTS CHARLESTON, SOUTH CAROLINA

1-1/2 pounds boneless skinless chicken breasts, cut into 3/4-inch cubes
1 tablespoon Greek seasoning
1 teaspoon pepper
1 tablespoon olive oil
4 green onions, thinly sliced
1 garlic clove, minced
1/4 cup white wine or chicken broth
7 cups reduced-sodium chicken broth
1/4 cup chopped sun-dried tomatoes (not packed in oil)
1/4 cup pitted Greek olives, sliced
1 tablespoon capers, drained
1-1/2 teaspoons minced fresh basil or 1/2 teaspoon dried basil
1-1/2 teaspoons minced fresh oregano or 1/2 teaspoon dried oregano
1-1/2 cups uncooked orzo pasta
2 tablespoons lemon juice
1-1/2 teaspoons minced fresh parsley

▢ Season chicken with Greek seasoning and pepper. In a Dutch oven, saute chicken in oil until no longer pink; remove and set aside. Add green onions and garlic to the pan; saute for 1 minute. Add wine, stirring to loosen browned bits from pan.

▢ Stir in the broth, tomatoes, olives, capers, basil, oregano and chicken. Bring to a boil. Reduce heat; cover and simmer for 15 minutes. Return to a boil. Stir in orzo. Cook 8-10 minutes longer or until pasta is tender. Stir in lemon juice and parsley.

Yield: 8 servings (2 quarts).

NUTRITION FACTS: 1 cup equals 285 calories, 5 g fat (1 g saturated fat), 47 mg cholesterol, 1,042 mg sodium, 31 g carbohydrate, 1 g fiber, 25 g protein.

russian borscht

Loaded with beets, carrots, onions and cabbage, this recipe is not only delicious, its brilliant red color is warm and eye-catching on the dinner table.
GINNY BETTIS MONTELLO, WISCONSIN

2	cups chopped fresh beets
2	cups chopped carrots
2	cups chopped onions
4	cups beef or vegetable broth
1	can (16 ounces) diced tomatoes, undrained
2	cups chopped cabbage
1/2	teaspoon salt
1/2	teaspoon dill weed
1/4	teaspoon pepper

Sour cream, optional

▢ In a large saucepan, combine the beets, carrots, onions and broth; bring to a boil. Reduce heat; cover and simmer for 30 minutes.

▢ Add tomatoes and cabbage; cover and simmer for 30 minutes or until cabbage is tender. Stir in salt, dill and pepper. Top each serving with sour cream if desired.

Yield: 8 servings (2 quarts).

NUTRITION FACTS: 1 cup (calculated without sour cream) equals 71 calories, 1 g fat (trace saturated fat), 0 cholesterol, 673 mg sodium, 14 g carbohydrate, 4 g fiber, 3 g protein.

award-winning chili

For an extra-spicy kick, use even more chili powder, but make sure you've got a cool drink close by!
EUGENE JARZAB JR. PHOENIX, ARIZONA

1	boneless beef chuck roast (3 pounds), cut into 1/2-inch cubes
1	pound pork stew meat, cut into 1/2-inch cubes
1/3	cup chili powder, divided
4	tablespoons canola oil, divided
1	large onion, finely chopped
1	celery rib, finely chopped
3	garlic cloves, minced
1	tablespoon chopped canned green chilies
1	carton (32 ounces) beef broth
3/4	cup beer
3/4	cup tomato sauce
2	tablespoons grated dark chocolate
3	teaspoons ground cumin
1	teaspoon dried oregano
1/2	teaspoon salt
1/2	teaspoon ground mustard
1/2	teaspoon cayenne pepper

▢ Sprinkle beef and pork with half of the chili powder. In a Dutch oven, brown meat in batches in 2 tablespoons oil; drain and set aside. In the same pan, saute onion and celery in remaining oil until crisp-tender. Add the garlic, chilies and remaining chili powder; cook 1 minute longer.

▢ Stir in the broth, beer, tomato sauce, chocolate, cumin, oregano, salt, mustard, cayenne and meat. Bring to a boil. Reduce heat; simmer, uncovered, for 1 to 1-1/2 hours or until meat is tender.

Yield: 6 servings.

NUTRITION FACTS: 1 cup equals 637 calories, 38 g fat (11 g saturated fat), 179 mg cholesterol, 1,285 mg sodium, 12 g carbohydrate, 4 g fiber, 57 g protein.

chili con carne

At chili suppers, this one always disappears first! It's nice at home, too, since the longer it sits in the refrigerator, the better this wonderful chili seems to taste.

JANIE TURNER TUTTLE, OKLAHOMA

2	pounds ground beef
2	tablespoons olive oil
2	medium onions, chopped
2	garlic cloves, minced
1	medium green pepper, chopped
1-1/2	teaspoons salt
2	tablespoons chili powder
1/8	teaspoon cayenne pepper
1/4	teaspoon ground cinnamon
1	teaspoon ground cumin
1	teaspoon dried oregano
2	cans (14-1/2 ounces each) diced tomatoes, undrained
3	teaspoons beef bouillon granules
1	cup boiling water
1	can (16 ounces) kidney beans, rinsed and drained

In a Dutch oven, cook beef over medium heat until no longer pink; drain and set aside.

In the same pot, heat oil; saute onions until tender. Add garlic; cook 1 minute longer. Stir in the green pepper, salt, chili powder, cayenne, cinnamon, cumin and oregano. Cook for 2 minutes, stirring until combined.

Add tomatoes and reserved beef. Dissolve bouillon in water and add to soup. Bring to a boil. Reduce heat; cover and simmer for about 1 hour. Add beans; simmer 30 minutes longer.

Yield: 10 servings (about 2-1/2 quarts).

NUTRITION FACTS: 1 cup equals 268 calories, 14 g fat (4 g saturated fat), 56 mg cholesterol, 835 mg sodium, 16 g carbohydrate, 5 g fiber, 20 g protein.

irish stew

This satisfying stew is chock-full of potatoes, turnips, carrots and lamb. Served with Irish soda bread, it makes a hearty St. Patrick's Day meal.
LOIS GELZER STANDISH, MAINE

1-1/2	pounds lamb stew meat
2	teaspoons olive oil
4	cups water
2	cups sliced peeled potatoes
1	medium onion, sliced
1/2	cup sliced carrot
1/2	cup cubed turnip
1	teaspoon salt
1/2	teaspoon each dried marjoram, thyme and rosemary, crushed
1/8	teaspoon pepper
2	tablespoons all-purpose flour
3	tablespoons fat-free milk
1/2	teaspoon browning sauce, optional
3	tablespoons minced fresh parsley

▢ In a Dutch oven, brown lamb in oil over medium-high heat. Add water; bring to a boil. Reduce heat; cover and simmer for 1 hour.

▢ Add the potatoes, onion, carrot, turnip and seasonings. Bring mixture to a boil. Reduce heat; cover and simmer for 30 minutes or until the vegetables are tender.

▢ In a small bowl, combine the flour, milk and browning sauce if desired until smooth; stir into stew. Add parsley. Bring to a boil; cook and stir for 2 minutes or until stew is thickened.

Yield: 6 servings.

NUTRITION FACTS: 1-1/2 cups equals 279 calories, 9 g fat (3 g saturated fat), 92 mg cholesterol, 469 mg sodium, 17 g carbohydrate, 2 g fiber, 31 g protein. **DIABETIC EXCHANGES:** 3 lean meat, 1 starch, 1 vegetable.

matzo ball soup

A variety of winter vegetables gives the broth for this classic Jewish soup an awesome flavor. Use a few green onions instead of the leek if you prefer.
TASTE OF HOME TEST KITCHEN

10	cups water
12	garlic cloves, peeled
3	medium carrots, cut into chunks
3	small turnips, peeled and cut into chunks
2	medium onions, cut into wedges
2	medium parsnips, peeled and cut into chunks
1	medium leek (white portion only), sliced
1/4	cup minced fresh parsley
2	tablespoons snipped fresh dill
1	teaspoon salt
1	teaspoon pepper
3/4	teaspoon ground turmeric
MATZO BALLS:	
3	eggs, separated
3	tablespoons water or chicken broth
3	tablespoons rendered chicken fat
1-1/2	teaspoons salt, divided
3/4	cup matzo meal
8	cups water

▢ For broth, in a stockpot, combine the first 12 ingredients. Bring to a boil. Reduce heat; cover and simmer for 2 hours.

▢ Meanwhile, in a large bowl, beat the egg yolks on high speed for 2 minutes or until thick and lemon-colored. Add the water, chicken fat and 1/2 teaspoon salt. In another bowl, beat egg whites on high until stiff peaks form; fold into yolk mixture. Fold in matzo meal. Cover and refrigerate for at least 1 hour or until thickened.

▢ In another stockpot, bring water to a boil; add remaining salt. Drop eight rounded tablespoonfuls of matzo ball dough into boiling water. Reduce heat; cover and simmer for 20-25 minutes or until a toothpick inserted into a matzo ball comes out clean (do not lift cover while simmering).

▢ Strain broth, discarding vegetables and seasonings. Carefully remove matzo balls from water with a slotted spoon; place one matzo ball in each soup bowl. Add the hot broth.

Yield: 8 servings (2 quarts).

NUTRITION FACTS: 1 cup equals 100 calories, 7 g fat (2 g saturated fat), 83 mg cholesterol, 322 mg sodium, 7 g carbohydrate, trace fiber, 3 g protein. **DIABETIC EXCHANGES:** 1-1/2 starch, 1-1/2 fat.

caribbean potato soup

(pictured at left)

An interesting blend of veggies including okra, kale and black-eyed peas go into this bright and hearty soup. No kale on hand? Use spinach instead.

CRYSTAL BRUNS ILIFF, COLORADO

- 2 medium onions, chopped
- 2 teaspoons canola oil
- 3 garlic cloves, minced
- 2 teaspoons minced fresh gingerroot
- 2 teaspoons ground coriander
- 1 teaspoon ground turmeric
- 1/2 teaspoon dried thyme
- 1/4 teaspoon ground allspice
- 5 cups vegetable broth
- 2 cups cubed peeled sweet potato
- 3 cups chopped fresh kale
- 1 cup frozen sliced okra
- 1 cup coconut milk
- 1 cup canned diced tomatoes, drained
- 1 cup canned black-eyed peas, rinsed and drained
- 2 tablespoons lime juice

▢ In a Dutch oven, saute onions in oil until tender. Add the garlic, ginger and spices; cook 1 minute longer.

▢ Stir in broth and potato. Bring to a boil. Reduce heat; cover and simmer for 5 minutes. Stir in kale and okra. Return to a boil; cover and simmer 10 minutes longer or until potato is tender. Add the milk, tomatoes, peas and lime juice; heat through.

Yield: 6 servings (2-1/4 quarts).

NUTRITION FACTS: 1-1/2 cups equals 213 calories, 10 g fat (7 g saturated fat), 0 cholesterol, 954 mg sodium, 28 g carbohydrate, 6 g fiber, 5 g protein.

new orleans gumbo

I've been making this gumbo for at least 30 years. I'm originally from New Orleans, and I think it's a nice taste of the Vieux Carre (French Quarter). Everyone who tastes my gumbo wants the recipe. My family requests it often.

DOLORES BRIDGES DANVILLE, KENTUCKY

- 2 cups chicken broth
- 1 cup uncooked converted rice
- 2 celery ribs, chopped
- 1 medium onion, chopped
- 2 garlic cloves, minced
- 1 can (28 ounces) diced tomatoes, undrained
- 1 pound boneless skinless chicken breasts, cut into 1/2-inch cubes
- 1/2 pound smoked kielbasa or Polish sausage, cut into 1/2-inch slices
- 1 teaspoon dried thyme
- 1 teaspoon pepper
- 2 bay leaves
- 1/4 teaspoon cayenne pepper
- 3 tablespoons all-purpose flour
- 1/4 cup cold water
- 1 pound uncooked medium shrimp, peeled and deveined
- 1 large green pepper, chopped
- 1/4 cup minced fresh parsley

▢ In a large saucepan, bring broth to a boil. Stir in the rice, celery, onion and garlic. Reduce heat; cover and simmer for 20 minutes.

▢ Meanwhile, in a Dutch oven, combine the tomatoes, chicken, kielbasa, thyme, pepper, bay leaves and cayenne. Bring to a boil. Reduce heat; cover and simmer for 10 minutes.

▢ Combine flour and water until smooth; gradually stir into chicken mixture. Stir in shrimp and green pepper. Cook, uncovered, over medium heat for 4-6 minutes or until shrimp turn pink and gumbo is thickened. Discard bay leaves.

▢ Remove rice from the heat and let stand for 5 minutes; stir in parsley. Serve with gumbo.

Yield: 8 servings.

NUTRITION FACTS: 1 cup gumbo with 1/2 cup rice equals 339 calories, 10 g fat (3 g saturated fat), 124 mg cholesterol, 841 mg sodium, 29 g carbohydrate, 2 g fiber, 29 g protein. **DIABETIC EXCHANGES:** 4 lean meat, 1-1/2 starch, 1 vegetable, 1/2 fat.

tuscan chicken soup

(pictured above)

Change up your traditional chicken soup by adding delicious white kidney beans. Soup is a great way to use up leftover chicken.
ROSEMARY GOETZ HUDSON, NEW YORK

1	small onion, chopped
1	small carrot, sliced
1	tablespoon olive oil
2	cans (14-1/2 ounces each) chicken broth
1	cup water
3/4	teaspoon salt
1/4	teaspoon pepper
1	can (15 ounces) white kidney or cannellini beans, rinsed and drained
2/3	cup uncooked small spiral pasta
3	cups thinly sliced fresh escarole or spinach
2	cups shredded cooked chicken

In a large saucepan, saute onion and carrot in oil until onion is tender. Add the broth, water, salt and pepper; bring to a boil. Stir in beans and pasta; return to a boil.

Reduce heat; cover and simmer for 15 minutes or until pasta and vegetables are tender, stirring occasionally. Add escarole and chicken; heat through.

Yield: 4 servings.

NUTRITION FACTS: 1-1/2 cups equals 329 calories, 10 g fat (2 g saturated fat), 67 mg cholesterol, 1,542 mg sodium, 30 g carbohydrate, 6 g fiber, 28 g protein.

chalupa (mexican stew)

We've lived in Arizona for decades, so we're experts on Southwestern fare. Nothing tastes better than this stew!
ANNE FATOUT PHOENIX, ARIZONA

1	bone-in pork loin roast (3 pounds), trimmed
1	package (16 ounces) dried pinto beans, soaked overnight
4	to 5 cloves garlic, minced
2	tablespoons chili powder
1	to 1-1/2 teaspoons ground cumin
1	teaspoon dried oregano
2	cans (4 ounces each) chopped green chilies
Pepper to taste	
5	medium carrots, sliced
4	celery ribs, sliced
1	can (14-1/2 ounces) diced tomatoes, undrained
3	small zucchini, sliced
Flour tortillas, warmed	

In a stockpot, combine the first eight ingredients. Cover with water. Bring to a boil. Reduce heat to low; cover and cook for 3 to 4 hours or until meat and beans are tender. Cool slightly; remove meat from bones. Cut meat into bite-size pieces; return to pan. Add the carrots, celery and tomatoes; cover and cook until vegetables are tender. During the last 10 minutes of cooking, add zucchini. Serve with warmed flour tortillas.

Yield: 16 servings (4 quarts).

NUTRITION FACTS: 1 cup equals 253 calories, 7 g fat (0 saturated fat), 41 mg cholesterol, 160 mg sodium, 26 g carbohydrate, 0 fiber, 22 g protein. **DIABETIC EXCHANGES:** 1-1/2 starch, 1-1/2 meat, 1 vegetable.

mulligatawny

You will love the wonderful aroma that fills your kitchen as this traditional curry-flavored soup simmers on the stovetop.
ESTHER NAFZIGER LA JUNTA, COLORADO

1	medium tart apple, peeled and diced
1/4	cup each chopped carrot, celery and onion
1/4	cup butter
1/3	cup all-purpose flour
1	teaspoon curry powder
1/2	teaspoon sugar
1/2	teaspoon salt
1/8	teaspoon pepper
1/8	teaspoon ground mace
6	cups chicken or turkey broth
1	cup cubed cooked chicken or turkey
1	medium tomato, peeled, seeded and chopped
1/2	cup chopped green pepper
2	whole cloves
1	tablespoon minced fresh parsley
1	cup cooked rice

▢ In a Dutch oven, saute the apple, carrot, celery and onion in butter for 5 minutes or until tender. Stir in the flour, curry, sugar, salt, pepper and mace until blended. Gradually add broth.

▢ Bring to a boil. Cook and stir for 2 minutes or until thickened. Add the chicken, tomato, green pepper, cloves and parsley; return to a boil. Reduce heat; cover and simmer for 20-30 minutes. Add rice; heat through. Discard cloves.

Yield: 8 servings (about 2 quarts).

NUTRITION FACTS: 1 cup equals 160 calories, 8 g fat (4 g saturated fat), 31 mg cholesterol, 925 mg sodium, 15 g carbohydrate, 1 g fiber, 8 g protein.

asian chicken noodle soup

One night I didn't have any noodles for my chicken soup, so I gave it an Asian twist with wonton wrappers. Don't skip the celery leaves; they bring great flavor to this soup.
NOELLE MYERS GRAND FORKS, NORTH DAKOTA

1-1/2	pounds boneless skinless chicken breasts, cut into 1-inch cubes
1	tablespoon sesame oil
3	medium carrots, sliced
2	celery ribs, chopped
1	medium onion, chopped
6	cups chicken broth
1/3	cup teriyaki sauce
1/4	cup chili garlic sauce
1	package (12 ounces) wonton wrappers, cut into 1/4-inch strips
2	cups sliced fresh shiitake mushrooms
1/3	cup chopped celery leaves
1/4	cup minced fresh basil
2	tablespoons minced fresh cilantro
2	green onions, sliced

▢ In a Dutch oven, cook chicken in oil over medium heat until no longer pink. Remove and keep warm. In the same pan, saute the carrots, celery and onion until tender. Stir in the broth, teriyaki sauce, garlic sauce and chicken. Bring to a boil. Reduce heat; simmer, uncovered, for 20 minutes.

▢ Add the wonton strips, mushrooms, celery leaves, basil and cilantro. Cook and stir for 4-5 minutes or until wonton strips and mushrooms are tender. Sprinkle with green onions.

Yield: 10 servings (2-1/2 quarts).

NUTRITION FACTS: 1 cup equals 227 calories, 4 g fat (1 g saturated fat), 44 mg cholesterol, 1,344 mg sodium, 27 g carbohydrate, 2 g fiber, 19 g protein.

cassoulet for the gang

Wine lends a warm background flavor to this lightened-up take on traditional French stew. Low-fat mashed beans thicken the broth and boost nutrition.
LYNN STEIN JOSEPH, OREGON

1	pork tenderloin (1 pound), cut into 1/2-inch pieces
1	pound smoked turkey kielbasa, cut into 1/2-inch pieces
1	tablespoon olive oil
3	medium carrots, chopped
1	large onion, cut into wedges
4	garlic cloves, minced
2	cans (14-1/2 ounces each) no-salt-added stewed tomatoes, cut up
1	can (14-1/2 ounces) reduced-sodium chicken broth
3	teaspoons herbes de Provence
1-1/2	teaspoons garlic powder
1-1/2	teaspoons dried basil
1/2	teaspoon dried oregano
1/4	teaspoon pepper
4	cans (15-1/2 ounces each) great northern beans, rinsed and drained, divided
3/4	cup white wine or additional chicken broth, divided

▢ In a Dutch oven coated with cooking spray, saute pork and kielbasa in oil until lightly browned; drain. Add carrots and onion; saute 4 minutes longer. Add garlic; cook for 1 minute longer. Stir in the tomatoes, broth and seasonings. Bring to a boil. Reduce heat; cover and simmer for 10 minutes.

▢ Place one can of beans in a food processor; add 1/4 cup wine or broth. Cover and process until pureed. Stir into meat mixture. Stir in the remaining beans and wine or broth. Bring to a boil. Reduce the heat; simmer, uncovered, for 8-10 minutes or until meat and vegetables are tender.

Yield: 10 servings (about 4 quarts).

NUTRITION FACTS: 1-1/2 cups equals 316 calories, 5 g fat (1 g saturated fat), 41 mg cholesterol, 959 mg sodium, 40 g carbohydrate, 11 g fiber, 25 g protein.

EDITOR'S NOTE: Look for herbes de Provence in the spice aisle.

ABOUT CASSOULET

Pronounced KASS-soo-lay. A French stew that contains white beans and a variety of meats. This version is a lightened-up take on the classic because it uses leaner meats and isn't thickened with butter and flour. With a variety of crowd-pleasing textures, cassoulet is perfect for a casually elegant fall get-together.

chicken egg drop soup

Who wants takeout when homemade is this easy and delicious? You'll love the addition of tender chicken.
TASTE OF HOME TEST KITCHEN

1-1/2	cups reduced-sodium chicken broth
1	slice peeled fresh gingerroot (1/4 inch thick)
1	small garlic clove, peeled
1-1/2	teaspoons cornstarch
1	tablespoon water
1/4	cup cubed cooked chicken
1	egg, lightly beaten
1	tablespoon sliced green onion

◻ In a small saucepan, combine the broth, ginger and garlic; bring to a boil. Reduce heat; simmer, uncovered, for 15 minutes. Remove and discard ginger and garlic.

◻ Combine cornstarch and water until smooth; gradually stir into broth. Bring to a boil; cook and stir for 2 minutes or until thickened. Add chicken; heat through. Reduce heat. Drizzle beaten egg into hot broth, stirring constantly. Remove from heat; stir in onion.

Yield: 1 serving.

NUTRITION FACTS: 1 cup equals 178 calories, 8 g fat (2 g saturated fat), 243 mg cholesterol, 956 mg sodium, 6 g carbohydrate, trace fiber, 21 g protein.

authentic cajun gumbo

I learned to cook in Louisiana and I love to cook Cajun food. This chicken oyster gumbo is one of my favorites.
PAUL MORRIS KELSO, WASHINGTON

6	quarts water
1	chicken (5 pounds), cut up
2	large onions, quartered
4	celery ribs, cut into 3-inch pieces
6	garlic cloves, coarsely chopped
2	tablespoons salt
1	teaspoon garlic powder
1/2	teaspoon poultry seasoning
1/2	teaspoon cayenne pepper
1/2	teaspoon pepper
1/4	teaspoon white pepper
1	cup canola oil
1-1/2	cups all-purpose flour
1	large onion, finely chopped
1	pound fully cooked andouille sausage links, chopped
2	pounds sliced okra
2	pints shucked oysters
3	tablespoons gumbo file powder

Hot cooked rice

◻ Place the first 11 ingredients in a stockpot; bring to a boil. Reduce heat; cover and simmer for 1-1/2 hours. Remove chicken and allow to cool. Strain broth, discarding vegetables; skim fat. Remove meat from bones; cut chicken into bite-size pieces and set aside. Discard bones.

◻ In the same pan, cook and stir oil and flour over medium heat until caramel-colored, about 14 minutes (do not burn). Add finely chopped onion; cook and stir 2 minutes longer. Gradually stir in broth. Bring to a boil.

◻ Carefully stir in sausage and reserved chicken. Reduce heat; simmer, uncovered, for 10 minutes. Stir in okra and oysters. Simmer, uncovered, 10-15 minutes longer or just until okra is tender. Stir in file powder. Serve with rice.

Yield: 20 servings (1-1/4 cups each).

NUTRITION FACTS: 1-1/4 cups (calculated without rice) equals 319 calories, 19 g fat (3 g saturated fat), 73 mg cholesterol, 990 mg sodium, 20 g carbohydrate, 3 g fiber, 19 g protein.

EDITOR'S NOTE: Gumbo file powder, used to thicken and flavor Creole recipes, is available in spice shops. If you don't want to use gumbo file powder, combine 2 tablespoons each cornstarch and cold water until smooth. Gradually stir into gumbo. Bring to a boil; cook and stir for 2 minutes or until slightly thickened.

jamaican ham and bean soup

(pictured at left)

An island vacation in a bowl might be the best way to describe this hearty soup. A splash of lime juice and a hint of jerk seasoning add tropical taste.
MARY LOU TIMPSON COLORADO CITY, ARIZONA

- 1   small onion, chopped
- 1   tablespoon canola oil
- 3   cups cubed fully cooked ham
- 2   cans (16 ounces each) vegetarian refried beans
- 1   can (14-1/2 ounces) chicken broth
- 1   can (11 ounces) Mexicorn, drained
- 1   can (7 ounces) white or shoepeg corn, drained
- 1   can (4 ounces) chopped green chilies
- 1/2 cup salsa
- 1   teaspoon Caribbean jerk seasoning
- 1   can (2-1/4 ounces) sliced ripe olives, drained
- 1/3 cup lime juice

Sour cream and lime

▨ In a Dutch oven, saute onion in oil for 3-4 minutes or until tender. Stir in the ham, refried beans, broth, corn, chilies, salsa and jerk seasoning; bring to a boil. Reduce heat; simmer, uncovered, for 5 minutes stirring occasionally.

▨ Stir in the olives and lime juice; heat through. Garnish servings with sour cream and lime slices.

Yield: 7 servings (2-3/4 quarts).

NUTRITION FACTS: 1-1/2 cups (calculated without garnishes) equals 312 calories, 9 g fat (2 g saturated fat), 33 mg cholesterol, 2,211 mg sodium, 38 g carbohydrate, 9 g fiber, 20 g protein.

slow-cooked hungarian stew

As the owner of a fitness center, I rely on a slow cooker many days to create a wonderful meal for my family. This hearty stew feels reminiscent of the old days.
SUSAN KAIN WOODBINE, MARYLAND

- 4   medium potatoes, cut into 1-inch cubes
- 2   medium onions, chopped
- 1   pound beef stew meat, cut into 1-inch cubes
- 2   tablespoons canola oil
- 1-1/2 cups water
- 3   teaspoons paprika
- 1   teaspoon salt
- 1   teaspoon caraway seeds
- 1   teaspoon tomato paste
- 1   garlic clove, minced
- 2   medium green peppers, cut into 1-inch pieces
- 2   medium tomatoes, peeled, seeded and chopped

- 3   tablespoons all-purpose flour
- 3   tablespoons cold water
- 1/2 cup sour cream

▨ Place potatoes and onions in a 3-qt. slow cooker. In a large skillet, brown meat in oil on all sides. Place over potato mixture.

▨ Pour off excess fat from skillet. Add water to the drippings, stirring to loosen browned bits from pan; heat through. Stir in the paprika, salt, caraway seeds, tomato paste and garlic. Pour into the slow cooker. Cover and cook on low for 6-8 hours.

▨ Add green peppers and tomatoes; cover and cook 1 hour longer or until meat and vegetables are tender. With a slotted spoon, transfer meat and vegetables to a large serving bowl; cover and keep warm.

▨ Pour cooking juices into a small saucepan. Combine flour and cold water until smooth; gradually whisk into the pan. Bring to a boil; cook and stir for 2 minutes or until thickened. Remove from the heat; whisk in sour cream. Stir into meat mixture.

Yield: 6 servings (2-1/4 quarts).

NUTRITION FACTS: 1-1/2 cups equals 358 calories, 14 g fat (5 g saturated fat), 60 mg cholesterol, 446 mg sodium, 39 g carbohydrate, 5 g fiber, 20 g protein.

fiesta chorizo-chicken soup

Just serve some crusty rolls with this soup and you'll have a hearty, comforting meal that will chase away winter's chill.
KATHY RODENBECK FORT WAYNE, INDIANA

1	pound uncooked chorizo, casings removed or bulk spicy pork sausage
2	cups sliced fresh carrots
1	medium onion, chopped
4	garlic cloves, minced
1	pound boneless skinless chicken breasts, cubed
1	teaspoon salt
1/4	teaspoon pepper
2	tablespoons olive oil
3	medium sweet potatoes, peeled and cubed
1	package (10 ounces) frozen corn
1	medium sweet red pepper, chopped
1	carton (32 ounces) reduced-sodium chicken broth
1	can (16 ounces) butter beans, rinsed and drained
1	can (15 ounces) black beans, rinsed and drained
1	can (14-1/2 ounces) fire-roasted diced tomatoes, undrained
1	can (5-1/2 ounces) reduced-sodium V8 juice
1	teaspoon hot pepper sauce
2	cups fresh spinach, chopped

▨ Crumble chorizo into a Dutch oven. Add the carrots, onion and garlic. Cook over medium heat until chorizo is fully cooked. Drain; remove and set aside.

▨ In the same pan, saute the chicken, salt and pepper in oil until no longer pink. Add sweet potatoes, corn and red pepper; cook 5 minutes longer.

▨ Stir in the chorizo mixture, broth, beans, tomatoes, V8 juice and pepper sauce. Bring to a boil. Reduce heat; simmer, uncovered, for 15 minutes or until vegetables are tender. Stir in spinach; cook until wilted.

Yield: 12 servings (4-1/2 quarts).

NUTRITION FACTS: 1-1/2 cups equals 336 calories, 15 g fat (5 g saturated fat), 54 mg cholesterol, 1,190 mg sodium, 29 g carbohydrate, 6 g fiber, 22 g protein.

cajun shrimp soup

My mom used to cut the corn off the cob to make this soup, but I use canned cream-style corn. This is a very good dish to come home to on a frosty day.
OLLIE JAMESON JEFFERSON, LOUISIANA

2	tablespoons canola oil
2	tablespoons all-purpose flour
3	celery ribs, thinly sliced
1	medium onion, chopped
1	small green pepper, chopped
2	green onions, thinly sliced
2	garlic cloves, minced
4	cans (14-3/4 ounces each) cream-style corn
1	can (10 ounces) diced tomatoes and green chilies, undrained
1	bay leaf
1/8	to 1/4 teaspoon white pepper
1/8	to 1/4 teaspoon cayenne pepper

Dash hot pepper sauce

3	cups cooked small shrimp
1/3	cup minced fresh parsley

▨ Heat oil in a heavy saucepan over medium heat. Carefully add flour; cook and stir until golden brown, about 6-8 minutes. Reduce heat to low. Add the celery, onion, green pepper and green onions; cook and stir for 5 minutes. Add garlic; cook 1 minute longer. Add the corn, tomatoes, bay leaf, white pepper, cayenne and pepper sauce; bring to a boil. Reduce heat; cover and simmer for 30-40 minutes.

▨ Stir in shrimp and parsley; heat through. Discard bay leaf.

Yield: 10 servings (2-1/2 quarts).

NUTRITION FACTS: 1 cup equals 131 calories, 3 g fat (trace saturated fat), 138 mg cholesterol, 1,026 mg sodium, 13 g carbohydrate, 2 g fiber, 14 g protein.

land of enchantment posole

We usually make this spicy soup over the holidays when we have lots of family over. We never have leftovers.
SUZANNE CALDWELL ARTESIA, NEW MEXICO

1-1/2	pounds pork stew meat, cut into 3/4-inch cubes
1	large onion, chopped
2	tablespoons canola oil
2	garlic cloves, minced
3	cups beef broth
2	cans (15-1/2 ounces each) hominy, rinsed and drained
2	cans (4 ounces each) chopped green chilies
1	to 2 jalapeno peppers, seeded and chopped, optional
1/2	teaspoon salt
1/2	teaspoon ground cumin
1/2	teaspoon dried oregano
1/4	teaspoon pepper
1/4	teaspoon cayenne pepper
1/2	cup minced fresh cilantro

Tortilla strips, optional

▨ In a Dutch oven, cook pork and onion in oil over medium heat until meat is no longer pink. Add garlic; cook 1 minute longer. Drain. Stir in the broth, hominy, chilies, jalapeno if desired, salt, cumin, oregano, pepper and cayenne.

▨ Bring to a boil. Reduce heat; cover and simmer for 45-60 minutes or until meat is tender. Stir in cilantro. Serve with tortilla strips if desired.

Yield: 5 servings.

NUTRITION FACTS: 1-1/3 cups (calculated without tortillas) equals 430 calories, 29 g fat (9 g saturated fat), 94 mg cholesterol, 1,266 mg sodium, 14 g carbohydrate, 3 g fiber, 27 g protein.

EDITOR'S NOTE: Wear disposable gloves when cutting hot peppers; the oils can burn skin. Avoid touching your face.

german sauerkraut soup

My mother used to make this soup often while I was growing up on a farm in Warwick, Alberta. I added my own touches.
THELMA LESCHENKO EDMONTON, ALBERTA

- 2 pounds pork spareribs
- 3 quarts water
- 2 cups diced peeled potatoes
- 2 carrots, chopped
- 1 teaspoon salt
- 1/2 teaspoon pepper
- 4 cups sauerkraut, rinsed and drained
- 1 pound smoked sausage, cut into 1-inch slices
- 5 bacon strips, diced
- 1 large onion, chopped

▨ In a Dutch oven, cook ribs in water until tender, about 1-1/2 hours. Skim off foam. Remove ribs from broth; strain broth and skim fat.

▨ Return broth to the heat. Add the potatoes, carrots, salt and pepper; simmer until vegetables are tender. Remove meat from bones and add to broth with the sauerkraut and sausage.

▨ Meanwhile, cook bacon until crisp; remove to paper towels to drain. Discard all but 1 tablespoon of the drippings. Cook onion in drippings until tender. Add to soup; cook 20-30 minutes longer. Ladle into bowls. Garnish with bacon.

Yield: 12 servings (3 quarts).

NUTRITION FACTS: 1 cup equals 325 calories, 23 g fat (9 g saturated fat), 72 mg cholesterol, 1,041 mg sodium, 10 g carbohydrate, 2 g fiber, 18 g protein.

thai shrimp soup

This tasty crowd-pleaser cooks up fast, and I like the fact that the ingredients are all available in my local grocery store.
JESSIE GREARSON-SAPAT FALMOUTH, MAINE

- 1 medium onion, chopped
- 1 tablespoon olive oil
- 3 cups reduced-sodium chicken broth
- 1 cup water
- 1 tablespoon brown sugar
- 1 tablespoon minced fresh gingerroot
- 1 tablespoon fish or soy sauce
- 1 tablespoon red curry paste
- 1 lemon grass stalk
- 1 pound uncooked large shrimp, peeled and deveined
- 1-1/2 cups frozen shelled edamame
- 1 can (13.66 ounces) light coconut milk
- 1 can (8-3/4 ounces) whole baby corn, drained and cut in half
- 1/2 cup bamboo shoots
- 1/4 cup fresh basil leaves, torn
- 1/4 cup minced fresh cilantro
- 2 tablespoons lime juice
- 1-1/2 teaspoons grated lime peel
- 1 teaspoon curry powder

▨ In a Dutch oven, saute onion in oil until tender. Add the broth, water, brown sugar, ginger, fish sauce, curry paste and lemon grass. Bring to a boil. Reduce heat; carefully stir in shrimp and edamame. Cook, uncovered, for 5-6 minutes or until shrimp turn pink.

▨ Add the coconut milk, corn, bamboo shoots, basil, cilantro, lime juice, lime peel and curry powder; heat through. Discard lemon grass.

Yield: 8 servings (2 quarts).

NUTRITION FACTS: 1 cup equals 163 calories, 7 g fat (3 g saturated fat), 69 mg cholesterol, 505 mg sodium, 9 g carbohydrate, 2 g fiber, 14 g protein. **DIABETIC EXCHANGES:** 2 lean meat, 1 vegetable, 1 fat.

gnocchi chicken minestrone

My Italian heritage—and my mom, who was an excellent soup maker—inspired my take on minestrone. Using frozen gnocchi saves time and adds extra heartiness to this chunky soup.
BARBARA ESTABROOK RHINELANDER, WISCONSIN

1-1/4	pounds chicken tenderloins, cut into 1/2-inch pieces
3/4	teaspoon dried oregano
1/4	teaspoon salt
1/4	teaspoon pepper
2	tablespoons olive oil, divided
1	each small green, sweet red and yellow peppers, finely chopped
1	medium zucchini, finely chopped
1	cup chopped fresh baby portobello mushrooms
1/3	cup chopped red onion
1/3	cup chopped prosciutto or deli ham
4	garlic cloves, minced
2	cans (14-1/2 ounces each) chicken broth
1	can (14-1/2 ounces) Italian diced tomatoes, undrained
3/4	cup canned white kidney or cannellini beans, rinsed and drained
1/2	cup frozen peas
3	tablespoons tomato paste
1	package (16 ounces) potato gnocchi
1/2	cup shredded Asiago cheese
8	fresh basil leaves, thinly sliced

▢ Sprinkle chicken with oregano, salt and pepper. In a Dutch oven, saute chicken in 1 tablespoon oil until no longer pink. Remove from the pan and set aside.

▢ In the same pan, cook the peppers, zucchini, mushrooms and onion in remaining oil until tender. Add prosciutto and garlic; cook 1 minute longer. Add the broth, tomatoes, beans, peas, tomato paste and chicken. Bring to a boil. Reduce heat; simmer, uncovered, for 20 minutes, stirring occasionally.

▢ Meanwhile, cook gnocchi according to package directions. Drain; stir into soup. Garnish each serving with cheese and basil.

Yield: 8 servings (2-3/4 quarts).

NUTRITION FACTS: 1-1/3 cups soup with 1 tablespoon cheese equals 324 calories, 8 g fat (2 g saturated fat), 59 mg cholesterol, 1,163 mg sodium, 38 g carbohydrate, 4 g fiber, 27 g protein.

EDITOR'S NOTE: Look for potato gnocchi in the pasta or frozen foods section.

guinness-lamb stew

(pictured at left)

My grandmother used to make this stew as a special Sunday meal and a memorable treat from Ireland.
VICKIE DESOURDY WASHINGTON, NORTH CAROLINA

2	pounds lamb stew meat, cut into 1-inch cubes
1	tablespoon butter
1	tablespoon olive oil
1	pound carrots, sliced
2	medium onions, thinly sliced
2	garlic cloves, minced
1-1/2	cups reduced-sodium chicken broth
1	bottle (12 ounces) Guinness stout or additional reduced-sodium chicken broth
6	medium red potatoes, peeled and cut into 1-inch cubes
4	bay leaves
2	fresh thyme sprigs
2	fresh rosemary sprigs
2	teaspoons salt
1-1/2	teaspoons pepper
1/4	cup heavy whipping cream

▢ In an ovenproof Dutch oven, brown lamb in butter and oil in batches. Remove and keep warm. In the same pan, saute carrots and onions in drippings until crisp-tender. Add garlic; cook 1 minute longer. Gradually add broth and beer. Stir in the lamb, potatoes, bay leaves, thyme, rosemary, salt and pepper.

▢ Cover and bake at 325° for 1-1/2 to 2 hours or until meat and vegetables are tender, stirring every 30 minutes. Discard bay leaves, thyme and rosemary. Stir in cream; heat through.

Yield: 8 servings (2-1/2 quarts).

NUTRITION FACTS: 1-1/4 cups equals 311 calories, 12 g fat (5 g saturated fat), 88 mg cholesterol, 829 mg sodium, 23 g carbohydrate, 4 g fiber, 26 g protein. **DIABETIC EXCHANGES:** 3 lean meat, 2 vegetable, 1 starch, 1 fat.

hot and sour soup

We tried several recipes for this soup and couldn't find one that resembled our favorite at the Chinese restaurant. So, I made my own, and I must say, it is on par with what you'll find when dining out. Regular or hot chili sauce can be used, according to taste.
VERA LEITOW MANCELONA, MICHIGAN

3/4	pound pork tenderloin, cut into 1-1/2-inch x 1/4-inch strips
1	tablespoon olive oil
1/2	pound sliced fresh mushrooms
6	cups chicken broth
1/4	cup soy sauce
2	tablespoons chili garlic sauce
3/4	teaspoon pepper
1	package (14 ounces) extra-firm tofu, drained and cut into 1/4-inch cubes
1	can (8 ounces) bamboo shoots, drained
1	can (8 ounces) sliced water chestnuts, drained
1/2	cup white vinegar
1/3	cup cornstarch
1/3	cup cold water
2	teaspoons sesame oil

Finely chopped green onions

▢ In a Dutch oven, brown pork in oil until no longer pink; remove meat and keep warm. Add mushrooms; saute until tender. Set aside and keep warm.

▢ Add the broth, soy sauce, chili garlic sauce and pepper to the pan. Bring to a boil. Reduce heat; cover and simmer for 10 minutes. Return the meat and mushrooms to the pan. Stir in the tofu, bamboo shoots, water chestnuts and vinegar. Simmer, uncovered, for 10 minutes.

▢ In a small bowl, combine cornstarch and water until smooth; gradually stir into soup. Bring to a boil; cook and stir for 2 minutes or until thickened. Remove from the heat; stir in sesame oil. Garnish servings with onions.

Yield: 6 servings (about 2 quarts).

NUTRITION FACTS: 1-1/2 cups equals 240 calories, 10 g fat (2 g saturated fat), 37 mg cholesterol, 1,779 mg sodium, 18 g carbohydrate, 2 g fiber, 21 g protein.

moroccan chickpea stew

When I served this spicy stew to guests, including three vegetarians, they were thrilled with the abundance of squash, potatoes, tomatoes and zucchini.

CINDY BEBERMAN ORLAND PARK, ILLINOIS

1	large onion, finely chopped
2	tablespoons olive oil
1	tablespoon butter
2	garlic cloves, minced
2	teaspoons ground cumin
1	cinnamon stick (3 inches)
1/2	teaspoon chili powder
4	cups vegetable broth
2	cups cubed peeled butternut squash
1	can (15 ounces) chickpeas or garbanzo beans, rinsed and drained
1	can (14-1/2 ounces) diced tomatoes, undrained
1	medium red potato, cut into 1-inch cubes
1	medium sweet potato, peeled and cut into 1-inch cubes
1	medium lemon, thinly sliced
1/4	teaspoon salt
2	small zucchini, cubed
3	tablespoons minced fresh cilantro

▨ In a Dutch oven, saute onion in oil and butter until tender. Add the garlic, cumin, cinnamon stick and chili powder; saute 1 minute longer.

▨ Stir in the broth, squash, chickpeas, tomatoes, potatoes, lemon and salt. Bring to a boil. Reduce heat; cover and simmer for 15-20 minutes or until potatoes and squash are almost tender.

▨ Add zucchini; return to a boil. Reduce heat; cover and simmer for 5-8 minutes or until vegetables are tender. Discard cinnamon stick and lemon slices. Stir in cilantro.

Yield: 9 servings (about 2 quarts).

NUTRITION FACTS: 1 cup equals 152 calories, 5 g fat (1 g saturated fat), 3 mg cholesterol, 621 mg sodium, 24 g carbohydrate, 5 g fiber, 4 g protein. **DIABETIC EXCHANGES:** 1 starch, 1 vegetable, 1 fat.

gazpacho for 2

Healthy vegetables are the basis of this tasty chilled soup. We recommend using spicy V8 juice for a spicier version.
TASTE OF HOME TEST KITCHEN

2	medium tomatoes, seeded and chopped
1/2	small green pepper, chopped
1/3	cup chopped peeled cucumber
1/3	cup chopped red onion
1-1/3	cups reduced-sodium tomato juice
1/4	teaspoon dried oregano
1/4	teaspoon dried basil
1/8	teaspoon salt
1	small garlic clove, minced

Dash pepper
Dash hot pepper sauce

1	tablespoon minced chives

Chopped sweet yellow pepper, optional

■ In a large bowl, combine the tomatoes, green pepper, cucumber and onion. In another bowl, combine the tomato juice, oregano, basil, salt, garlic, pepper and pepper sauce; pour over vegetables.

■ Cover and refrigerate for at least 4 hours or overnight. Just before serving, sprinkle with chives and yellow pepper if desired.

Yield: 2 servings.

NUTRITION FACTS: 1-1/2 cups equals 81 calories, trace fat (trace saturated fat), 0 cholesterol, 252 mg sodium, 17 g carbohydrate, 4 g fiber, 3 g protein. **DIABETIC EXCHANGE:** 3 vegetable.

italian wedding soup

After one taste, you'll find that this soup is absolutely delicious. Lean ground beef and reduced-sodium broth help keep it light. For variety, substitute garbanzo beans for the kidney beans.
PAULA SULLIVAN BARKER, NEW YORK

1	egg, lightly beaten
1	tablespoon dry bread crumbs
1	tablespoon dried parsley flakes
1	tablespoon plus 1/4 cup grated Parmesan cheese, divided
1/2	teaspoon onion powder
1/2	teaspoon salt, divided
1/8	teaspoon plus 1/4 teaspoon pepper, divided
1/2	pound lean ground beef (90% lean)
1/4	cup uncooked orzo pasta or acini di pepe pasta
1	medium onion, finely chopped
3	celery ribs, chopped
1	tablespoon olive oil
2	garlic cloves, minced
4	cans (14-1/2 ounces each) reduced-sodium chicken broth
1	can (16 ounces) kidney beans, rinsed and drained
4	cups chopped fresh spinach

■ In a large bowl, combine the egg, bread crumbs, parsley, 1 tablespoon Parmesan cheese, onion powder, 1/4 teaspoon salt and 1/8 teaspoon pepper. Crumble beef over mixture and mix well. Shape mixture into 3/4-in. meatballs.

■ Place in a 15-in. x 10-in. x 1-in. baking pan coated with cooking spray. Bake at 350° for 8-10 minutes or until juices run clear; drain.

■ Cook pasta according to package directions; drain. In a large saucepan, saute onion and celery in oil until tender. Add garlic; cook 1 minute longer. Stir in the broth, beans and spinach. Stir in pasta, meatballs and remaining salt and pepper.

■ Cook until spinach is tender and meatballs are heated through. Garnish with remaining Parmesan cheese.

Yield: 7 servings.

NUTRITION FACTS: 1-1/3 cups soup with about 1-1/2 teaspoons cheese equals 205 calories, 6 g fat (2 g saturated fat), 49 mg cholesterol, 1,024 mg sodium, 20 g carbohydrate, 4 g fiber, 17 g protein. **DIABETIC EXCHANGES:** 2 lean meat, 1 starch, 1 vegetable.

cioppino

If you're looking for a great seafood recipe to create in your slow cooker, this classic fish stew is just the ticket. It's full to the brim with clams, crab, fish and shrimp, and is fancy enough to be an elegant meal.

LISA MORIARTY WILTON, NEW HAMPSHIRE

1	can (28 ounces) diced tomatoes, undrained
2	medium onions, chopped
3	celery ribs, chopped
1	bottle (8 ounces) clam juice
1	can (6 ounces) tomato paste
1/2	cup white wine or vegetable broth
5	garlic cloves, minced
1	tablespoon red wine vinegar
1	tablespoon olive oil
1	to 2 teaspoons Italian seasoning
1/2	teaspoon sugar
1	bay leaf
1	pound haddock fillets, cut into 1-inch pieces
1	pound uncooked small shrimp, peeled and deveined
1	can (6 ounces) lump crabmeat, drained
1	can (6 ounces) chopped clams
2	tablespoons minced fresh parsley or 2 teaspoons dried parsley flakes

◻ In a 4- or 5-qt. slow cooker, combine the first twelve ingredients. Cover and cook on low for 4-5 hours. Stir in the haddock, shrimp, crabmeat and clams. Cover and cook 30 minutes longer or until fish flakes easily with a fork and shrimp turn pink. Stir in parsley. Discard bay leaf.

Yield: 8 servings (2-1/2 quarts).

NUTRITION FACTS: 1-1/4 cups equals 205 calories, 3 g fat (1 g saturated fat), 125 mg cholesterol, 483 mg sodium, 15 g carbohydrate, 3 g fiber, 29 g protein. **DIABETIC EXCHANGES:** 3 lean meat, 2 vegetable.

SO-EASY CIOPPINO

Pronounced chuh-PEE-noh. This flavorful seafood stew originated with Italian immigrants in San Francisco, where fresh fish is abundant. This version uses canned tomatoes, clams and crab and cooks in a slow cooker for delicious convenience. Cioppino is sometimes served with angel hair pasta.

bean & lentil

refried bean soup

(pictured above)

You'll love the way my recipe combines the ease of soup with the heartiness of chili. It's a perfect filler-upper on cold afternoons and a great last-minute lunch. If you like it spicier, use medium or hot green chilies instead of mild.
DARLENE BRENDEN SALEM, OREGON

1	can (16 ounces) spicy fat-free refried beans
1	can (15-1/4 ounces) whole kernel corn, drained
1	can (15 ounces) black beans, rinsed and drained
1	can (14-1/2 ounces) chicken broth
1	can (14-1/2 ounces) stewed tomatoes, cut up
1/2	cup water
1	can (4 ounces) chopped green chilies
1/4	cup salsa

Tortilla chips

▨ In a large saucepan, combine the first eight ingredients. Bring to a boil. Reduce heat; simmer, uncovered, for 8-10 minutes to allow flavors to blend. Serve with tortilla chips.

Yield: 8 servings (2 quarts).

NUTRITION FACTS: 1 cup (calculated without chips) equals 117 calories, 1 g fat (trace saturated fat), 1 mg cholesterol, 720 mg sodium, 21 g carbohydrate, 4 g fiber, 5 g protein.

mixed legume soup

My brother began growing legumes a few years back, so I've been trying many different recipes. Everyone enjoys the comforting old-fashioned flavor of this soup.
MARLENE PENNO EDEN, MANITOBA

1/2	pound sliced bacon, diced
1	cup dried lentils, rinsed
3/4	cup dried yellow split peas
3/4	cup dried green split peas
3	quarts beef broth
1	large onion, chopped
1	cup chopped celery
1	cup chopped carrot
1/4	teaspoon pepper

▨ In a Dutch oven, cook bacon until crisp; drain. Add the remaining ingredients and bring to a boil. Reduce heat; cover and simmer for 1 to 1-1/2 hours or until the lentils and peas are tender.

Yield: 14 servings (about 3-1/2 quarts).

NUTRITION FACTS: 1 cup equals 177 calories, 4 g fat (1 g saturated fat), 5 mg cholesterol, 802 mg sodium, 24 g carbohydrate, 7 g fiber, 13 g protein.

lentil soup for the soul

You'll never miss the meat when you serve this wonderful soup. It's so rich and satisfying!
ATHENA RUSSELL FLORENCE, SOUTH CAROLINA

1/3	cup chopped peeled parsnip
1/3	cup diced peeled potato
1/4	cup chopped green onions
1/4	cup chopped leek (white portion only)
1/4	cup chopped carrot
1/4	cup chopped celery
2	teaspoons olive oil
1	can (14-1/2 ounces) vegetable broth
1	cup no-salt-added diced tomatoes
1/3	cup dried lentils, rinsed
1/4	cup dry red wine or additional vegetable broth
1	teaspoon Worcestershire sauce
1	bay leaf
1/3	cup minced fresh cilantro

▨ In a large saucepan, saute the parsnip, potato, onions, leek, carrot and celery in oil for 3 minutes. Add the broth, tomatoes, lentils, wine, Worcestershire sauce and bay leaf. Bring to a boil. Reduce heat; cover and simmer for 25-30 minutes or until lentils are tender.

▨ Just before serving, discard bay leaf; stir in cilantro.

Yield: 3 servings.

NUTRITION FACTS: 1-1/3 cups equals 183 calories, 4 g fat (trace saturated fat), 0 cholesterol, 631 mg sodium, 28 g carbohydrate, 9 g fiber, 9 g protein. **DIABETIC EXCHANGES:** 1-1/2 starch, 1 lean meat, 1 vegetable, 1/2 fat.

split pea soup

Slow cook your split pea soup while you are out for the day, and a delicious dinner will be ready when you arrive back home! This is a real stick-to-your-ribs soup. Ham hocks give it a great smoky flavor.
TASTE OF HOME TEST KITCHEN

1	can (49-1/2 ounces) chicken broth
1-1/2	pounds smoked ham hocks
2	cups each chopped onions, celery and carrots
1	package (16 ounces) dried green split peas
2	bay leaves

Salad croutons, optional

▨ In a 4- or 5-qt. slow cooker, combine the broth, ham hocks, vegetables, peas and bay leaves. Cover and cook on low for 8-10 hours or until ham hocks and peas are tender.

▨ Discard bay leaves. Remove meat from bones when cool enough to handle; cut ham into small pieces and set aside. Cool soup slightly.

▨ In a blender, cover and process soup in batches until smooth. Return soup to slow cooker; stir in reserved ham. Heat through. Garnish with croutons if desired.

Yield: 7 servings (about 2 quarts).

NUTRITION FACTS: 1-1/4 cups equals 592 calories, 24 g fat (8 g saturated fat), 106 mg cholesterol, 933 mg sodium, 49 g carbohydrate, 19 g fiber, 46 g protein.

taco bean soup

(pictured above)

This satisfying three-bean soup is very easy to fix. You can add a can of green chilies if you like it hotter. I increase the amount of tomatoes and beans for large get-togethers at my church.
SHARON THOMPSON HUNTER, KANSAS

1	pound bulk pork sausage
1	pound ground beef
1	envelope taco seasoning
4	cups water
2	cans (16 ounces each) kidney beans, rinsed and drained
2	cans (15 ounces each) pinto beans, rinsed and drained
2	cans (15 ounces each) garbanzo beans or chickpeas, rinsed and drained
2	cans (14-1/2 ounces each) stewed tomatoes
2	cans (14-1/2 ounces each) Mexican diced tomatoes, undrained
1	jar (16 ounces) chunky salsa

Sour cream, shredded cheddar cheese and sliced ripe olives, optional

▢ In a stockpot, cook sausage and beef over medium heat until no longer pink; drain. Add taco seasoning and mix well. Stir in the water, beans, tomatoes and salsa. Bring to a boil. reduce heat; simmer, uncovered, for 30 minutes, stirring occasionally. Garnish with sour cream, cheese and olives if desired.

Yield: 14 servings (3-1/2 quarts).

NUTRITION FACTS: 1 cup (calculated without garnishes) equals 236 calories, 10 g fat (3 g saturated fat), 28 mg cholesterol, 838 mg sodium, 23 g carbohydrate, 6 g fiber, 13 g protein.

lentil barley stew

You can have your comfort food and nutrition, too, when you stir up this scrumptious stew. We love this dish! Filled with wholesome lentils and barley, it's a hearty meal that tastes even better the next day.
SANDY STARKS AMHERST, NEW YORK

1/2	cup chopped celery
1/3	cup chopped onion
1	tablespoon butter
3	cups V8 juice
2-1/2	cups chopped seeded plum tomatoes (about 8)
1-1/2	cups water
3/4	cup dried lentils, rinsed
1/2	cup medium pearl barley
1/2	teaspoon salt
1/2	teaspoon pepper
1/2	teaspoon dried rosemary, crushed
1/2	cup shredded carrot
3/4	cup shredded reduced-fat cheddar cheese

▢ In a large saucepan, saute celery and onion in butter until tender. Add the V8 juice, tomatoes, water, lentils, barley and seasonings. Bring to a boil. Reduce heat; cover and simmer for 45 minutes.

▢ Add carrot; cook 10 minutes longer or until barley and lentils are tender. If desired, stir in additional water for a thinner stew. Sprinkle with cheese.

Yield: 6 servings.

NUTRITION FACTS: 1 cup stew with 2 tablespoons cheese equals 231 calories, 4 g fat (2 g saturated fat), 8 mg cholesterol, 631 mg sodium, 38 g carbohydrate, 6 g fiber, 13 g protein. **DIABETIC EXCHANGES:** 2 starch, 1 medium-fat meat, 1 vegetable.

bart's black bean soup for 2

Every cook can appreciate a fresh, simple soup that's ready in minutes. Add a salad and dinner rolls or quesadillas for a complete meal that's really tasty.

SHARON ULLYOT LONDON, ONTARIO

3/4	cup canned black beans, rinsed and drained
3/4	cup chicken broth
1/3	cup salsa
1/4	cup whole kernel corn
Dash	hot pepper sauce
1	teaspoon lime juice
1/2	cup shredded cheddar cheese
1	tablespoon chopped green onion

▢ In a microwave-safe bowl, combine the first five ingredients. Cover and microwave on high for 2 minutes or until heated through. Pour into two serving bowls; drizzle each with lime juice. Sprinkle with cheese and green onions.

Yield: 2 servings.

NUTRITION FACTS: 1 cup equals 218 calories, 8 g fat (6 g saturated fat), 32 mg cholesterol, 964 mg sodium, 22 g carbohydrate, 4 g fiber, 11 g protein.

EDITOR'S NOTE: This recipe was tested in a 1,100-watt microwave.

southwestern refried bean soup

My daughter gave me this soup recipe, and I'm glad she did. It's become a family favorite!

GRACE NORDANG METHOW, WASHINGTON

4	bacon strips
3/4	cup chopped onion
3/4	cup chopped celery
1/8	teaspoon garlic powder
1	can (16 ounces) refried beans
1/4	cup picante sauce or salsa
1	can (14-1/2 ounces) chicken broth
1	tablespoon chopped fresh parsley
Hot pepper sauce, optional	
Tortilla chips and shredded cheddar cheese	

▢ In a large saucepan, cook bacon over medium heat until crisp. Remove to paper towels; drain, reserving drippings. Crumble bacon and set aside. In the drippings, saute the onion, celery and garlic powder until vegetables are tender.

▢ Add the beans, picante sauce, broth, parsley and bacon; bring to a boil. Reduce heat; simmer, uncovered, for 10-15 minutes or until flavors are blended. Season to taste with pepper sauce if desired. Ladle into bowls and top with cheese. Serve with tortilla chips.

Yield: 4 servings.

NUTRITION FACTS: 1 serving equals 260 calories, 15 g fat (5 g saturated fat), 24 mg cholesterol, 1,012 mg sodium, 23 g carbohydrate, 7 g fiber, 10 g protein.

italian vegetable soup

(pictured at left)

Laced with a splash of white wine, this soup is packed with garden-fresh nutrition and veggies! Leafy escarole adds color and plenty of vitamin A. You could substitute spinach or kale for the escarole if you wish.
LEA REITER THOUSAND OAKS, CALIFORNIA

- 2 celery ribs, sliced
- 1 medium onion, chopped
- 1 medium carrot, halved and sliced
- 1 tablespoon olive oil
- 2 cups water
- 1 can (15 ounces) white kidney or cannellini beans, rinsed and drained
- 1 can (14-1/2 ounces) diced tomatoes, undrained
- 1 can (14-1/2 ounces) reduced-sodium chicken broth
- 1/2 cup Marsala wine or additional reduced-sodium chicken broth
- 1 teaspoon each dried basil, marjoram, oregano and thyme
- 1/4 teaspoon salt
- 1/4 teaspoon pepper
- 1 cup uncooked bow tie pasta
- 6 cups torn escarole (about 1 small head)

▢ In a Dutch oven, saute the celery, onion and carrot in oil until tender. Stir in the water, beans, tomatoes, broth, wine and seasonings. Bring to a boil. Stir in pasta.

▢ Reduce heat; simmer, uncovered, for 13-15 minutes or until pasta is tender, adding escarole during last 3 minutes of cooking.

Yield: 7 servings.

NUTRITION FACTS: 1 cup equals 164 calories, 3 g fat (trace saturated fat), 0 cholesterol, 426 mg sodium, 26 g carbohydrate, 5 g fiber, 6 g protein. **DIABETIC EXCHANGES:** 1-1/2 starch, 1 vegetable, 1/2 fat.

southwest chicken-black bean soup

Cook up a big pot of this hearty soup on Sunday, then reheat it for quick lunches during the week!
WILL SMITH BEEBE, ARKANSAS

- 1/2 pound boneless skinless chicken breast, cut into 3/4-inch pieces
- 2 teaspoons canola oil
- 1 small sweet red pepper, finely chopped
- 1 medium onion, chopped
- 1 garlic clove, minced
- 2 cans (14-1/2 ounces each) reduced-sodium chicken broth
- 1 can (15 ounces) black beans, rinsed and drained
- 1 cup frozen corn
- 1 medium lime, peeled, seeded and finely chopped
- 1 jalapeno pepper, seeded and chopped
- 1/4 teaspoon pepper
- 1/8 to 1/4 teaspoon cayenne pepper
- 1 small tomato, peeled, seeded and chopped
- 2 green onions, sliced

▢ In a large nonstick saucepan, saute chicken in oil until no longer pink. Remove and keep warm.

▢ In the same pan, saute red pepper and onion until tender. Add garlic; cook 1 minute longer. Stir in the broth, beans, corn, lime, jalapeno, black pepper and cayenne; bring to a boil. Reduce heat; cover and simmer for 10 minutes.

▢ Add the tomato, green onions and chicken; cook and stir until heated through.

Yield: 5 servings.

NUTRITION FACTS: 1-1/2 cups equals 199 calories, 3 g fat (trace saturated fat), 25 mg cholesterol, 621 mg sodium, 26 g carbohydrate, 6 g fiber, 17 g protein. **DIABETIC EXCHANGES:** 2 lean meat, 1-1/2 starch, 1 vegetable.

EDITOR'S NOTE: Wear disposable gloves when cutting hot peppers; the oils can burn skin. Avoid touching your face.

white chili

(pictured above)

A friend and I came up with this delicious slow-cooked chicken chili. It's unusual because it calls for Alfredo sauce. You'll want to make it again and again!
CINDI MITCHELL ST. MARYS, KANSAS

3	cans (15-1/2 ounces each) great northern beans, rinsed and drained
3	cups cubed cooked chicken breast
1	jar (15 ounces) Alfredo sauce
2	cups chicken broth
1	to 2 cans (4 ounces each) chopped green chilies
1-1/2	cups frozen gold and white corn
1	cup (4 ounces) shredded Monterey Jack cheese
1	cup (4 ounces) shredded pepper jack cheese
1	cup sour cream
1	small sweet yellow pepper, chopped
1	small onion, chopped
3	garlic cloves, minced
1	tablespoon ground cumin
1-1/2	teaspoons white pepper
1	to 1-1/2 teaspoons cayenne pepper

Salsa verde and chopped fresh cilantro, optional

In a 5- or 6-qt. slow cooker, combine the first 15 ingredients. Cover and cook on low for 3-4 hours or until heated though, stirring once. Serve with salsa verde and cilantro if desired.

Yield: 12 servings (3 quarts).

NUTRITION FACTS: 1 cup (calculated without optional ingredients) equals 336 calories, 15 g fat (9 g saturated fat), 69 mg cholesterol, 772 mg sodium, 27 g carbohydrate, 7 g fiber, 24 g protein.

echo valley bean soup

I came up with this recipe after sampling some excellent bean soup at a sandwich shop in a neighboring town.
PATRICIA CRANDALL INCHELIUM, WASHINGTON

10	bacon strips, diced
1	medium onion, diced
2	garlic cloves, minced
1	can (14-1/2 ounces) stewed tomatoes
2	cans (15 ounces each) pork and beans
2	cans (14-1/2 ounces each) beef broth

In a saucepan, cook bacon until crisp. Set bacon aside; drain, reserving 1-2 tablespoons drippings. In the drippings, saute the onion and garlic until tender.

Meanwhile, in a blender, process tomatoes until smooth. Add to the onion mixture. Stir in pork and beans and broth. Bring to a boil. Reduce heat; simmer, uncovered, for 15 minutes to allow flavors to blend. Stir in bacon.

Yield: 6 servings.

NUTRITION FACTS: 1 cup equals 307 calories, 23 g fat (8 g saturated fat), 25 mg cholesterol, 877 mg sodium, 21 g carbohydrate, 4 g fiber, 8 g protein.

potato-lentil stew

Jam-packed with nutritious veggies, this hearty main-dish soup makes a rib-sticking meatless meal the whole family will love. Serve with a crusty loaf of bread and dinner's done!
KRISTA GOODWIN YPSILANTI, MICHIGAN

1	large onion, chopped
2	medium carrots, chopped
2	teaspoons olive oil
4	teaspoons chili powder
3	garlic cloves, minced
3	teaspoons ground cumin
1	teaspoon dried oregano
1	carton (32 ounces) vegetable broth
3/4	cup dried lentils, rinsed
2	cans (10 ounces each) diced tomatoes and green chilies
3-1/2	cups frozen cubed hash brown potatoes
1	can (16 ounces) kidney beans, rinsed and drained
1/2	teaspoon salt
1/4	teaspoon pepper

▨ In a Dutch oven, saute onion and carrots in oil for 3 minutes. Add the chili powder, garlic, cumin and oregano; cook 1 minute longer.

▨ Stir in broth and lentils. Bring to a boil. Reduce heat; cover and simmer for 18-22 minutes or until lentils are tender. Stir in the tomatoes, potatoes, beans, salt and pepper. Return to a boil. Reduce heat; cover and simmer 10-15 minutes longer or until potatoes are tender.

Yield: 6 servings (2-1/2 quarts).

NUTRITION FACTS: 1-2/3 cups equals 295 calories, 2 g fat (trace saturated fat), 0 cholesterol, 1,478 mg sodium, 56 g carbohydrate, 16 g fiber, 15 g protein.

cannellini orzo soup

This budget-friendly bean soup with orzo and veggies is so hearty, you won't even notice it's meatless. It really satisfies.
GILDA LESTER MILLSBORO, DELAWARE

1	medium onion, thinly sliced
1	small potato, peeled and finely chopped
1	celery rib, chopped
2	tablespoons olive oil
3	garlic cloves, minced
3	cans (14-1/2 ounces each) reduced-sodium chicken broth
1	can (15 ounces) white kidney or cannellini beans, rinsed and drained
1	can (14-1/2 ounces) Italian stewed tomatoes, undrained
1/4	cup minced fresh parsley
1	tablespoon prepared pesto
1/4	cup uncooked orzo pasta
1	cup fresh baby spinach
1/4	cup grated Romano cheese

▨ In a Dutch oven, saute the onion, potato and celery in oil until tender. Add garlic; cook 1 minute longer. Stir in the broth, beans, tomatoes, parsley and pesto. Bring to a boil. Stir in pasta. Reduce heat; cover and simmer for 10-15 minutes or until pasta is tender.

▨ Add spinach and cook just until wilted. Sprinkle each serving with cheese.

Yield: 6 servings (about 2 quarts).

NUTRITION FACTS: 1-1/3 cups soup with 2 teaspoons cheese equals 224 calories, 8 g fat (2 g saturated fat), 6 mg cholesterol, 1,029 mg sodium, 29 g carbohydrate, 5 g fiber, 11 g protein.

easy low-fat chili

Here's a simple chili that will really warm you on cool fall days. It's so quick to make that you can enjoy it any time.
JANET MOORE OGDENSBURG, NEW YORK

1	medium onion, chopped
1/4	cup chopped green pepper
2	cups water, divided
1	can (15-1/2 ounces) great northern beans, rinsed and drained
1	can (15 ounces) navy beans, rinsed and drained
1	can (14-1/2 ounces) reduced-salt diced tomatoes, undrained
1	can (6 ounces) salt-free tomato paste
2	to 4 teaspoons chili powder
1	teaspoon salt, optional
1/2	teaspoon pepper

▢ In a large saucepan, cook the onion and green pepper in 1/2 cup water until tender. Add beans, tomatoes and tomato paste. Stir in chili powder, salt if desired, pepper and remaining water; bring to a boil. Reduce heat; cover and simmer for 20 minutes.

Yield: 7 servings.

NUTRITION FACTS: 1 cup (calculated without added salt) equals 198 calories, 1 g fat (0 saturated fat), 0 cholesterol, 295 mg sodium, 38 g carbohydrate, 0 fiber, 11 g protein. **DIABETIC EXCHANGES:** 2 starch, 1-1/2 vegetable.

lentil soup with brown rice

Lentils, like beans, are part of the legume family and add cholesterol-reducing fiber to this tasty soup. Adjust the amount of red pepper flakes according to how much heat you like.
MARYBETH GESSELE GASTON, OREGON

1	medium onion, chopped
1	tablespoon olive oil
2	garlic cloves, minced
3-1/4	cups water
1	can (14-1/2 ounces) vegetable broth
1	cup dried lentils, rinsed
1	medium carrot, shredded
1	small green pepper, finely chopped
1	teaspoon dried oregano
1/2	teaspoon dried basil
1/4	teaspoon crushed red pepper flakes, optional
1	can (14-1/2 ounces) no-salt-added diced tomatoes
1	can (6 ounces) tomato paste
1	tablespoon lemon juice
2	cups cooked brown rice

▢ In a Dutch oven, saute onion in oil until tender. Add garlic; cook 1 minute longer. Add the water, broth, lentils, carrot, green pepper, oregano, basil and pepper flakes if desired. Bring to a boil. Reduce heat; cover and simmer for 20-25 minutes or until lentils are tender.

▢ Stir in the tomatoes, tomato paste and lemon juice. Bring to a boil. Reduce the heat; cover and simmer 10 minutes longer or until lentils are tender. Serve with rice.

Yield: 6 servings (2 quarts).

NUTRITION FACTS: 1-1/3 cups soup with 1/3 cup rice equals 269 calories, 3 g fat (trace saturated fat), 0 cholesterol, 383 mg sodium, 48 g carbohydrate, 14 g fiber, 13 g protein.

grandma's pea soup

Monday was always washday at our house when I was a child, and because of it being such a busy day, it was always "soup day." My grandma's pea soup was a family favorite. What makes it different from other pea soups I have tried is the addition of whole peas, spaetzle-like "dumplings" and sausage.
CAROLE TALCOTT DAHINDA, ILLINOIS

1/2	pound dried whole peas
1/2	pound dried green split peas
1	meaty ham bone
3	quarts water
1	large onion, chopped
1	medium carrot, chopped
2	celery ribs, chopped
1/2	cup chopped celery leaves
1	teaspoon bouquet garni (mixed herbs)
1	tablespoon minced fresh parsley
1	bay leaf
1	teaspoon salt
1/4	teaspoon pepper
1/2	pound smoked sausage, chopped, optional

SPAETZLE DUMPLINGS:

1	cup all-purpose flour
1	egg, beaten
1/3	cup water

▨ Cover peas with water and soak overnight. Drain; rinse and place in a Dutch oven.

▨ Add ham bone, water and remaining soup ingredients except sausage and dumplings. Bring to a boil. Reduce heat; cover and simmer for 2 to 2-1/2 hours.

▨ Remove ham bone and skim fat. Remove meat from bone; dice. Add ham and sausage if desired to pan.

▨ For dumplings, place flour in a small bowl; make a depression in the center of the flour; add egg and water and stir until smooth.

▨ Place a colander with 3/16-in.-diameter holes over simmering soup; transfer dough to the colander and press through with a wooden spoon. Cook, uncovered, for 10-15 minutes. Discard bay leaf.

Yield: 4 quarts.

NUTRITION FACTS: 1 cup equals 155 calories, 2 g fat (1 g saturated fat), 20 mg cholesterol, 171 mg sodium, 26 g carbohydrate, 6 g fiber, 9 g protein.

black bean-pumpkin soup

This is such a healthy recipe, packed with protein from the beans and vitamins from the pumpkin. The dollop of light sour cream adds a satisfying touch that feels indulgent.
JENNIFER FISHER AUSTIN, TEXAS

2	cans (15 ounces each) black beans, rinsed and drained
1	can (14-1/2 ounces) diced tomatoes, drained
2	medium onions, finely chopped
1	teaspoon olive oil
3	garlic cloves, minced
1	teaspoon ground cumin
3	cups vegetable broth
1	can (15 ounces) solid-pack pumpkin
2	tablespoons cider vinegar
1/2	teaspoon pepper
2	tablespoons bourbon, optional
1/2	cup reduced-fat sour cream
1/2	cup thinly sliced green onions
1/2	cup roasted salted pumpkin seeds

▨ Place beans and tomatoes in a food processor; cover and process until blended. Set aside.

▨ In a Dutch oven, saute onions in oil until tender. Add garlic and cumin; saute 1 minute longer. Stir in the broth, pumpkin, vinegar, pepper and bean mixture. Bring to a boil. Reduce heat; cover and simmer for 20 minutes.

▨ Stir in bourbon if desired. Garnish each serving with sour cream, green onions and pumpkin seeds.

Yield: 8 servings (2 quarts).

NUTRITION FACTS: 1 cup equals 238 calories, 8 g fat (2 g saturated fat), 5 mg cholesterol, 716 mg sodium, 30 g carbohydrate, 9 g fiber, 13 g protein. **DIABETIC EXCHANGES:** 1-1/2 starch, 1-1/2 fat, 1 lean meat, 1 vegetable.

hominy taco chili
(pictured at left)

Made with hominy, seasonings and two kinds of beans, my chili offers an exciting change of pace. This recipe makes enough for dinner with leftovers to freeze.
BARBARA WHELESS SHELDON, SOUTH CAROLINA

1	pound ground beef
1	large onion, chopped
2	cans (15-1/2 ounces each) hominy, drained
2	cans (14-1/2 ounces each) stewed tomatoes, undrained
1	can (15-1/4 ounces) whole kernel corn, drained
1	can (15 ounces) pinto beans, rinsed and drained
1	can (15 ounces) black beans, rinsed and drained
1	cup water
1	envelope taco seasoning
1	envelope ranch salad dressing mix
2	teaspoons ground cumin
1/2	teaspoon garlic salt
1/2	teaspoon pepper

Corn chips, optional

In a Dutch oven, cook beef and onion over medium heat until meat is no longer pink; drain. Stir in the next 11 ingredients. Bring to a boil. Reduce heat; cover and simmer for 30 minutes.

Serve half of the chili with corn chips if desired. Freeze remaining chili in a freezer container for up to 3 months.

TO USE FROZEN CHILI: Thaw in the refrigerator. Transfer to a large saucepan; heat through, adding water if desired.

Yield: 2 batches (5 servings each).

NUTRITION FACTS: 1 cup (calculated without chips) equals 274 calories, 6 g fat (2 g saturated fat), 28 mg cholesterol, 1,439 mg sodium, 39 g carbohydrate, 7 g fiber, 14 g protein.

sweet potato & black bean chili

My whole family enjoys this vegetarian chili, but my daughter especially loves it. I like to make it because it's so easy and very flavorful. It's the perfect comfort food for the chilly fall and winter months.
JOY PENDLEY ORTONVILLE, MICHIGAN

3	large sweet potatoes, peeled and cut into 1/2-inch cubes
1	large onion, chopped
1	tablespoon olive oil
2	tablespoons chili powder
3	garlic cloves, minced
1	teaspoon ground cumin
1/4	teaspoon cayenne pepper
2	cans (15 ounces each) black beans, rinsed and drained
1	can (28 ounces) diced tomatoes, undrained
1/4	cup brewed coffee
2	tablespoons honey
1/2	teaspoon salt
1/4	teaspoon pepper
1/2	cup shredded reduced-fat Monterey Jack cheese or reduced-fat Mexican cheese blend

In a nonstick Dutch oven coated with cooking spray, saute sweet potatoes and onion in oil until crisp-tender. Add the chili powder, garlic, cumin and cayenne; cook 1 minute longer. Stir in the beans, tomatoes, coffee, honey, salt and pepper.

Bring to a boil. Reduce heat; cover and simmer for 30-35 minutes or until sweet potatoes are tender. Sprinkle with cheese.

Yield: 8 servings (2 quarts).

NUTRITION FACTS: 1 cup chili with 1 tablespoon cheese equals 252 calories, 4 g fat (1 g saturated fat), 5 mg cholesterol, 554 mg sodium, 47 g carbohydrate, 9 g fiber, 10 g protein.

black-eyed pea soup

(pictured above)

I had eaten this soup countless times at a small restaurant in our town. When the owner retired, he said I deserved the secret recipe and passed it along!
ALICE JARRELL DEXTER, MISSOURI

1	pound bulk pork sausage
1	pound ground beef
1	large onion, chopped
4	cups water
3	cans (15-1/2 ounces each) black-eyed peas, rinsed and drained
1	can (28 ounces) diced tomatoes, undrained
1	can (10 ounces) diced tomatoes and green chilies, undrained
1	can (4 ounces) chopped green chilies
4	beef bouillon cubes
4	teaspoons molasses
1	teaspoon Worcestershire sauce
3/4	teaspoon garlic salt
1/2	teaspoon salt
1/4	teaspoon pepper
1/4	teaspoon ground cumin

▢ In a Dutch oven, cook the sausage, beef and onion over medium heat until meat is no longer pink; drain. Add the remaining ingredients; bring to a boil. Reduce heat; cover and simmer for 45 minutes.

Yield: 16 servings (4 quarts).

NUTRITION FACTS: 1 serving equals 145 calories, 8 g fat (3 g saturated fat), 24 mg cholesterol, 731 mg sodium, 9 g carbohydrate, 2 g fiber, 9 g protein.

ham and lentil soup

This delicious soup is a great way to use up leftover ham. The hearty broth makes it perfect for a cold day. Just serve with fresh crusty bread and butter.
CONNIE JONES PIXLEY ROXBORO, NORTH CAROLINA

1	cup chopped celery
1	cup chopped carrots
1/2	cup chopped onion
1	tablespoon butter
8	cups water
2	cups dried lentils, rinsed
1	cup cubed fully cooked ham
2	teaspoons salt
1	teaspoon dried marjoram
1/2	teaspoon pepper

▢ In a large skillet, saute the celery, carrots and onion in butter for 3-4 minutes or until crisp-tender. In a 5-qt. slow cooker, combine the water, lentils, ham, salt, marjoram and pepper. Stir in the celery mixture. Cover and cook on low for 4-5 hours or until lentils are tender.

Yield: 11 servings (2-3/4 quarts).

NUTRITION FACTS: 1 cup equals 158 calories, 2 g fat (1 g saturated fat), 10 mg cholesterol, 620 mg sodium, 23 g carbohydrate, 11 g fiber, 12 g protein.

lentil-barley ham soup

This hearty veggie-and-herb soup is light and easy to prepare, yet with all the delicious homemade taste of my grandmother's original recipe. Also try it with leftover turkey instead of ham.
PRISCILLA GILBERT INDIAN HARBOUR BEACH, FLORIDA

1/2	cup chopped onion
1/2	cup chopped celery
1	garlic clove, minced
1	tablespoon butter
4	cups reduced-sodium chicken broth
1/2	cup dried lentils, rinsed
1/2	teaspoon each dried basil, oregano and rosemary, crushed
1/4	teaspoon pepper
1-1/2	cups cubed fully cooked ham
3/4	cup sliced fresh carrots
1/2	cup quick-cooking barley
1	can (14-1/2 ounces) diced tomatoes, undrained

▨ In a large saucepan, saute the onion, celery and garlic in butter until tender. Stir in the broth, lentils, basil, oregano, rosemary and pepper. Bring to a boil. Reduce heat; cover and simmer for 20 minutes.

▨ Add ham and carrots. Cover and simmer 10 minutes longer. Return to a boil; stir in the barley. Reduce heat; cover and simmer for 15 minutes or until barley and lentils are tender. Stir in tomatoes; heat through.

Yield: 5 servings.

NUTRITION FACTS: 1-1/3 cups equals 247 calories, 5 g fat (2 g saturated fat), 22 mg cholesterol, 1,172 mg sodium, 33 g carbohydrate, 12 g fiber, 19 g protein. **DIABETIC EXCHANGES:** 2 lean meat, 1-1/2 starch, 1 vegetable.

hearty vegetarian chili

Rich and flavorful, my chili is absolutely packed with veggies, beans and sun-dried tomatoes. It's so satisfying, you'll fool any meat lover.
PAM IVBULS OMAHA, NEBRASKA

1-3/4	cups chopped baby portobello mushrooms
1	medium onion, finely chopped
1/2	cup chopped sun-dried tomatoes (not packed in oil)
2	tablespoons olive oil
2	garlic cloves, minced
1	package (12 ounces) frozen vegetarian meat crumbles
2	cans (16 ounces each) chili beans, undrained
2	cans (14-1/2 ounces each) no-salt-added diced tomatoes
1/2	cup water
1/2	cup vegetable broth
4-1/2	teaspoons chili powder
2	teaspoons brown sugar
1/2	teaspoon celery salt
1/2	teaspoon ground cumin
1	medium ripe avocado, peeled and finely chopped
9	tablespoons reduced-fat sour cream

▨ In a Dutch oven, saute the mushrooms, onion and sun-dried tomatoes in oil until tender. Add garlic; cook 1 minute longer. Add meat crumbles; heat through.

▨ Stir in the chili beans, tomatoes, water, broth, chili powder, brown sugar, celery salt and cumin. Bring to a boil. Reduce heat; simmer, uncovered, for 10 minutes. Ladle chili into bowls. Top each with avocado and sour cream.

Yield: 9 servings (2-1/4 quarts).

NUTRITION FACTS: 1 cup equals 275 calories, 10 g fat (2 g saturated fat), 5 mg cholesterol, 768 mg sodium, 37 g carbohydrate, 12 g fiber, 17 g protein. **DIABETIC EXCHANGES:** 2 lean meat, 2 vegetable, 1-1/2 starch, 1 fat.

EDITOR'S NOTE: Vegetarian meat crumbles are a nutritious protein source made from soy. Look for them in the natural foods freezer section.

slow-cooked cannellini turkey soup

(pictured at left)

All you have to do is add the ingredients to the slow cooker and let them cook! Nothing could be simpler.

GARY FENSKI HURON, SOUTH DAKOTA

2	cans (15 ounces each) white kidney or cannellini beans, rinsed and drained
2	cups cubed cooked turkey
1	can (14-1/2 ounces) chicken broth
1	can (10 ounces) diced tomatoes and green chilies, undrained
1	cup salsa
1/2	teaspoon ground cumin
1/4	teaspoon curry powder
1/4	teaspoon ground ginger
1/4	teaspoon paprika

▨ In a 3-qt. slow cooker, combine all ingredients. Cover and cook on low for 5-6 hours or until the soup is heated through.

Yield: 4 servings.

NUTRITION FACTS: 1-1/2 cups equals 322 calories, 5 g fat (1 g saturated fat), 55 mg cholesterol, 1,283 mg sodium, 37 g carbohydrate, 9 g fiber, 30 g protein.

emily's bean soup

Served with thick slices of warm homemade bread, my soup makes a wonderful fall or winter meal. The recipe evolved over the years as I added to it. I often double it and freeze what we don't eat. That way, I can throw some in a pot for a quick meal or if unexpected guests drop by.

EMILY CHANEY PENOBSCOT, MAINE

1/2	cup each dried great northern beans, kidney beans, navy beans, lima beans, butter beans, split green or yellow peas, pinto beans and lentils
	Water
1	meaty ham bone
2	teaspoons chicken bouillon granules
1	can (28 ounces) tomatoes with liquid, quartered
1	can (6 ounces) tomato paste
1	large onion, chopped
3	celery ribs, chopped
4	medium carrots, sliced
2	garlic cloves, minced
1/4	cup minced chives
3	bay leaves
2	tablespoons dried parsley flakes
1	teaspoon dried thyme
1	teaspoon ground mustard
1/2	teaspoon cayenne pepper

▨ Wash all beans thoroughly; drain and place in a large saucepan. Add 5 cups of water. Bring to a rapid boil; boil for 2 minutes. Remove from the heat; cover and let stand for 1 hour.

▨ Meanwhile, place ham bone and 3 qts. of water in a stockpot. Simmer until beans have stood for 1 hour.

▨ Drain beans and add to the ham stock; add remaining ingredients. Simmer for 2-3 hours or until beans are tender. Cut meat from ham bone; discard bone. Add additional water to soup if desired.

Yield: about 5-1/2 quarts.

NUTRITION FACTS: 1 cup equals 149 calories, 2 g fat (trace saturated fat), 5 mg cholesterol, 210 mg sodium, 25 g carbohydrate, 9 g fiber, 10 g protein.

three-bean soup

This is a terrific recipe for cold days. Even my young son asks for it! I like it because it's so easy to make.
MARILYN COY ST. HELENA, CALIFORNIA

1	pound ground beef
1	can (28 ounces) crushed tomatoes
1	can (10-1/2 ounces) condensed beef consomme, undiluted
1	cup water
1/2	cup medium pearl barley
1/4	cup chopped onion
1	teaspoon salt
1/4	teaspoon dried marjoram
1/4	teaspoon dried thyme
1	can (16 ounces) kidney beans, rinsed and drained
1	can (15-1/4 ounces) lima beans or 1 can (14-1/2 ounces) cut wax beans, drained
1	can (14-1/2 ounces) cut green beans or Italian-style green beans, drained

Grated Parmesan or Romano cheese

▢ In a Dutch oven, cook beef over medium heat until no longer pink; drain. Add the tomatoes, consomme, water, barley, onion, salt, marjoram and thyme; bring to a boil. Reduce heat; cover and simmer for 50 minutes.

▢ Stir in all the beans and bring to a boil. Reduce heat and simmer for 10 minutes. Sprinkle individual bowls with cheese.

Yield: Yield: 10 servings (2-1/2 quarts).

NUTRITION FACTS: 1 cup (calculated without cheese) equals 229 calories, 5 g fat (2 g saturated fat), 26 mg cholesterol, 1,096 mg sodium, 29 g carbohydrate, 7 g fiber, 17 g protein.

sausage lentil soup

I found this good-for-you recipe in a men's magazine and lightened it up. It's so tasty and loaded with fiber, vitamins and iron. It uses low-fat ingredients without sacrificing taste.
SUZANNE DABKOWSKI BLYTHEWOOD, SOUTH CAROLINA

1	medium onion, chopped
1	celery rib, chopped
1/4	pound reduced-fat smoked sausage, halved and thinly sliced
1	medium carrot, halved and thinly sliced
2	garlic cloves, minced
2	cans (14-1/2 ounces each) reduced-sodium chicken broth
1/3	cup water
1	cup dried lentils, rinsed
1/2	teaspoon dried oregano
1/4	teaspoon ground cumin
1/4	teaspoon pepper
1	can (14-1/2 ounces) stewed tomatoes, cut up
1	tablespoon Worcestershire sauce
1	cup chopped fresh spinach

▢ In a large saucepan coated with cooking spray, cook and stir onion and celery over medium-high heat for 2 minutes. Add the sausage, carrot and garlic; cook 2-3 minutes longer or until onion is tender.

▢ Stir in the broth, water, lentils, oregano, cumin and pepper. Bring to a boil. Reduce heat; cover and simmer for 25-30 minutes or until lentils and vegetables are tender.

▢ Stir in the tomatoes, Worcestershire sauce and spinach; cook until heated through and spinach is wilted.

Yield: 6 servings.

NUTRITION FACTS: 1 cup equals 180 calories, 1 g fat (trace saturated fat), 7 mg cholesterol, 639 mg sodium, 31 g carbohydrate, 12 g fiber, 14 g protein.

FIBER SMARTS

Foods high in fiber, like beans and lentils, help you feel fuller longer, which can help you eat less. Adding them to your favorite soup is a healthy and economical way to stretch the meat in the recipe. You can even omit the meat altogether for a still-satisfying vegetarian meal.

vegetable

cremini & butternut squash soup

This wholesome soup tastes like autumn, with vitamin-rich squash and the earthy flavor of mushrooms. Adding cream makes it velvety smooth.

GILDA LESTER MILLSBORO, DELAWARE

1	large butternut squash (about 5 pounds)
1	carton (32 ounces) reduced-sodium chicken broth, divided
1	large onion, chopped
1	tablespoon olive oil
1/2	pound chopped baby portobello (cremini) mushrooms
3	garlic cloves, minced
1	teaspoon minced fresh thyme
1/2	teaspoon rubbed sage
1/8	teaspoon ground nutmeg
1/4	cup heavy whipping cream
1/4	cup grated Romano cheese

▢ Cut squash in half lengthwise; discard seeds. Place squash, cut side down, in a 15-in. x 10-in. x 1-in. baking pan coated with cooking spray. Bake at 400° for 55-65 minutes or until tender.

▢ Cool slightly; carefully scoop out pulp. Place in a food processor with 1 cup broth; cover and process until smooth.

▢ In a large saucepan over medium heat, cook onion in oil until tender. Add mushrooms; cook 3-4 minutes longer or until tender. Add the garlic, thyme and sage; cook 1 minute longer. Stir in the nutmeg, squash puree and remaining broth. Bring to a boil. Reduce heat; simmer, uncovered, for 20 minutes.

▢ Stir in cream; heat through (do not boil). Ladle soup into bowls; sprinkle with cheese.

Yield: 8 servings (2 quarts).

NUTRITION FACTS: 1 cup with 1-1/2 teaspoons cheese equals 167 calories, 6 g fat (3 g saturated fat), 14 mg cholesterol, 403 mg sodium, 26 g carbohydrate, 7 g fiber, 6 g protein. **DIABETIC EXCHANGES:** 1-1/2 starch, 1 lean meat, 1/2 fat.

CREMINI MUSHROOMS

Creminis, or baby portobello mushrooms, are a cousin of the familiar button mushrooms available in most stores. Use creminis instead of button mushrooms any time you'd like a flavor boost. Because they're affordable, you can also use them to save money when preparing recipes that use gourmet or wild mushrooms. Just substitute cremini mushrooms for half of the more expensive mushrooms called for in the recipe.

all-day soup

I start this soup in the morning, and by evening, dinner's ready to go! My family loves all of the hearty vegetable and steak pieces in a zesty tomato broth.
CATHY LOGAN SPARKS, NEVADA

1	beef flank steak (1-1/2 pounds), cut into 1/2-inch cubes
1	medium onion, chopped
1	tablespoon olive oil
5	medium carrots, thinly sliced
4	cups shredded cabbage
4	medium red potatoes, diced
2	celery ribs, diced
2	cans (14-1/2 ounces each) diced tomatoes, undrained
2	cans (14-1/2 ounces each) beef broth
1	can (10-3/4 ounces) condensed tomato soup, undiluted
1	tablespoon sugar
2	teaspoons Italian seasoning
1	teaspoon dried parsley flakes

▢ In a large skillet, brown steak and onion in oil; drain. Transfer to a 5-qt. slow cooker. Stir in the remaining ingredients. Cover and cook on low for 8-10 hours or until meat is tender.

Yield: 8 servings.

NUTRITION FACTS: 1-3/4 cups equals 274 calories, 8 g fat (3 g saturated fat), 41 mg cholesterol, 679 mg sodium, 29 g carbohydrate, 5 g fiber, 21 g protein. **DIABETIC EXCHANGES:** 2 starch, 2 lean meat, 1 vegetable.

lima bean okra soup

This soup's unique flavor comes from the wonderful combination of vegetables with a hint of sweet spices. Every serving is loaded with nutrition and color.
CLARA COULSON MINNEY
WASHINGTON COURT HOUSE, OHIO

1	medium green pepper, chopped
1	medium onion, chopped
1/4	teaspoon whole cloves
1	tablespoon butter
3	cups vegetable broth
3	cups chopped tomatoes
2-1/2	cups sliced fresh or frozen okra, thawed
1	cup frozen lima beans, thawed
1/2	cup fresh or frozen corn, thawed
1/2	to 1 teaspoon salt
1/4	to 1/2 teaspoon ground allspice
1/4	teaspoon pepper
1/8	teaspoon cayenne pepper

▢ In a large saucepan, saute the green pepper, onion and cloves in butter until vegetables are tender. Discard cloves.

▢ Stir in the remaining ingredients. Bring to a boil. Reduce heat; cover and simmer for 15-20 minutes or until beans are tender.

Yield: 7 servings.

NUTRITION FACTS: 1 cup equals 96 calories, 2 g fat (1 g saturated fat), 4 mg cholesterol, 601 mg sodium, 17 g carbohydrate, 5 g fiber, 4 g protein. **DIABETIC EXCHANGES:** 1 starch, 1 vegetable.

lemony mushroom-orzo soup

(pictured at left)

Here's a versatile soup that works as an appetizer or side for a sandwich lunch. It's loaded with mushrooms and orzo pasta, with a hint of lemon to brighten the flavor.

EDRIE O'BRIEN DENVER, COLORADO

2-1/2	cups sliced fresh mushrooms
2	green onions, chopped
1	tablespoon olive oil
1	garlic clove, minced
1-1/2	cups chicken broth
1-1/2	teaspoons minced fresh parsley
1/4	teaspoon dried thyme
1/8	teaspoon pepper
1/4	cup uncooked orzo pasta
1-1/2	teaspoons lemon juice
1/8	teaspoon grated lemon peel

▢ In a small saucepan, saute mushrooms and onions in oil until tender. Add garlic; cook 1 minute longer. Stir in the broth, parsley, thyme and pepper.

▢ Bring to a boil. Stir in the orzo, lemon juice and peel. Cook for 5-6 minutes or until pasta is tender.

Yield: 2 servings.

NUTRITION FACTS: 1 cup equals 194 calories, 8 g fat (1 g saturated fat), 4 mg cholesterol, 744 mg sodium, 25 g carbohydrate, 2 g fiber, 7 g protein.

four-cheese french onion soup

This beef broth is slightly sweet...not too salty like so many other soups. Serve this as a first course on special occasions or as a meal by itself with a green salad.

GAIL VAN OSDELL ST. CHARLES, ILLINOIS

1/3	cup butter, cubed
2	tablespoons olive oil
12	cups thinly sliced onions
2	teaspoons salt
1	teaspoon sugar
1/4	cup all-purpose flour
2	cartons (32 ounces each) reduced-sodium beef broth
1-1/2	cups white wine or additional reduced-sodium beef broth
8	slices French bread (1/2 inch thick)
1-1/3	cups shredded Swiss cheese
2/3	cup shredded cheddar cheese
1/2	cup shredded part-skim mozzarella cheese
2	tablespoons grated Parmesan cheese

▢ In a Dutch oven, melt butter with oil. Add the onions, salt and sugar; cook over medium heat for 15-20 minutes or until lightly browned, stirring frequently.

▢ Sprinkle flour over onion mixture; stir until blended. Gradually stir in broth and wine. Bring to a boil; cook and stir for 2 minutes. Reduce heat; cover and simmer for 30 minutes, stirring occasionally.

▢ Place bread slices on an ungreased baking sheet. Broil 3-4 in. from the heat for 3-5 minutes on each side or until lightly browned; set aside. Combine the cheeses.

▢ Ladle soup into ovenproof bowls. Top each with a slice of toast; sprinkle with cheese mixture. Place bowls on a baking sheet. Broil for 2-3 minutes or until cheese is lightly golden.

Yield: 8 servings.

NUTRITION FACTS: 1 serving equals 388 calories, 21 g fat (12 g saturated fat), 56 mg cholesterol, 1,293 mg sodium, 29 g carbohydrate, 3 g fiber, 15 g protein.

Cool slightly. In a blender, process soup in batches until smooth. Return all to the pan; stir in milk and heat through.

Yield: 6 servings.

NUTRITION FACTS: 1 cup equals 113 calories, 2 g fat (1 g saturated fat), 6 mg cholesterol, 513 mg sodium, 20 g carbohydrate, 5 g fiber, 5 g protein. **DIABETIC EXCHANGES:** 1 starch, 1/2 fat.

fresh tomato soup

When tomatoes are in season, my family knows they can expect to see this soup on the dinner table.
EDNA HOFFMAN HEBRON, INDIANA

1/2	cup chopped onion
1/4	cup butter
1/4	cup all-purpose flour
2	cups water
6	medium tomatoes, peeled and diced
1	tablespoon minced fresh parsley
1-1/2	teaspoon salt
1	teaspoon sugar
1	teaspoon minced fresh thyme or 1/2 teaspoon dried thyme
1	bay leaf
1/4	teaspoon pepper

In a large saucepan, cook onion in butter until tender. Stir in flour until blended. Gradually add water, stirring constantly until thickened. Add the tomatoes, parsley, salt, sugar, thyme, bay leaf and pepper; bring to a boil.

Reduce heat; cover and simmer for 20-30 minutes or until tomatoes are tender. Discard bay leaf.

Yield: 4 servings.

NUTRITION FACTS: 1-1/4 cups equals 188 calories, 12 g fat (7 g saturated fat), 31 mg cholesterol, 1,022 mg sodium, 19 g carbohydrate, 3 g fiber, 3 g protein.

curried parsnip soup

My mum used to make this soup at home in England, where parsnips are more widely used than here. It's very aromatic and has a nice bite from the curry and pepper.
JULIE MATHIESON BRISTOL, TENNESSEE

1	large onion, chopped
1	large carrot, chopped
1	tablespoon butter
1	pound parsnips, peeled and chopped
2	cans (14-1/2 ounces each) reduced-sodium chicken broth
1	teaspoon curry powder
1/4	teaspoon salt
1/4	teaspoon pepper
1	cup fat-free milk

In a large saucepan, saute onion and carrot in butter until onion is tender. Add parsnips; cook 2 minutes longer. Stir in broth and seasonings. Bring to a boil. Reduce heat; cover and simmer for 12-15 minutes or until parsnips are tender.

PARSNIPS

Parsnips are root vegetables that look like white carrots. They're less sweet than carrots and have a brighter, more herbal flavor. Look for small to medium parsnips that are firm and smooth, not shriveled, cracked or spotted. Try using them in any recipe in place of some or all of the carrots called for. Together, the two veggies make a lovely flavor contrast.

rustic autumn soup

This recipe is a great way to use the harvest of fall. The flavors of root vegetables really shine when combined with the subtle sweetness of apple.
GREG HAGELI ELMHURST, ILLINOIS

5	medium parsnips, chopped
5	medium carrots, chopped
2	medium onions, chopped
1	medium sweet potato, peeled and chopped
1	medium turnip, peeled and chopped
1/2	medium tart apple, peeled and chopped
2	tablespoons chopped roasted sweet red pepper
2	celery ribs, chopped
3	cans (14-1/2 ounces each) reduced-sodium chicken broth
2	bay leaves
1	garlic clove, minced
1	teaspoon dried tarragon
1/2	teaspoon salt
1/2	teaspoon pepper
2	cups half-and-half cream

Optional garnish: additional cooked finely chopped carrots, parsnips and/or apples, fresh chives

▢ In a Dutch oven, combine the first 14 ingredients. Bring to a boil. Reduce heat; cover and simmer for 20-25 minutes or until tender. Discard bay leaves. Cool slightly.

▢ In a blender, process soup in batches until smooth. Return all to the pan; add cream and heat through. Garnish with additional cooked vegetables and/or apples and chives.

Yield: 13 servings (3-1/4 quarts).

NUTRITION FACTS: 1 cup equals 134 calories, 4 g fat (3 g saturated fat), 18 mg cholesterol, 384 mg sodium, 20 g carbohydrate, 4 g fiber, 4 g protein. **DIABETIC EXCHANGES:** 1 starch, 1 fat.

smoky & spicy vegetable bisque

I like to make my bisque a complete meal by serving it with a side of bruschetta or a Caprese salad.
JULIANA INHOFER ROCKLIN, CALIFORNIA

2	large onions, cut into eight wedges
4	large tomatoes, cut into eight wedges
1	large sweet red pepper, cut into eight wedges
4	garlic cloves, halved
1/4	cup olive oil
2	cans (14-1/2 ounces each) reduced-sodium chicken broth
1/2	cup fat-free half-and-half
1/2	cup coarsely chopped fresh basil
1	small chipotle pepper in adobo sauce, seeded
1/2	teaspoon pepper
1/4	teaspoon salt

Fresh basil leaves, optional

▢ Line a 15-in. x 10-in. x 1-in. baking pan with foil and coat the foil with cooking spray. Place the onions, tomatoes, red pepper and garlic in pan. Drizzle with oil and toss to coat.

▢ Bake, uncovered, at 425° for 40-45 minutes or until tender and browned, stirring occasionally.

▢ In a large saucepan, combine the broth, half-and-half, chopped basil, chipotle pepper, pepper, salt and roasted vegetables. Bring to a boil. Reduce heat; simmer, uncovered, for 20-25 minutes. Cool slightly.

▢ In a blender, process soup in batches until smooth. Return all to the pan; heat through. Garnish with basil leaves if desired.

Yield: 6 servings.

NUTRITION FACTS: 1 cup equals 157 calories, 9 g fat (1 g saturated fat), 0 cholesterol, 528 mg sodium, 15 g carbohydrate, 3 g fiber, 5 g protein.

marjoram mushroom soup

This creamy and rich soup features fresh mushrooms, potato and the pleasant flavoring of marjoram.

MICHELE ODSTRCILEK LEMONT, ILLINOIS

1	large potato, peeled and diced
1	large leek (white portion only), chopped
1	medium onion, diced
2	tablespoons canola oil
1/2	pound sliced fresh mushrooms
4	cups chicken broth or vegetable broth
1	tablespoon minced fresh marjoram or 1 teaspoon dried marjoram, divided
1	cup (8 ounces) sour cream
2	tablespoons butter

Salt and pepper to taste

▢ In a Dutch oven, saute the potato, leek and onion in oil for 4 minutes. Add mushrooms and cook for 2 minutes. Stir in broth and half of the marjoram. Cover and simmer for 10 minutes or until potato is tender. Cool slightly.

▢ Puree in small batches in a blender; return all to pan. Whisk in sour cream and butter; season with salt and pepper. Heat through (do not boil). Just before serving, sprinkle with remaining marjoram.

Yield: 6 servings.

NUTRITION FACTS: 1 cup equals 213 calories, 16 g fat (8 g saturated fat), 37 mg cholesterol, 685 mg sodium, 13 g carbohydrate, 2 g fiber, 5 g protein.

garlic fennel bisque

I usually serve this in the spring as a wonderful first course. The fennel in this bisque is so refreshing.
JANET ONDRICH THAMESVILLE, ONTARIO

4	cups water
2-1/2	cups half-and-half cream
24	garlic cloves, peeled and halved
3	medium fennel bulbs, cut into 1/2-inch pieces
2	tablespoons chopped fennel fronds
1/2	teaspoon salt
1/8	teaspoon pepper
1/2	cup pine nuts, toasted

▢ In a Dutch oven, bring the water, cream and garlic to a boil. Reduce heat; cover and simmer for 15 minutes or until garlic is very soft. Add fennel and fennel fronds; cover and simmer 15 minutes longer or until fennel is very soft.

▢ Cool slightly. In a blender, process soup in batches until blended. Return all to the pan. Season with salt and pepper; heat through. Sprinkle each serving with pine nuts.

Yield: 14 servings (1/2 cup each).

NUTRITION FACTS: 1/2 cup soup with about 1-1/2 teaspoons pine nuts equals 108 calories, 7 g fat (3 g saturated fat), 21 mg cholesterol, 133 mg sodium, 8 g carbohydrate, 2 g fiber, 4 g protein. **DIABETIC EXCHANGES:** 1-1/2 fat, 1 vegetable.

easy carrot-beef soup

My husband's grandmother passed this recipe along to us, and it's just wonderful! This soup also freezes well.
WENDY WILKINS PRATTVILLE, ALABAMA

1	pound ground beef, browned and drained
1/2	cup chopped celery
1/2	cup chopped onion
1	cup chopped green pepper
2-1/2	cups grated carrots
1	can (32 ounces) tomato juice
2	cans (10-3/4 ounces each) condensed cream of celery soup, undiluted
1-1/2	cups water
1/2	teaspoon garlic salt
1/2	teaspoon dried marjoram
1	teaspoon sugar
1/2	teaspoon salt

Shredded Monterey Jack cheese

▢ In a Dutch oven, combine all ingredients except the cheese. Bring to a boil; reduce heat and simmer, uncovered, about 1 hour or until the vegetables are tender. Sprinkle each serving with cheese.

Yield: 10 servings (2-1/2 quarts).

NUTRITION FACTS: 1 cup (calculated without cheese) equals 130 calories, 5 g fat (2 g saturated fat), 23 mg cholesterol, 803 mg sodium, 11 g carbohydrate, 2 g fiber, 10 g protein.

roasted tomato soup with fresh basil for 2

Here's a delicious way to use up an abundance of fresh garden tomatoes. The thyme makes it taste extra fresh.
MARIE FORTE RARITAN, NEW JERSEY

1-1/4	pounds tomatoes (about 4 medium), halved
1	small onion, quartered
1	garlic clove, peeled and halved
1	tablespoon olive oil
1	tablespoon minced fresh thyme
1/2	teaspoon salt
1/8	teaspoon pepper
4	fresh basil leaves

Salad croutons and additional fresh basil leaves, optional

▢ Place the tomatoes, onion and garlic in a greased 15-in. x 10-in. x 1-in. baking pan; drizzle with oil. Sprinkle with thyme, salt and pepper; toss to coat. Bake at 400° for 25-30 minutes or until tender, stirring once. Cool slightly.

▢ In a blender, process tomato mixture and basil leaves until blended. Transfer to a saucepan and heat through. Top each serving with croutons and additional basil leaves if desired.

Yield: 2 servings.

NUTRITION FACTS: 1 cup (calculated without croutons) equals 129 calories, 7 g fat (1 g saturated fat), 0 cholesterol, 606 mg sodium, 15 g carbohydrate, 4 g fiber, 3 g protein. **DIABETIC EXCHANGES:** 3 vegetable, 1 fat.

curried acorn squash soup

Here is an easy soup that highlights the sweet flavor of acorn squash. The curry powder gives it a unique taste.
MARILOU ROBINSON PORTLAND, OREGON

3	medium acorn squash, halved and seeded
1/2	cup chopped onion
3	to 4 teaspoons curry powder
2	tablespoons butter
3	cups chicken broth
1	cup half-and-half cream
1/2	teaspoon ground nutmeg

Salt and pepper to taste
Crumbled cooked bacon, optional

▢ Place squash, cut side down, in a greased shallow baking pan. Bake at 350° for 35-40 minutes or until the squash is almost tender.

▢ In a large saucepan, saute onion and curry powder in butter until onion is tender. Remove from the heat; set aside. Carefully scoop out squash; add pulp to saucepan. Gradually add broth. Cook over medium heat for 15-20 minutes or until squash is very tender. Cool slightly.

▢ In a food processor, process the squash mixture until smooth; return to saucepan. Stir in the cream, nutmeg, salt and pepper. Cook over low heat until heated through (do not boil). Garnish with bacon if desired.

Yield: 6 servings.

NUTRITION FACTS: 1 cup (calculated without bacon) equals 196 calories, 8 g fat (5 g saturated fat), 30 mg cholesterol, 531 mg sodium, 28 g carbohydrate, 4 g fiber, 5 g protein.

savory root vegetable soup

Instead of the usual side dishes, consider serving a vegetable-laden soup at your next holiday meal. Each spoonful will warm the body and soul.

ZAN BROCK JASPER, ALABAMA

4	bacon strips
2	celery ribs, chopped
1	medium onion, chopped
1	medium green pepper, chopped
2	medium leeks (white portion only), chopped
2	cups frozen shredded hash brown potatoes
1	cup cubed peeled sweet potato
2	medium parsnips, peeled and chopped
2	medium carrots, peeled and chopped
2	small turnips, peeled and chopped
3	cans (14-1/2 ounces each) chicken broth
2	tablespoons minced fresh parsley
2	teaspoons herbes de Provence
1	garlic clove, minced
1/2	teaspoon white pepper
1/2	teaspoon ground coriander
1	cup (8 ounces) sour cream
1	cup (4 ounces) shredded Swiss cheese

In a Dutch oven, cook bacon over medium heat until crisp. Remove to paper towels; drain, reserving drippings. Crumble bacon and set aside. Saute the celery, onion, green pepper and leeks in drippings until tender.

Add the hash browns, sweet potato, parsnips, carrots and turnips; cook and stir over medium heat for 10 minutes.

Add the broth, parsley, herbes de Provence, garlic, white pepper and coriander; bring to a boil. Reduce heat; cover and simmer for 15-20 minutes or until vegetables are tender. Ladle soup into bowls. Top each serving with sour cream, cheese and crumbled bacon.

Yield: 8 servings (2 quarts).

NUTRITION FACTS: 1 cup equals 255 calories, 14 g fat (8 g saturated fat), 43 mg cholesterol, 855 mg sodium, 21 g carbohydrate, 4 g fiber, 9 g protein.

EDITOR'S NOTE: Look for herbes de Provence in the spice aisle.

roasted yellow pepper soup

We got this recipe from a good friend in New Hampshire. My husband and our two small children liked it so much that I started raising yellow peppers. We enjoy it in the middle of summer or on a cool fall day.

AMY SPURRIER WELLSBURG, WEST VIRGINIA

6	large sweet yellow peppers
1	large onion, chopped
1	cup chopped leeks (white portion only)
1/4	cup butter
3	small potatoes, peeled and cubed
5	cups chicken broth
1/2	teaspoon salt
1/2	teaspoon pepper

Shredded Parmesan cheese, optional

▢ Halve peppers; remove and discard tops and seeds. Broil peppers 4 in. from the heat until skins blister, about 4 minutes. Immediately place peppers in a bowl; cover and let stand for 15-20 minutes.

▢ Meanwhile, in a large saucepan, saute onion and leeks in butter until tender. Add the potatoes, broth, salt and pepper. Bring to a boil. Reduce heat; cover and simmer for 30 minutes or until potatoes are tender.

▢ Peel off and discard charred skins from peppers. Finely chop peppers; add to potato mixture. Cool mixture slightly.

▢ In a blender, cover and process soup in batches until smooth. Return to the pan; heat through (do not boil). Serve with Parmesan cheese if desired.

Yield: 8 cups (2 quarts).

NUTRITION FACTS: 1 cup (calculated without cheese) equals 124 calories, 6 g fat (4 g saturated fat), 18 mg cholesterol, 807 mg sodium, 16 g carbohydrate, 2 g fiber, 3 g protein.

morel mushroom soup

Some years, we have an abundance of morel mushrooms growing wild on our farm. I came up with this rich and flavorful soup to use these rare mushrooms.
GERALDINE DAVENPORT MADISON, WISCONSIN

1	pound fresh morel or other mushrooms, sliced
2	tablespoons lemon juice
1	large onion, chopped
3	tablespoons butter
2	tablespoons all-purpose flour
4	cups milk
3	teaspoons chicken bouillon granules
1/2	teaspoon dried thyme
1/2	teaspoon salt
1/8	teaspoon pepper

▨ Sprinkle mushrooms with lemon juice. In a saucepan, saute the mushrooms and onion in butter until tender. Sprinkle with flour; stir well. Gradually add milk, bouillon, thyme, salt and pepper. Bring to a boil; boil and stir for 2 minutes. Reduce heat; simmer for 10-15 minutes.

Yield: 6 servings.

NUTRITION FACTS: 1 cup equals 198 calories, 12 g fat (7 g saturated fat), 38 mg cholesterol, 896 mg sodium, 16 g carbohydrate, 2 g fiber, 9 g protein.

chilled cream of cucumber soup

We grow lots of cukes, but plenty are available from friends if you don't happen to have your own garden. This is a good make-ahead summer soup that is so cool and refreshing.
DORIS HEATH FRANKLIN, NORTH CAROLINA

1	medium onion, chopped
2	tablespoons butter
2	pounds cucumbers, peeled
5	cups chicken broth
1/4	cup minced fresh dill or 1 tablespoon dill weed
1	tablespoon balsamic vinegar
1/4	teaspoon salt
1/4	cup quick-cooking farina
1	cup (8 ounces) reduced-fat sour cream, divided

▨ In a large saucepan, saute onion in butter until tender. Slice 1/3 cup cucumbers; refrigerate. Chop the remaining cucumbers and add to onion mixture. Add the broth, dill, vinegar and salt; bring to a boil. Gradually add farina, stirring constantly. Reduce heat; simmer, uncovered, for 20 minutes, stirring occasionally. Cool slightly.

▨ In a blender, process soup in batches until pureed.

Pour into a container; refrigerate until chilled. Just before serving, whisk in 1/2 cup sour cream. Garnish each serving with reserved cucumber slices and a dollop of sour cream.

Yield: 8 servings (2 quarts).

NUTRITION FACTS: 1 cup equals 116 calories, 6 g fat (4 g saturated fat), 18 mg cholesterol, 707 mg sodium, 11 g carbohydrate, 1 g fiber, 5 g protein. **DIABETIC EXCHANGES:** 1 lean meat, 1 vegetable, 1/2 starch.

zesty gazpacho

When I have a taste for something different, or something with a little zip, gazpacho always hits the spot!
FRANCES DAWSON ORLANDO, FLORIDA

2	cans (28 ounces each) whole tomatoes
1	medium cucumber, peeled, seeded and cut into chunks
1	medium green pepper, cut into chunks
1	small onion, cut into chunks
1/3	cup red wine vinegar
2	slices rye bread, cubed
3	tablespoons olive oil
1/2	teaspoon salt
1/2	teaspoon garlic powder
1/4	teaspoon pepper
1/4	teaspoon hot pepper sauce

▨ Drain tomatoes, reserving juice. In a blender, cover and process the tomatoes, cucumber, green pepper and onion in batches until chopped. Transfer to a bowl.

▨ Place the vinegar, bread cubes and reserved tomato juice in blender; cover and process until smooth. Pour over vegetable mixture.

▨ Stir in the oil, salt, garlic powder, pepper and pepper sauce. Cover and refrigerate for 1-2 hours before serving.

Yield: 8 servings (2 quarts).

NUTRITION FACTS: 1 cup equals 122 calories, 5 g fat (1 g saturated fat), 0 cholesterol, 563 mg sodium, 16 g carbohydrate, 3 g fiber, 3 g protein.

tip!

GAZPACHO GARNISH

For an easy garnish, try topping your gazpacho with a sprinkling of finely chopped veggies and herbs. Chopped boiled egg is a classic Spanish garnish. Make the soup more rich and satisfying with a garnish of croutons and chopped egg.

special french onion soup

(pictured at left)

Combined with a salad, this rich soup is a meal for my husband and me. I top it with Brie, prosciutto and garlic on French bread to make it extra tasty.
LAURA MCALLISTER MORGANTON, NORTH CAROLINA

1/4	cup butter, cubed
1/4	cup plus 1 tablespoon olive oil, divided
6	large sweet onions, thinly sliced (about 12 cups)
1	whole garlic bulb
1/4	cup dry red wine or beef broth
6	cups beef broth
1-1/2	teaspoons Worcestershire sauce
1	bay leaf

Dash cayenne pepper
Pepper to taste

9	slices French bread (1 inch thick)
1	round (8 ounces) Brie cheese, rind removed, softened
6	thin slices prosciutto or deli ham, chopped
2	cups grated Parmesan cheese

▢ In Dutch oven over medium heat, melt butter with 1/4 cup oil; add onions. Cook, stirring, occasionally, for 15 minutes. Reduce heat to low. Cook 45 minutes longer or until onions are golden, stirring occasionally.

▢ Meanwhile, remove papery outer skin from garlic (do not peel or separate cloves). Cut top off garlic bulb; brush with remaining oil. Wrap in heavy-duty foil.

▢ Bake at 425° for 30-35 minutes or until softened. Cool for 10-15 minutes. Squeeze softened garlic into a small bowl; mash and set aside.

▢ Add wine to the onion mixture; cook for 2 minutes. Stir in the broth, Worcestershire sauce, bay leaf, cayenne and pepper. Bring to a boil. Reduce heat; simmer, uncovered, for 15-20 minutes.

▢ Place bread on a baking sheet. Bake at 425° for 3-5 minutes or until golden brown, turning once. Spread each slice with Brie and mashed garlic; sprinkle with prosciutto.

▢ Discard bay leaf from soup; ladle 1 cup each into nine ovenproof bowls. Top with one slice of toast; sprinkle with Parmesan cheese. Place bowls on a baking sheet. Bake for 10 minutes or until cheese is melted.

Yield: 9 servings.

NUTRITION FACTS: 1 serving equals 396 calories, 27 g fat (12 g saturated fat), 63 mg cholesterol, 1,348 mg sodium, 20 g carbohydrate, 2 g fiber, 19 g protein.

german vegetable soup

My sister-in-law gave me this recipe—it's a nice thick soup. It does call for quite a few ingredients, but the taste is worth it!
GUDRUN BRAKER BURNETT, WISCONSIN

1-1/2	pounds ground beef
2	medium onions, diced
2	tablespoons beef bouillon granules
1	cup water

Salt and pepper to taste

1/2	to 1 teaspoon garlic powder
1	bay leaf
1	can (46 ounces) tomato or vegetable juice
3	celery ribs, diced
6	medium carrots, sliced
3	medium potatoes, peeled and diced
3	cups shredded cabbage
1	small green pepper, chopped
1	can (15-1/4 ounces) whole kernel corn, drained
1	can (8-1/2 ounces) peas, drained
1	can (8 ounces) cut green beans, drained

▢ In a Dutch oven, cook beef and onions over medium heat until meat is no longer pink; drain.

▢ Dissolve bouillon in water; add to the beef mixture. Add the salt, pepper, garlic, bay leaf, tomato juice, celery, carrots, potatoes, cabbage and green pepper.

▢ Simmer, uncovered, for 25 minutes or until vegetables are tender. Stir in the corn, peas and beans; heat through. Discard bay leaf before serving.

Yield: 16 servings (4 quarts).

NUTRITION FACTS: 1 cup equals 167 calories, 4 g fat (2 g saturated fat), 21 mg cholesterol, 730 mg sodium, 21 g carbohydrate, 4 g fiber, 11 g protein.

buttery onion soup

(pictured above)

I developed this recipe when I had an abundance of sweet onions. I like making it for guests. Sometimes I'll halve the recipe and make some just for me!
SHARON BERTHELOTE SUNBURST, MONTANA

2	cups thinly sliced onions
1/2	cup butter
1/4	cup all-purpose flour
2	cups chicken broth
2	cups milk
1-1/2	to 2 cups (6 to 8 ounces) shredded part-skim mozzarella cheese

Salt and pepper to taste
Croutons, optional

▢ In a large saucepan, cook onions in butter over low heat until tender and transparent, about 20 minutes.

▢ Stir in flour. Gradually add broth and milk; cook and stir over medium heat until bubbly. Cook and stir for 1 minute longer; reduce heat to low. Add mozzarella cheese and stir constantly until melted (do not boil). Season to taste with salt and pepper. Serve with croutons if desired.

Yield: 6 servings.

NUTRITION FACTS: 1 cup equals 294 calories, 23 g fat (14 g saturated fat), 66 mg cholesterol, 600 mg sodium, 12 g carbohydrate, 1 g fiber, 11 g protein.

cream of celery soup

This rich celery soup will warm up any family gathering or quiet evening at home. With just the right amount of onion flavor, it's creamy and crowd-pleasing.
JANET JAMES BLUFF CITY, TENNESSEE

4	cups chopped onions
3-1/3	cups water
6	celery ribs, chopped
4	teaspoons beef bouillon granules
1-1/2	teaspoons salt
1/2	teaspoon pepper
1/2	cup all-purpose flour
1	cup milk
1	cup (4 ounces) shredded reduced-fat Mexican cheese blend

▢ In a large saucepan, combine onions, water, celery, bouillon, salt and pepper. Bring to a boil. Reduce heat; cover and simmer for 10 minutes or until vegetables are tender.

▢ Combine the flour and milk until smooth; gradually stir into onion mixture. Bring to a boil; cook and stir for 2 minutes or until thickened. Reduce heat; stir in cheese until melted.

Yield: 7 servings.

NUTRITION FACTS: 1 cup equals 144 calories, 5 g fat (3 g saturated fat), 16 mg cholesterol, 1,120 mg sodium, 19 g carbohydrate, 3 g fiber, 8 g protein.

apres-ski soup

Apres-ski, French for "after skiing," refers to the social time directly after getting off the slopes, and this microwave soup is perfect for the occasion. Chock-full of healthful veggies, this one will warm you from head to toe.
NANCY HAMLIN LITTLETON, COLORADO

1	tablespoon butter
1-1/4	cups cubed acorn squash
1	carrot, thinly sliced
1	medium leek (white portion only), thinly sliced
3	cans (14-1/2 ounces each) reduced-sodium chicken broth
1	small zucchini, halved and sliced
1/2	cup uncooked elbow macaroni
1	bay leaf
1/2	teaspoon dried basil
1/4	teaspoon dried thyme
1/8	teaspoon salt
1/8	teaspoon pepper

▨ Place butter in a 3-qt. microwave-safe bowl; microwave on high for 20-30 seconds or until melted. Add the squash, carrot and leek; stir to coat. Cover and cook on high for 6 minutes.

▨ Stir in the remaining ingredients; cover and cook on high for 12-14 minutes or until vegetables and macaroni are tender, stirring twice. Discard bay leaf.

Yield: 6 servings.

NUTRITION FACTS: 1 cup equals 92 calories, 2 g fat (1 g saturated fat), 5 mg cholesterol, 594 mg sodium, 15 g carbohydrate, 3 g fiber, 4 g protein. DIABETIC EXCHANGES: 1 vegetable, 1/2 starch, 1/2 fat.

EDITOR'S NOTE: This recipe was tested in a 1,100-watt microwave.

zucchini soup

When there's an abundance of zucchini in our garden, I know it's time for this fresh-tasting soup.
SUE FRIEND LYNDEN, WASHINGTON

1	cup chopped onion
1	cup thinly sliced celery
1	garlic clove, minced
1/4	cup chopped green pepper
1	tablespoon canola oil
2	pounds zucchini, chopped
2	medium tomatoes, chopped
3	cups chicken or vegetable broth
1/2	teaspoon dried basil
1/4	teaspoon dried thyme
1	cup half-and-half cream or milk

▨ In a large saucepan, saute onion, celery, garlic and green pepper in oil until tender. Add zucchini, tomatoes, broth, basil and thyme; bring to a boil. Reduce heat; simmer, uncovered, for 20-30 minutes or until the vegetables are tender. Stir in cream; heat through. Serve hot or cold.

Yield: 8 servings (2 quarts).

NUTRITION FACTS: 1 cup equals 98 calories, 5 g fat (2 g saturated fat), 17 mg cholesterol, 409 mg sodium, 9 g carbohydrate, 2 g fiber, 3 g protein. DIABETIC EXCHANGES: 2 vegetable, 1 fat.

chipotle butternut squash soup

(pictured at left)

Here's a rich and satisfying vegetarian main-dish soup. It's a great way to use your garden veggies and herbs.

ROXANNE CHAN ALBANY, CALIFORNIA

- 2 cups diced peeled butternut squash
- 1 small carrot, finely chopped
- 1 green onion, sliced
- 1/2 teaspoon ground cumin
- 1 tablespoon olive oil
- 2 garlic cloves, minced
- 2 cups vegetable broth, divided
- 1 can (14-1/2 ounces) diced tomatoes, undrained
- 1 package (3 ounces) cream cheese, cubed
- 1/4 cup chopped fresh basil
- 1 chipotle pepper in adobo sauce, chopped
- 1 can (15 ounces) black beans, rinsed and drained
- 1 can (11 ounces) Mexicorn, drained
- 2 cups fresh baby spinach, chopped

▢ In a large saucepan, saute the squash, carrot, onion and cumin in oil for 10 minutes. Add garlic; cook 1 minute longer. Add 1-1/2 cups broth; bring to a boil. Reduce heat. Cover and simmer for 10-12 minutes or until vegetables are tender; cool slightly.

▢ Transfer mixture to a blender; add the tomatoes, cream cheese, basil, chipotle pepper and remaining broth. Cover and process for 1-2 minutes or until smooth.

▢ Return to the saucepan; stir in the beans, corn and spinach. Cook and stir until spinach is wilted and soup is heated through.

Yield: 5 servings.

NUTRITION FACTS: 1-1/3 cups equals 279 calories, 9 g fat (4 g saturated fat), 19 mg cholesterol, 1,097 mg sodium, 43 g carbohydrate, 10 g fiber, 10 g protein.

tomato soup with cheese tortellini

Tortellini gives this garden-fresh tomato soup a stick-to-your-ribs goodness. This recipe is a regular in my repertoire.

SUSAN PECK REPUBLIC, MISSOURI

- 1 large onion, chopped
- 1 tablespoon butter
- 2 pounds plum tomatoes, seeded and quartered
- 3 cups reduced-sodium chicken broth or vegetable broth
- 1 can (8 ounces) tomato sauce
- 1 tablespoon minced fresh basil
- 1/4 teaspoon salt
- Dash pepper
- 1 cup dried cheese tortellini
- 1/3 cup shredded Parmesan cheese

▢ In a large saucepan, saute onion in butter until tender. Add the tomatoes, broth, tomato sauce, basil, salt and pepper. Bring to a boil. Reduce heat; cover and simmer for 30 minutes. Cool slightly.

▢ Cook tortellini according to package directions; drain well and set aside. In a blender, cover and process soup in batches until smooth. Return to the saucepan; add tortellini and heat through. Garnish with cheese.

Yield: 8 servings (2 quarts).

NUTRITION FACTS: 1-1/3 cups equals 114 calories, 4 g fat (2 g saturated fat), 14 mg cholesterol, 609 mg sodium, 15 g carbohydrate, 2 g fiber, 6 g protein. **DIABETIC EXCHANGES:** 2 vegetable, 1/2 starch, 1/2 fat.

corn soup with pico de gallo

This Southwestern soup has a wonderful aroma that quickly lures my family to the dinner table. The blend of seasonings and succulent pico de gallo add to its fabulous flavor.
ELAINE SWEET DALLAS, TEXAS

3	corn tortillas (6 inches), cut into 1-inch strips
4	medium ears sweet corn, husks removed
1/2	teaspoon canola oil
1/2	teaspoon each salt, pepper and paprika
1	medium red onion, chopped
1	bacon strip, chopped
6	garlic cloves, minced
1/4	cup all-purpose flour
3	cups reduced-sodium chicken broth
1	cup fat-free milk
1	can (4 ounces) chopped green chilies
1	teaspoon ground cumin
1	teaspoon dried oregano
1/2	cup minced fresh cilantro
1/4	cup lime juice

PICO DE GALLO:

2	plum tomatoes, chopped
1	medium ripe avocado, peeled and chopped
1	small serrano pepper, seeded and chopped
1	garlic clove, minced
1/4	teaspoon salt
1/4	teaspoon pepper

▢ Place tortilla strips on a baking sheet coated with cooking spray; bake at 350° for 8-10 minutes or until crisp.

▢ Rub corn with canola oil; sprinkle with seasonings. Moisten a paper towel with cooking oil; using long-handled tongs, lightly coat the grill rack.

▢ Grill corn, covered, over medium heat for 10-12 minutes or until tender, turning frequently. Cool slightly; cut corn from cobs and set aside.

▢ In a large saucepan, saute onion and bacon for 5 minutes; add garlic, cook 1 minute longer. Stir in flour until blended; gradually add broth. Bring to a boil; cook and stir for 2 minutes or until thickened. Add corn, milk, chilies, cumin and oregano; heat through. Remove from heat; stir in cilantro and lime juice.

▢ Combine pico de gallo ingredients. Serve with soup and tortilla strips.

Yield: 6 servings.

NUTRITION FACTS: 3/4 cup soup with 1/4 cup pico de gallo and 3 tortilla strips equals 217 calories, 8 g fat (1 g saturated fat), 3 mg cholesterol, 740 mg sodium, 33 g carbohydrate, 6 g fiber, 8 g protein. **DIABETIC EXCHANGES:** 2 starch, 1-1/2 fat.

EDITOR'S NOTE: Wear disposable gloves when cutting hot peppers; the oils can burn skin. Avoid touching your face.

pea soup with quinoa

This soup is low in fat, high in fiber, has a fantastically fresh flavor and a wonderful texture. Plus, it's so simple to make!
JANE HACKER MILWAUKEE, WISCONSIN

- 1 cup water
- 1/2 cup quinoa, rinsed
- 1 medium onion, chopped
- 2 teaspoons canola oil
- 2 cans (14-1/2 ounces each) reduced-sodium chicken broth or vegetable broth
- 2 packages (10 ounces each) frozen peas
- 1/2 teaspoon salt
- 1/4 teaspoon pepper
- 2 teaspoons reduced-fat plain yogurt

▢ In a small saucepan, bring water to a boil. Add quinoa. Reduce heat; cover and simmer for 12-15 minutes or until water is absorbed.

▢ Meanwhile, in a large saucepan, saute onion in oil until tender. Stir in broth and peas. Bring to a boil. Reduce heat; simmer, uncovered, for 5 minutes or until peas are tender. Cool slightly.

▢ In a blender, process soup in batches until smooth. Return all to the pan. Stir in the salt, pepper and quinoa; heat through. Garnish each serving with 1/2 teaspoon yogurt.

Yield: 4 servings.

NUTRITION FACTS: 1-1/2 cups equals 236 calories, 4 g fat (trace saturated fat), trace cholesterol, 858 mg sodium, 38 g carbohydrate, 9 g fiber, 13 g protein. **DIABETIC EXCHANGES:** 2-1/2 starch, 1/2 fat.

EDITOR'S NOTE: Look for quinoa in the cereal, rice or organic food aisle.

makeover cauliflower soup

Creamy soups can be soul-warming and satisfying, and this cauliflower soup is no exception. The Taste of Home Test Kitchen made a healthier version of this recipe that I received from a friend.
DORIS WATT DAVIS HELLERTOWN, PENNSYLVANIA

- 2 celery ribs, chopped
- 1 small onion, chopped
- 1 medium carrot, chopped
- 2 tablespoons butter
- 1 large head cauliflower (2 pounds), broken into florets
- 6 cups reduced-sodium chicken broth
- 1/2 cup all-purpose flour
- 2 cups 2% milk
- 3/4 cup fat-free half-and-half
- 1 tablespoon minced fresh parsley
- 1 teaspoon salt
- 1 teaspoon dill weed
- 1/4 teaspoon white pepper

▢ In a Dutch oven, saute the celery, onion and carrot in butter for 3-5 minutes or until crisp-tender. Stir in cauliflower and broth; bring to a boil. Reduce heat; cover and simmer for 15-20 minutes or until tender. Cool slightly.

▢ In a blender, process vegetable mixture in batches until smooth. Return all to the pan and heat through over medium heat.

▢ In a small bowl, whisk flour and milk until smooth; stir into puree. Bring to a boil; cook and stir for 2 minutes or until thickened. Reduce heat; stir in the half-and-half, parsley, salt, dill and pepper. Heat through.

Yield: 11 servings (2-3/4 quarts).

NUTRITION FACTS: 1 cup equals 106 calories, 3 g fat (2 g saturated fat), 9 mg cholesterol, 641 mg sodium, 14 g carbohydrate, 3 g fiber, 6 g protein. **DIABETIC EXCHANGES:** 1 vegetable, 1/2 starch, 1/2 fat.

pureed carrot soup

This bright and creamy soup is my son's favorite. I like that it's fast, easy and makes a perfect amount for the two of us when my husband is away at work.
ROBYN LARABEE LUCKNOW, ONTARIO

2	cups chopped carrots
1/4	cup chopped onion
1	tablespoon butter
1	can (14-1/2 ounces) chicken broth
1/4	teaspoon ground ginger
1/2	cup buttermilk

In a small saucepan, saute carrots and onion in butter until crisp-tender. Add broth and ginger. Bring to a boil. Reduce heat; cover and simmer for 10-15 minutes or until carrots are very tender. Cool slightly.

Puree soup in a blender; return to the pan. Stir in buttermilk; heat through (do not boil).

Yield: 2-1/2 cups.

NUTRITION FACTS: 3/4 cup equals 100 calories, 5 g fat (3 g saturated fat), 15 mg cholesterol, 721 mg sodium, 12 g carbohydrate, 3 g fiber, 3 g protein.

vegetarian polka dot stew

Here's a speedy and satisfying version of traditional minestrone. The fun polka-dot shapes of the couscous, black beans and sliced baby carrots give this stew its name.
TEAGAN O'TOOLE BOSTON, MASSACHUSETTS

2	cups water
1	cup uncooked Israeli couscous
2	medium carrots, sliced
1	plum tomato, chopped
1/4	cup chopped onion
1	garlic clove, minced
2	cans (19 ounces each) ready-to-serve tomato soup
1	can (15 ounces) black beans, rinsed and drained
1	package (10 ounces) frozen chopped spinach, thawed and squeezed dry
1	tablespoon minced fresh basil or 1 teaspoon dried basil
1/2	teaspoon salt
1/2	teaspoon dried oregano
1/2	teaspoon dried marjoram
1/4	teaspoon pepper

Shredded Parmesan cheese

In a saucepan, bring water to a boil. Stir in the couscous, carrots, tomato, onion and garlic. Bring to a boil. Reduce heat; simmer, uncovered, for 10-15 minutes or until tender and water is absorbed. Stir in the remaining ingredients; heat through. Sprinkle with cheese.

Yield: 5 servings.

NUTRITION FACTS: 1-1/2 cups (calculated without cheese) equals 309 calories, 2 g fat (trace saturated fat), 0 cholesterol, 879 mg sodium, 60 g carbohydrate, 10 g fiber, 14 g protein.

EDITOR'S NOTE: You may substitute 1 cup quick-cooking barley for the couscous if desired.

cabbage patch soup

People are always glad to see this nutritious soup on the menu. Loaded with veggies, meat and beans, it's high in protein and flavor, but low in fat.
FRAN STROTHER WASILLA, ALASKA

1/2	pound ground beef
1-1/2	cups chopped onion
1/2	cup sliced celery
2	cups water
1	can (16 ounces) kidney beans, rinsed and drained
1	can (14-1/2 ounces) stewed tomatoes
1	cup shredded cabbage
1	teaspoon chili powder
1/2	teaspoon salt

Hot mashed potatoes, optional

In a large saucepan over medium heat, brown beef until no longer pink; drain. Add onion and celery; cook until tender. Stir in the water, beans, tomatoes, cabbage, chili powder and salt; bring to a boil. Reduce heat; cover and simmer for 20-30 minutes or until cabbage is tender. Top each bowl with mashed potatoes if desired.

Yield: 4-6 servings.

NUTRITION FACTS: 1 cup equals 180 calories, 5 g fat (2 g saturated fat), 25 mg cholesterol, 476 mg sodium, 22 g carbohydrate, 5 g fiber, 14 g protein.

veggie tortellini soup

Make great use of tortellini and frozen veggies with this no-fuss recipe. If you'd like, add a sprinkle of Parmesan cheese to the top or a small drizzle of balsamic vinegar.

HELEN REHBERGER PEWAUKEE, WISCONSIN

5	cups chicken broth
1	package (16 ounces) frozen California-blend vegetables
1	package (8 ounces) dried cheese tortellini
1	can (14-1/2 ounces) Italian diced tomatoes, undrained

☐ In a Dutch oven, bring broth to a boil. Stir in vegetables and tortellini. Return to a boil. Reduce heat; simmer, uncovered, for 10-12 minutes or until vegetables are tender, stirring occasionally. Stir in tomatoes. Cover and cook for 5-6 minutes or until heated through.

Yield: 6 servings.

NUTRITION FACTS: 1-1/2 cups equals 215 calories, 6 g fat (3 g saturated fat), 31 mg cholesterol, 1,431 mg sodium, 32 g carbohydrate, 4 g fiber, 9 g protein.

best broccoli soup

(pictured at left)

Here's a creamy, comforting soup that beautifully showcases broccoli. It's a delicious way to eat your vegetables!
CAROLYN WEINBERG HARDIN, MONTANA

2	cups water
4	cups chopped fresh broccoli (about 1-1/2 pounds)
1	cup chopped celery
1	cup chopped carrots
1/2	cup chopped onion
6	tablespoons butter
6	tablespoons all-purpose flour
3	cups chicken broth
2	cups 2% milk
1	tablespoon minced fresh parsley
1	teaspoon onion salt
1/2	teaspoon garlic powder
1/2	teaspoon salt

In a Dutch oven, bring water to boil. Add the broccoli, celery and carrots; boil 2-3 minutes or until crisp-tender. Drain; set vegetables aside.

In the same pot, saute onion in butter until tender. Stir in flour until blended. Gradually stir in broth and milk until smooth. Bring to a boil; cook and stir for 1 minute or until thickened.

Stir in reserved vegetables and remaining ingredients. Reduce heat; cook, stirring occasionally, for 15 minutes or until vegetables are tender.

Yield: 6-8 servings (2 quarts).

NUTRITION FACTS: 1 cup equals 164 calories, 11 g fat (7 g saturated fat), 31 mg cholesterol, 868 mg sodium, 13 g carbohydrate, 2 g fiber, 5 g protein.

mushroom barley soup

Here's a hearty soup that is delicious and full of vegetables. I like to eat it with warm bread smothered in butter.
CONSTANCE SULLIVAN OCEANSIDE, CALIFORNIA

1/2	cup dried great northern beans
1	pound sliced fresh mushrooms
2	cups chopped onions
1	medium leek (white portion only), sliced
2	tablespoons butter
1	to 2 garlic cloves, minced
2	cartons (32 ounces each) chicken broth
3	celery ribs, thinly sliced
3	large carrots, chopped
1/2	cup medium pearl barley
2	teaspoons dried parsley flakes
1-1/2	teaspoons salt
1	bay leaf
1/4	teaspoon white pepper

Soak beans according to package directions. In a large skillet, cook the mushrooms, onions and leek in butter over medium heat until tender. Add garlic; cook 1 minute longer.

Transfer to a 6-quart slow cooker. Drain and rinse beans, discarding liquid. Add the beans, broth, celery, carrots, barley, parsley, salt, bay leaf and pepper. Cover and cook on low for 5-6 hours or until beans and vegetables are tender. Discard bay leaf.

Yield: 12 servings (3 quarts).

NUTRITION FACTS: 1 cup equals 116 calories, 3 g fat (1 g saturated fat), 8 mg cholesterol, 988 mg sodium, 19 g carbohydrate, 5 g fiber, 5 g protein.

italian-style onion soup

On a chilly winter's day, warm everyone with a steaming pot of this veggie soup. Each bowlful is crowned with a slice of cheesy tomato-topped toast.

DEBBIE MILLER OLDSMAR, FLORIDA

2	tablespoons butter
1	tablespoon olive oil
6	medium sweet onions, thinly sliced (about 6 cups)
1/2	teaspoon minced fresh rosemary
1/4	teaspoon salt, divided
1/4	teaspoon pepper, divided
6	cups beef broth
1/2	cup white wine or additional beef broth
1	tablespoon balsamic vinegar
1	cup grape tomatoes, quartered
1/2	cup fresh basil leaves, thinly sliced
1/4	cup grated Parmesan cheese
1/2	teaspoon garlic powder
5	slices day-old French bread (1-1/2 inches thick), toasted
5	slices part-skim mozzarella cheese

☐ In a Dutch oven over medium heat, melt butter with the oil. Add the onions, rosemary, 1/8 teaspoon salt and 1/8 teaspoon pepper. Cook for 30 minutes or until lightly browned, stirring occasionally. Add the broth, wine and vinegar; heat through.

☐ Meanwhile, in a small bowl, combine the tomatoes, basil, Parmesan cheese, garlic powder and remaining salt and pepper. Spoon tomato mixture over bread slices; top with mozzarella. Place on a baking sheet.

☐ Broil 3-4 in. from the heat for 2-3 minutes or until cheese is melted. Ladle soup into bowls; top with toast. Serve immediately.

Yield: 5 servings.

NUTRITION FACTS: 1 serving equals 349 calories, 16 g fat (8 g saturated fat), 31 mg cholesterol, 1,579 mg sodium, 33 g carbohydrate, 4 g fiber, 16 g protein.

pumpkin corn soup

My family loves this soup, especially on cold winter nights. It's definitely not your normal pumpkin soup! If you have fresh cilantro, it's a nice garnish.
MELISSA EVERY AUSTIN, TEXAS

- 1 large onion, chopped
- 1 medium sweet red pepper, chopped
- 2 tablespoons butter
- 2 cups fresh or frozen corn, thawed
- 1 jalapeno pepper, seeded and chopped
- 2 garlic cloves, minced
- 2 teaspoons chili powder
- 2 cans (14-1/2 ounces each) vegetable broth
- 1 can (15 ounces) solid-pack pumpkin
- 1/2 teaspoon salt
- Dash cayenne pepper
- 2 tablespoons lime juice

▢ In a large saucepan, saute onion and red pepper in butter until almost tender. Add the corn, jalapeno, garlic and chili powder; saute 2 minutes longer.

▢ Stir in the broth, pumpkin, salt and cayenne until blended. Bring to a boil. Reduce heat; cover and simmer for 10 minutes. Stir in lime juice.

Yield: 7 servings.

NUTRITION FACTS: 1 cup equals 120 calories, 5 g fat (2 g saturated fat), 9 mg cholesterol, 714 mg sodium, 20 g carbohydrate, 5 g fiber, 4 g protein. **DIABETIC EXCHANGES:** 1 starch, 1/2 fat.

EDITOR'S NOTE: Wear disposable gloves when cutting hot peppers; the oils can burn skin. Avoid touching your face.

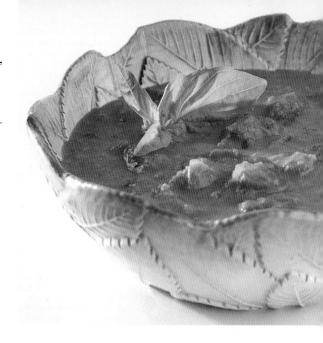

tomato-basil bisque

My husband makes this wonderful creamy bisque. Sweet red pepper enhances the lovely tomato-basil flavor.
VERONIQUE DEBLOIS MINE HILL, NEW JERSEY

- 6 celery ribs, chopped
- 1 large onion, chopped
- 1 medium sweet red pepper, chopped
- 1/4 cup butter
- 3 cans (14-1/2 ounces each) diced tomatoes, undrained
- 1 tablespoon tomato paste
- 3/4 cup loosely packed basil leaves, coarsely chopped
- 3 teaspoons sugar
- 2 teaspoons salt
- 1/2 teaspoon pepper
- 1-1/2 cups heavy whipping cream

▢ In a large saucepan, saute the celery, onion and red pepper in butter for 5-6 minutes or until tender. Add tomatoes and tomato paste. Bring to a boil. Reduce heat; cover and simmer for 40 minutes.

▢ Remove from the heat. Stir in the basil, sugar, salt and pepper; cool slightly. Transfer half of the soup mixture to a blender. While processing, gradually add cream; process until pureed. Return to the pan; heat through (do not boil).

Yield: 5 servings.

NUTRITION FACTS: 1-1/3 cups equals 383 calories, 36 g fat (22 g saturated fat), 122 mg cholesterol, 1,214 mg sodium, 15 g carbohydrate, 4 g fiber, 3 g protein.

butternut soup with parmesan croutons

Roasting creates a rich, caramelized flavor, but you can cook the squash cubes directly in the broth if you're short on time. They should pierce easily with a fork when they're done.
JEN LEHNER SEATTLE, WASHINGTON

1	medium butternut squash (about 3 pounds), peeled, seeded and cut into 1-inch cubes
2	tablespoons olive oil, divided
1/4	teaspoon pepper
1	large onion, chopped
3	celery ribs, chopped
2	tablespoons minced fresh sage or 2 teaspoons rubbed sage
3	cans (14-1/2 ounces each) reduced-sodium chicken broth

CROUTONS:

2	tablespoons grated Parmesan cheese
2	tablespoons olive oil
1	tablespoon minced fresh sage or 1 teaspoon rubbed sage
2	garlic cloves, minced
2	cups cubed French bread (1/2-inch cubes)

Cooking spray
Additional grated Parmesan cheese, optional

▢ Place squash in a 15-in. x 10-in. x 1-in. baking pan lightly coated with cooking spray. Drizzle with 1 tablespoon oil; sprinkle with pepper. Toss to coat. Bake, uncovered, at 425° for 30-35 minutes or until tender, stirring every 15 minutes. Set aside.

▢ In a Dutch oven, saute the onion, celery and sage in remaining oil until tender. Stir in the broth and squash. Bring to a boil. Reduce heat; cover and simmer for 15-20 minutes to allow flavors to blend. Cool slightly.

▢ In a blender, puree soup in batches until smooth. Return to the pan; heat through.

▢ For croutons, in a small bowl, combine the cheese, oil, sage and garlic. Add bread cubes and spritz with cooking spray; toss to coat. Place on a baking sheet coated with cooking spray.

▢ Bake at 425° for 5-8 minutes or until golden brown, stirring occasionally.

▢ Sprinkle each serving of soup with croutons and additional cheese if desired.

Yield: 8 servings (2 quarts).

NUTRITION FACTS: 1 cup soup with 1/4 cup croutons equals 179 calories, 8 g fat (1 g saturated fat), 1 mg cholesterol, 541 mg sodium, 25 g carbohydrate, 6 g fiber, 5 g protein. **DIABETIC EXCHANGES:** 1-1/2 starch, 1 fat.

bread right now

red onion focaccia

(pictured above)

Cooking the onions in oil before using them to top this quick focaccia gives them a mellow flavor with just a hint of crispness.

TASTE OF HOME TEST KITCHEN

2	small red onions, sliced and separated into rings
3	tablespoons olive oil, divided
1	tube (13.8 ounces) refrigerated pizza crust
2	tablespoons grated Parmesan cheese
2	tablespoons grated Romano cheese
1	teaspoon dried rosemary, crushed
1	teaspoon garlic powder

◻ In a large skillet, saute onions in 1 tablespoon oil for 4 minutes; set aside.

◻ On a greased baking sheet, roll out pizza crust into a 12-in. x 8-in. rectangle. Brush with remaining oil. Sprinkle with the cheeses, rosemary and garlic powder. Top with onions.

◻ Bake at 425° for 14-16 minutes or until lightly browned.

Yield: 6 servings.

NUTRITION FACTS: 1 serving equals 213 calories, 10 g fat (2 g saturated fat), 4 mg cholesterol, 382 mg sodium, 25 g carbohydrate, 1 g fiber, 6 g protein.

three-cheese flatbread

I use refrigerated pizza dough to make a crowd-sized batch of flatbread that's table-ready in just 20 minutes. Try it with warm spaghetti sauce for dipping.

TOM HILLIKER LAKE HAVASU CITY, ARIZONA

1	tube (13.8 ounces) refrigerated pizza crust
1/4	cup butter, melted
4	garlic cloves, minced
1	tablespoon minced fresh basil
1	cup (4 ounces) shredded cheddar cheese
1/2	cup grated Romano cheese
1/4	cup grated Parmesan cheese

◻ Press dough onto a greased 15-in. x 10-in. x 1-in. baking pan. In a small bowl, combine butter, garlic and basil; drizzle over dough. Sprinkle with the cheeses.

◻ Bake at 400° for 10-12 minutes or until crisp. Cut into squares. Serve warm.

Yield: 12-15 servings.

NUTRITION FACTS: 1 piece equals 145 calories, 8 g fat (5 g saturated fat), 21 mg cholesterol, 331 mg sodium, 13 g carbohydrate, trace fiber, 6 g protein.

beer 'n' brat biscuits

My husband, our three girls and I all love to cook, so we're always coming up with something new to try. These yummy biscuits require just four ingredients, including leftover brats. Serve them with mustard and a big bowl of bean soup.
NANCY BOURGET ROUND ROCK, TEXAS

- 2 fully cooked bratwurst links
- 4 cups biscuit/baking mix
- 2 to 3 teaspoons caraway seeds
- 1 can (12 ounces) beer or nonalcoholic beer

▢ Cut bratwurst into bite-size pieces. In a large bowl, combine the biscuit mix, caraway seeds and bratwurst; stir in beer just until moistened. Fill greased muffin cups two-thirds full.

▢ Bake at 400° for 18-20 minutes or until golden brown. Cool for 5 minutes before removing from pans to wire racks. Serve warm. Refrigerate leftovers.

Yield: 16 biscuits.

NUTRITION FACTS: 1 biscuit equals 164 calories, 7 g fat (2 g saturated fat), 6 mg cholesterol, 438 mg sodium, 20 g carbohydrate, 1 g fiber, 4 g protein.

apricot-date mini loaves

By using a prepared quick bread mix, it's easy to make a loaf of this apricot-date bread for yourself and extras to give to family and friends.
MARILYN MINER SANTA MARGARITA, CALIFORNIA

- 1 package (18.3 ounces) cinnamon streusel quick bread mix
- 1/2 teaspoon baking powder
- 2 eggs, lightly beaten
- 2/3 cup orange juice
- 1/2 cup chopped dried apricots
- 1/2 cup chopped dates

▢ Set aside streusel topping packet from quick bread mix. In a large bowl, combine quick bread mix and baking powder. Make a well in the center; add eggs and orange juice. Stir just until moistened. Fold in apricots and dates.

▢ Pour into four greased 5-in. x 3-in. x 2-in. loaf pans. Top with half of the streusel; cut through with a knife to swirl. Sprinkle with remaining streusel; press gently.

▢ Bake at 350° for 25-28 minutes or until a toothpick inserted near the center comes out clean. Cool for 10 minutes before removing from pans to wire racks.

Yield: 4 loaves (5 slices each).

NUTRITION FACTS: 1 slice equals 151 calories, 4 g fat (1 g saturated fat), 21 mg cholesterol, 124 mg sodium, 28 g carbohydrate, 1 g fiber, 1 g protein.

chocolate-pecan sticky buns

You won't believe how delicious these super-easy, four-ingredient rolls are! They have surprise chocolate kisses inside that guests will love. Try them as an impromptu dessert or for a special brunch.
TAMMY LOGAN OAK RIDGE, TENNESSEE

1	can (15 ounces) coconut-pecan frosting
1	cup pecan halves
2	tubes (12 ounces each) refrigerated buttermilk biscuits
20	milk chocolate kisses

▢ Spread frosting over the bottom of a greased 9-in. square baking pan. Arrange pecans over frosting; set aside.

▢ Flatten each biscuit to 1/4-in. thickness. Place a chocolate kiss in the center of each biscuit. Bring up edges of dough and pinch to seal. Arrange biscuits, flat side down, over pecans.

▢ Bake at 400° for 25-30 minutes or until golden brown. Cool on a wire rack for 5 minutes. Invert onto a serving plate; serve immediately.

Yield: 20 servings.

NUTRITION FACTS: 1 bun equals 229 calories, 11 g fat (3 g saturated fat), 1 mg cholesterol, 325 mg sodium, 30 g carbohydrate, 1 g fiber, 4 g protein.

biscuits italiano

These biscuits couldn't be much simpler to make! And with from-scratch flavor and a golden-brown cheese topping, they're sure to be a hit.
LYNN TICE OSAGE CITY, KANSAS

1	tube (12 ounces) refrigerated buttermilk biscuits
1/4	cup prepared Italian salad dressing
1/3	cup grated Parmesan cheese
1/2	cup shredded part-skim mozzarella cheese

▢ Separate biscuits; dip the top of each in salad dressing, then in Parmesan cheese. Place cheese side up on an ungreased baking sheet; sprinkle with mozzarella cheese.

▢ Bake at 400° for 9-11 minutes or until golden brown. Serve warm.

Yield: 10 biscuits.

NUTRITION FACTS: 1 biscuit equals 130 calories, 5 g fat (1 g saturated fat), 6 mg cholesterol, 459 mg sodium, 17 g carbohydrate, trace fiber, 5 g protein.

crab crescent loaf

Golden crescent roll slices are scrumptious filled with dilled cream cheese and tender crab. You're sure to appreciate this recipe's rich flavor and easy preparation.
MAUREEN DONGOSKI PETERSBURG, WEST VIRGINIA

1	tube (8 ounces) refrigerated crescent rolls
2	packages (3 ounces each) cream cheese, softened
1/3	cup chopped onion
1/2	teaspoon dill weed
1	cup imitation crabmeat or 1 can (6 ounces) lump crabmeat, drained
1	egg yolk, lightly beaten

▣ On a greased baking sheet, unroll crescent dough into one long rectangle; seal seams and perforations. In a small bowl, beat the cream cheese, onion and dill until blended. Spread mixture lengthwise over half of the dough to within 1/2 in. of edges. Top with crab.

▣ Fold dough over filling; pinch seam to seal. Brush the top with egg yolk. Bake at 375° for 18-22 minutes or until golden brown. Cut into slices.

Yield: 1 loaf (12 slices).

NUTRITION FACTS: 1 slice equals 144 calories, 10 g fat (4 g saturated fat), 45 mg cholesterol, 239 mg sodium, 8 g carbohydrate, trace fiber, 6 g protein.

spinach flatbreads

I always seemed to have spinach that would spoil before I could use it all. So I started making these delicious flatbreads. They're low-fat and can double as a light lunch.
KRISTEN WESTBROOK PITTSBURGH, PENNSYLVANIA

2/3	cup sliced onion
4	teaspoons olive oil, divided
4	whole pita breads
2	cups fresh baby spinach
1-1/2	cups (6 ounces) shredded part-skim mozzarella cheese
1/4	teaspoon pepper

▣ In a small skillet, saute onion in 2 teaspoons oil until tender; set aside.

▣ Place pitas on an ungreased baking sheet; brush with remaining oil. Layer with spinach, onion and cheese. Sprinkle with pepper. Bake at 425° for 6-8 minutes or until cheese is melted.

Yield: 4 servings.

NUTRITION FACTS: 1 serving equals 322 calories, 12 g fat (5 g saturated fat), 24 mg cholesterol, 528 mg sodium, 37 g carbohydrate, 2 g fiber, 16 g protein. **DIABETIC EXCHANGES:** 2 starch, 2 lean meat, 1 vegetable.

fresh tomato flatbread

(pictured at left)

Looking for an easy appetizer or side? You'll need just a can of refrigerated crescent rolls, fresh tomatoes, olive oil, and a sprinkling of cheese and seasonings.

MARLENE MOHR CINCINNATI, OHIO

2	plum tomatoes
1	tube (8 ounces) refrigerated crescent rolls
1	small onion, thinly sliced
2	tablespoons olive oil
1	teaspoon Italian seasoning
1	garlic clove, minced
1/4	teaspoon salt
1/8	teaspoon pepper
1	tablespoon grated Parmesan cheese

▣ Thinly slice the tomatoes; place on paper towels to drain. Unroll crescent dough; place on an ungreased baking sheet. Roll into a 14-in. x 10-in. rectangle; seal seams and perforations.

▣ Arrange tomatoes and onion over crust. In a small bowl, combine the oil, Italian seasoning, garlic, salt and pepper; brush over top. Sprinkle with cheese.

▣ Bake at 375° for 10-14 minutes or until flatbread is lightly browned.

Yield: 12 servings.

NUTRITION FACTS: 1 piece equals 101 calories, 6 g fat (1 g saturated fat), trace cholesterol, 205 mg sodium, 9 g carbohydrate, trace fiber, 2 g protein. **DIABETIC EXCHANGES:** 1 fat, 1/2 starch.

cheddar-parm loaf

People love the rich and cheesy topping on this garlic bread that's ready after just a few minutes under the broiler. It's also great with a main-dish salad or soup.

TAMMY GRIFFIN FRANKSTON, TEXAS

1/2	cup grated Parmesan cheese
1/2	cup shredded cheddar cheese
1/2	cup mayonnaise
1/4	teaspoon garlic powder
1	loaf (8 ounces) French bread, split

▣ In a small bowl, combine the cheeses, mayonnaise and garlic powder. Spread over cut sides of bread. Place on an ungreased baking sheet. Broil 4 in. from the heat for 2-3 minutes or until lightly browned. Cut each piece in half. Serve warm.

Yield: 4 servings.

NUTRITION FACTS: 1 serving equals 458 calories, 30 g fat (8 g saturated fat), 34 mg cholesterol, 756 mg sodium, 33 g carbohydrate, 1 g fiber, 14 g protein.

blue cheese garlic bread

This is a great way to dress up an ordinary loaf of bread for special occasions. Serve as an appetizer or with a meal.

KEVALYN HENDERSON HAYWARD, WISCONSIN

1/2	cup butter, softened
4	ounces crumbled blue cheese
2	tablespoons grated Parmesan cheese
1	tablespoon minced chives
1	teaspoon garlic powder
1	loaf (1 pound) unsliced French bread

▣ In a small bowl, combine the first five ingredients. Cut bread into 1-in.-thick slices, but not all the way through, leaving slices attached at the bottom. Spread cheese mixture between slices.

▣ Wrap loaf in a large piece of heavy-duty foil (about 28-in. x 18-in.). Fold foil around bread and seal tightly. Bake at 350° for 20 minutes or until heated through. Serve warm.

Yield: 10 servings.

NUTRITION FACTS: 1 slice equals 250 calories, 14 g fat (8 g saturated fat), 34 mg cholesterol, 546 mg sodium, 24 g carbohydrate, 1 g fiber, 7 g protein.

green olive focaccia

(pictured above left)

Green olives complement my speedy version of this beloved Italian bread. Try the focaccia with minestrone or Italian wedding soup, or serve it with an antipasto tray for a hearty appetizer the guys will love.
IVY LAFFOON CERES, CALIFORNIA

1	loaf (1 pound) frozen bread dough, thawed
1/2	cup sliced pimiento-stuffed olives
1/2	cup shredded Colby-Monterey Jack cheese
1/2	cup shredded Parmesan cheese
1	teaspoon Italian seasoning
2	tablespoons olive oil

On an ungreased baking sheet, pat dough into a 12-in. x 6-in. rectangle. Build up edges slightly. Top with olives, cheeses and Italian seasoning; press gently into dough. Drizzle with oil.

Bake at 350° for 15-20 minutes or until cheese is melted and golden brown. Let stand for 5 minutes before slicing.

Yield: 8 servings.

NUTRITION FACTS: 1 piece equals 249 calories, 11 g fat (3 g saturated fat), 10 mg cholesterol, 623 mg sodium, 31 g carbohydrate, 2 g fiber, 9 g protein.

sweet potato biscuits

(pictured above right)

Just four ingredients make these tender biscuits a snap. I modified my grandma's recipe to make it shorter and quicker. These are my husband's favorites.
PAM BOUILLION RAYNE, LOUISIANA

2-1/2	cups biscuit/baking mix
1-1/2	cups canned sweet potatoes
6	tablespoons milk
1/3	cup butter, melted

Place biscuit mix in a large bowl. In a small bowl, mash sweet potatoes; stir in milk and butter. Stir into biscuit mix just until moistened.

Drop by heaping tablespoonfuls 2 in. apart onto a greased baking sheet. Bake at 425° for 8-10 minutes or until golden brown. Serve warm.
Yield: about 1 dozen.

NUTRITION FACTS: 1 biscuit equals 132 calories, 7 g fat (3 g saturated fat), 11 mg cholesterol, 287 mg sodium, 16 g carbohydrate, 1 g fiber, 2 g protein.

nutty gouda rolls

Here's a quick take on crescents that feels special enough for company. With Gouda, pecans and honey, these super-simple rolls will complement a variety of weeknight meals.
TASTE OF HOME TEST KITCHEN

- 2 ounces Gouda cheese
- 1 tube (8 ounces) refrigerated crescent rolls
- 2 tablespoons finely chopped pecans
- 1 tablespoon honey

◻ Cut cheese into eight 1/2-in.-wide strips. Separate crescent dough into eight triangles; sprinkle with pecans. Place a cheese strip on the shortest side of each triangle; roll up. Pinch ends to seal.

◻ Place on an ungreased baking sheet. Bake at 375° for 10-12 minutes or until golden brown. Immediately brush with honey. Serve warm.

Yield: 8 servings.

NUTRITION FACTS: 1 roll equals 158 calories, 9 g fat (3 g saturated fat), 8 mg cholesterol, 281 mg sodium, 14 g carbohydrate, trace fiber, 4 g protein.

blueberry corn muffins

Sweet blueberries really jazz up an ordinary box of corn bread mix. These are perfect for on-the-go snacking or as an addition to any summer potluck.
DIANE HIXON NICEVILLE, FLORIDA

- 1 package (8-1/2 ounces) corn bread/muffin mix
- 1 tablespoon brown sugar
- 1 egg, lightly beaten
- 1/3 cup milk
- 1/2 cup fresh or frozen blueberries

◻ In a large bowl, combine the muffin mix and brown sugar. Combine the egg and milk; stir into dry ingredients just until moistened. Fold in blueberries.

◻ Coat muffin cups with cooking spray or use paper liners. Fill half full with batter. Bake at 400° for 12-15 minutes or until a toothpick inserted in muffin comes out clean. Cool for 5 minutes before removing from pan to a wire rack. Serve warm.

Yield: 8 muffins.

NUTRITION FACTS: 1 muffin equals 146 calories, 4 g fat (1 g saturated fat), 33 mg cholesterol, 264 mg sodium, 25 g carbohydrate, 1 g fiber, 3 g protein. **DIABETIC EXCHANGES:** 1-1/2 starch, 1/2 fat.

EDITOR'S NOTE: If using frozen blueberries, use without thawing to avoid discoloring the batter.

- 1/2 cup seasoned bread crumbs
- 1/3 cup grated Parmesan cheese
- 1/3 cup reduced-fat mayonnaise
- 2 garlic cloves, minced
- 1 cup (4 ounces) shredded part-skim mozzarella cheese

▢ Bake loaf according to package directions; cool. Cut bread in half lengthwise; place on an ungreased baking sheet.

▢ In a small bowl, combine the artichokes, bread crumbs, Parmesan cheese, mayonnaise and garlic; spread evenly over cut sides of bread. Sprinkle with mozzarella cheese.

▢ Bake at 350° for 15-20 minutes or until cheese is melted. Slice and serve warm.

Yield: 1 loaf (12 slices).

NUTRITION FACTS: 1 slice equals 151 calories, 5 g fat (2 g saturated fat), 10 mg cholesterol, 456 mg sodium, 18 g carbohydrate, 1 g fiber, 7 g protein.

herbed pita chips

Instead of simply serving bread alongside soup, why not whip up a batch of these seasoned pita chips? They're a fun and flavorful addition to any meal!
TASTE OF HOME TEST KITCHEN

- 4 pita breads (6 inches)
- 1 tablespoon butter, melted
- 1/2 teaspoon dried basil
- 1/2 teaspoon dried thyme

▢ Place pita breads on an ungreased baking sheet; brush with butter. Combine basil and thyme; sprinkle over pitas. Cut each into eight wedges. Bake at 400° for 8-10 minutes or until crisp.

Yield: 6 servings.

NUTRITION FACTS: 5 or 6 chips equals 127 calories, 2 g fat (1 g saturated fat), 5 mg cholesterol, 234 mg sodium, 22 g carbohydrate, 1 g fiber, 4 g protein.

artichoke bread

A creamy rich artichoke spread tops these warm crusty bites that folks just love. You won't find a quicker or more delicious way to round out your menu. It's especially good with Italian food.
SHERRY CAMPBELL ST. AMANT, LOUISIANA

- 1 tube (11 ounces) refrigerated crusty French loaf
- 1 can (14 ounces) water-packed artichoke hearts, rinsed, drained and chopped

so-easy spinach crescents

These spinach-stuffed rolls are a great way to get my son to eat his vegetables! I experimented with the recipe many times after tasting similar bundles years ago.
SUSAN JAMES MANHATTAN, KANSAS

1/2	cup sliced almonds
1	package (10 ounces) frozen chopped spinach, thawed and squeezed dry
1/2	cup grated Parmesan cheese
1/4	cup chopped onion
2	teaspoons olive oil
1/4	teaspoon salt
1/8	teaspoon pepper
1	package (8 ounces) refrigerated crescent rolls

▢ In a food processor, finely chop the almonds. Add the spinach, cheese, onion, oil, salt and pepper; cover and process until well blended.

▢ Unroll and separate the crescent dough into eight pieces. Spread spinach mixture evenly over dough to within 1/8 in. of edges. Roll up and place on a greased baking sheet. Bake at 375° for 15-18 minutes or until golden brown. Serve warm.

Yield: 8 servings.

NUTRITION FACTS: 1 serving equals 189 calories, 12 g fat (3 g saturated fat), 4 mg cholesterol, 416 mg sodium, 14 g carbohydrate, 2 g fiber, 6 g protein.

parmesan breadsticks

These tender and flavorful breadsticks make the perfect accompaniment to any meal. You'll love the jazzed-up taste that cumin and paprika provide.
LINDA FINCHMAN SPENCER, WEST VIRGINIA

1/2	cup grated Parmesan cheese
1/4	teaspoon paprika
1/8	teaspoon ground cumin
3	tablespoons butter, melted
1	tube (11 ounces) refrigerated breadsticks

▢ In a shallow bowl, combine the cheese, paprika and cumin. Place butter in another shallow bowl.

▢ Separate the dough into individual breadsticks. Dip each in butter, then in cheese mixture. Twist breadsticks two to three times and place on an ungreased baking sheet.

▢ Bake at 375° for 10-12 minutes or until golden brown. Serve immediately.

Yield: 1 dozen.

NUTRITION FACTS: 1 breadstick equals 110 calories, 5 g fat (3 g saturated fat), 10 mg cholesterol, 256 mg sodium, 13 g carbohydrate, trace fiber, 3 g protein. **DIABETIC EXCHANGES:** 1 starch, 1/2 fat.

melty swiss bread

(pictured at left)

I like to serve slices of this dressed-up French bread with a chef's salad. It's also a great complement to a hearty soup on cold days.
LAURA MURPHY VENTURA, CALIFORNIA

2	cups (8 ounces) shredded Swiss cheese
1/3	cup mayonnaise
1	tablespoon minced fresh oregano
1	tablespoon grated onion
1	tablespoon cider vinegar
1	loaf (1 pound) French bread, split

▢ In a small bowl, combine the cheese, mayonnaise, oregano, onion and vinegar. Spread over bread.

▢ Place on an ungreased baking sheet. Bake at 400° for 8-10 minutes or until cheese is melted and lightly browned. Serve warm.

Yield: 16 slices.

NUTRITION FACTS: 1 slice equals 162 calories, 8 g fat (3 g saturated fat), 14 mg cholesterol, 233 mg sodium, 15 g carbohydrate, 1 g fiber, 6 g protein.

italian breadsticks

These soft breadsticks are so easy to make and have wonderful homemade flavor. We enjoy them warm from the oven dipped in pizza sauce.
MARLENE MUCKENHIRN DELANO, MINNESOTA

3/4	cup grated Parmesan cheese
1-1/2	teaspoons Italian seasoning
1	loaf (1 pound) frozen white bread dough, thawed
1/4	cup butter, melted

Warm pizza sauce, optional

▢ Combine cheese and Italian seasoning in a shallow bowl; set aside. Divide dough into 32 sections; roll each into a 5-in. rope. Twist two pieces together. Moisten ends with water and pinch to seal. Dip in butter, then in cheese mixture.

▢ Place on a greased baking sheet. Bake at 400° for 10-14 minutes or until golden brown. Serve with pizza sauce for dipping if desired.

Yield: 16 servings.

NUTRITION FACTS: 1 breadstick equals 121 calories, 5 g fat (2 g saturated fat), 11 mg cholesterol, 236 mg sodium, 14 g carbohydrate, 1 g fiber, 4 g protein.

ranch biscuits

I dress up biscuit mix with ranch salad dressing mix, then brush the golden bites with garlic butter after baking. I bake several dozen at once and store them in the freezer. The parsley-flecked biscuits go well with any entree.
CHRISTI GILLENTINE TULSA, OKLAHOMA

2	cups biscuit/baking mix
4	teaspoons dry ranch salad dressing mix
2/3	cup milk
2	tablespoons butter, melted
1	teaspoon dried parsley flakes
1/8	teaspoon garlic powder

▢ In a large bowl, stir the biscuit mix, salad dressing mix and milk until combined. Drop 2 in. apart onto a greased baking sheet.

▢ Bake at 425° for 10-15 minutes or until golden brown. In a small bowl, combine the butter, parsley and garlic powder; brush over warm biscuits. Serve warm.

Yield: 9 biscuits.

NUTRITION FACTS: 1 biscuit equals 150 calories, 7 g fat (3 g saturated fat), 8 mg cholesterol, 641 mg sodium, 19 g carbohydrate, trace fiber, 3 g protein.

onion swiss loaf

(pictured above)

This rich, oniony bread is one of our favorites. I hope you enjoy it just as much as our family and friends do. Try it with French onion or lentil soup. Simply delicious!
PAT BREMSON KANSAS CITY, MISSOURI

1/2	cup butter, cubed
1	large sweet or yellow onion, halved and thinly sliced
1/2	teaspoon prepared mustard
1/4	teaspoon lemon juice
1	loaf (1 pound) French bread, halved lengthwise
12	slices Swiss cheese

▢ Melt butter in a large skillet over medium heat. Add the onion, mustard and lemon juice; cook and stir for 10-12 minutes or until tender. Remove from the heat.

▢ Brush cut sides of bread with some of the butter from the pan. Spoon onion mixture onto bread bottom; top with cheese. Replace bread top.

▢ Wrap loaf in foil; place on a baking sheet. Bake at 350° for 15 minutes or until cheese is melted.

Yield: 8 servings.

NUTRITION FACTS: 1 slice equals 413 calories, 23 g fat (15 g saturated fat), 68 mg cholesterol, 516 mg sodium, 35 g carbohydrate, 2 g fiber, 16 g protein.

pull-apart bacon bread

I made this tasty bread for my husband, and he just loved it!
TERRI CHRISTENSEN MONTAGUE, MICHIGAN

12	bacon strips, diced
2	tubes (12 ounces each) refrigerated buttermilk biscuits
2	cups (8 ounces) shredded part-skim mozzarella cheese
1	tablespoon Italian salad dressing mix
2	teaspoons olive oil

▢ In a large skillet, cook bacon over medium heat until cooked but not crisp. Using a slotted spoon, remove to paper towels to drain. Separate biscuits; cut each biscuit into quarters.

▢ In a bowl, combine the cheese, dressing mix, oil and bacon. Place half of the biscuit pieces in a greased 10-in. fluted tube pan; sprinkle with half of the cheese mixture. Top with remaining biscuit pieces and cheese mixture.

▢ Bake at 375° for 25-30 minutes or until golden brown. Cool for 5 minutes before inverting onto a serving plate. Serve immediately.

Yield: 12 servings.

NUTRITION FACTS: 1 slice equals 227 calories, 8 g fat (3 g saturated fat), 18 mg cholesterol, 800 mg sodium, 28 g carbohydrate, 0 fiber, 11 g protein.

garlic poppy seed spirals

Here is a fast, easy way to transform crescent rolls. Adjust the seasoning to your family's taste...or use a little powdered ranch dressing mix as an alternative.
STACEY SCHERER MACOMB, MICHIGAN

3	tablespoons butter, melted
1	teaspoon garlic powder
1	teaspoon dried minced onion
1/2	teaspoon poppy seeds
1	tube (8 ounces) refrigerated crescent rolls

▢ In a small bowl, combine the butter, garlic powder, onion and poppy seeds; set aside. Remove crescent dough from tube; do not unroll. Cut dough into 10 slices; dip one side in butter mixture.

▢ Place buttered side up in an ungreased 9-in. round baking pan. Brush with remaining butter mixture. Bake at 350° for 14-16 minutes or until golden brown. Serve warm.

Yield: 10 servings.

NUTRITION FACTS: 1 spiral equals 121 calories, 8 g fat (3 g saturated fat), 9 mg cholesterol, 213 mg sodium, 9 g carbohydrate, trace fiber, 2 g protein.

cranberry bran muffins

Apple-cinnamon and cranberry flavors make these muffins the perfect treat for chilly autumn mornings and evenings. With just four ingredients, you can whip them up fast.
TASTE OF HOME TEST KITCHEN

1	package (8.1 ounces) apple cinnamon muffin mix
1/2	cup All-Bran, crushed
1/2	cup dried cranberries
1/2	cup milk

▢ In a large bowl, combine the muffin mix, cereal and cranberries. Stir in milk just until moistened. Fill greased or paper-lined muffin cups three-fourths full.

▢ Bake at 400° for 16-18 minutes or until a toothpick inserted in muffin comes out clean. Cool muffins for 5 minutes before removing from the pan to a wire rack. Serve warm.

Yield: 6 muffins.

NUTRITION FACTS: 1 muffin equals 210 calories, 5 g fat (1 g saturated fat), 4 mg cholesterol, 567 mg sodium, 41 g carbohydrate, 2 g fiber, 3 g protein.

tip!

TENDER MUFFINS AND QUICK BREADS

To ensure tender muffins and quick breads, mix all of the dry ingredients well before adding wet ingredients, including already-beaten eggs. This cuts the risk of overmixing so your baked goods will be tender, not tough or chewy.

Place crust on a pizza pan or baking sheet. Spread with pesto; sprinkle with garlic salt and cheeses. Bake at 325° for 12-15 minutes or until cheese is melted. Cut into wedges.

Yield: 6-8 servings.

NUTRITION FACTS: 1 wedge equals 221 calories, 10 g fat (4 g saturated fat), 17 mg cholesterol, 505 mg sodium, 22 g carbohydrate, 1 g fiber, 11 g protein.

corn dog muffins

Our three boys were always asking for corn dogs, so I came up with this fast way to deliver the same flavor. Try them with a not-too-spicy chili for a fun meal the whole family will love.
LYNITA ARTEBERRY PLANKINTON, SOUTH DAKOTA

  2   packages (8-1/2 ounces each) corn bread/muffin mix
  2   tablespoons brown sugar
  2   eggs
  1   cup milk
  1   can (11 ounces) whole kernel corn, drained
  5   hot dogs, chopped

In a large bowl, combine corn bread mix and brown sugar. Combine eggs and milk; stir into dry ingredients until moistened. Stir in corn and hot dogs (batter will be thin).

Fill greased or paper-lined muffin cups three-fourths full. Bake at 400° for 14-18 minutes or until a toothpick inserted in muffin comes out clean. Serve warm.

Yield: 1-1/2 dozen.

NUTRITION FACTS: 1 muffin equals 130 calories, 6 g fat (2 g saturated fat), 35 mg cholesterol, 300 mg sodium, 14 g carbohydrate, trace fiber, 4 g protein.

chive corn bread

"Busy" is my middle name, so I love easy recipes that make meal prep simpler. They help me juggle working, volunteering, and keeping my family's schedule running smoothly.
TERRI KEENEY GREELEY, COLORADO

  1   package (8-1/2 ounces) corn bread/muffin mix
  1/2 cup shredded cheddar cheese
  1   tablespoon minced chives

Prepare corn bread batter according to package directions. Stir in cheese and chives. Pour into a greased 8-in. square baking dish. Bake at 400° for 20-25 minutes or until lightly browned. Serve warm.

Yield: 9 servings.

NUTRITION FACTS: 1 piece equals 144 calories, 5 g fat (2 g saturated fat), 37 mg cholesterol, 271 mg sodium, 20 g carbohydrate, trace fiber, 4 g protein.

cheesy pesto bread

I topped a prebaked pizza crust with pesto and cheese for dinner one night when I was in a rush. Now it's expected whenever I make pasta and salad! Any leftovers are also great heated up for lunch the next day.
KAREN GRANT TULARE, CALIFORNIA

  1   prebaked 12-inch pizza crust
  3   tablespoons prepared pesto
  1/8 teaspoon garlic salt
  1   cup (4 ounces) shredded mozzarella cheese
  1/2 cup shredded Parmesan cheese

sausage pinwheels

These spirals are simple to make but look special on a buffet. Our guests eagerly help themselves—sometimes the eye-catching pinwheels never even make it to their plates!
GAIL SYKORA MENOMONEE FALLS, WISCONSIN

- 1 tube (8 ounces) refrigerated crescent rolls
- 1/2 pound uncooked bulk pork sausage
- 2 tablespoons minced chives

▢ Unroll crescent roll dough on a lightly floured surface; press seams and perforations together. Roll into a 14-in. x 10-in. rectangle. Spread sausage to within 1/2 in. of edges. Sprinkle with chives.

▢ Carefully roll up from a long side; cut into 12 slices. Place 1 in. apart in an ungreased 15-in. x 10-in. x 1-in. baking pan. Bake at 375° for 12-16 minutes or until golden brown.

Yield: 1 dozen.

NUTRITION FACTS: 1 pinwheel equals 113 calories, 8 g fat (2 g saturated fat), 7 mg cholesterol, 226 mg sodium, 8 g carbohydrate, trace fiber, 3 g protein.

biscuit bites

These savory mini biscuits are wonderful with soup, a main dish or even as a snack. We like to munch on them instead of popcorn while watching television.
JOY BECK CINCINNATI, OHIO

- 1 tube (12 ounces) refrigerated buttermilk biscuits
- 2 tablespoons grated Parmesan cheese
- 1 teaspoon onion powder

▢ Cut each biscuit into thirds; place on a greased baking sheet. Combine cheese and onion powder; sprinkle over biscuits. Bake at 400° for 7-8 minutes or until golden brown.

Yield: 5 servings.

NUTRITION FACTS: 1 serving equals 175 calories, 2 g fat (1 g saturated fat), 2 mg cholesterol, 619 mg sodium, 33 g carbohydrate, trace fiber, 6 g protein.

tip!

STORING ONION & GARLIC POWDERS

Garlic and onion powders tend to absorb moisture from the air, especially during warm weather months. Store them in airtight spice jars to keep them as free from moisture and humidity as possible.

General Index

Alphabetical Index